DESIGNING INTERIOR ARCHITECTURE

SYLVIA LEYDECKER (Ed.)

DESIGNING INTERIOR ARCHITECTURE

CONCEPT
TYPOLOGY
MATERIAL
CONSTRUCTION

BIRKHÄUSER
BASEL

The Publisher and the Editor wish to thank the following
companies for their participation in this book:

AGROB BUCHTAL

burgbad

nora systems GmbH

Sto AG

Trevira GmbH

Translation from German into English (chapters
by Leydecker, Wachs, Catoir, Ippolito, Blaschitz,
Stumpf, Welter):
Julian Reisenberger, Weimar

Copyediting of English version:
Raymond Peat, Alford, Aberdeenshire

Editor for the Publisher: Andreas Müller, Berlin

Layout, cover design and typography:
Rein Steger, Proxi, Barcelona

Cover illustration: Translucent back-lit concrete
(manufactured by Lucem); photo: Sylvia Leydecker

A CIP catalogue record for this book is available from
the Library of Congress, Washington D.C., USA.

Bibliographic information published by the German
National Library:
The German National Library lists this publication in the
Deutsche Nationalbibliografie; detailed bibliographic data
are available on the Internet at http://dnb.d-nb.de.

This book is also available in a German language edition
(ISBN 978-3-0346-1579-2 hardcover,
ISBN 978-3-0346-1300-2 softcover)

© 2013 Birkhäuser Verlag GmbH, Basel
P.O. Box 44, 4009 Basel, Switzerland
Part of De Gruyter

Printed on acid-free paper produced from chlorine-free pulp.
TCF ∞

Printed in Germany

ISBN 978-3-0346-0680-6 hardcover
ISBN 978-3-0346-1302-6 softcover

9 8 7 6 5 4 3 2 1
www.birkhauser.com

CONTENT

FOREWORD

BY SIMON HAMILTON

Simon Hamilton & Associates Ltd; International Director,
British Institute of Interior Design (BIID)

Working within the interior design industry is a privilege and an ever-changing experience. As design students we are taught that anything can be created and not to give up on our ideas. Reality kicks in once the theory days of study are over. However, I believe it is still possible to be inspiring, innovative and different within the constraints of budgets, regulations, client's requirements and timescale.

During my career as an interior designer, spanning more than two decades, I have worked across several sectors including workplace, hotel, restaurant, offices, exhibition, residential and healthcare. Whatever the brief, the fundamental elements of the design process remain the same.

The challenge that exists on the international market is to produce designs that are relevant, responsible and appropriate. As International Director for the British Institute of Interior Design, I have been fortunate enough to personally meet and connect with design communities around the world. Despite cultural and language differences, there is a common bond between them. We share very familiar problems, issues and obstacles, in a way that is both refreshing and frustrating. Interior design is good and will enhance your life, this is the message we deliver and that does not always get heard.

A trend that has become evident to me through my travels is the ubiquitous desire to be part of the interior design circuit. The list of countries now staging regular large-scale interior design-focused events includes India, Singapore, Russia, Brazil and China. They are more than keen to take on the established events such as the Salone Internazionale del Mobile in Milan, Neocon in Chicago, Orgatec in Cologne, 100% Design in London and Maison et Objet in Paris. With so much competition, are we in danger of design overload?

The increase in our appetite for interior design on a global basis has resulted in positive acceptance of the idea that interior design has meaning and purpose. While the image of being a quick fix on a budget will not disappear overnight, the media are better informed and perhaps a little less cynical today. The importance and influence of good design is widely recognised, particularly in the retail and hospitality sectors. Increasing the financial bottom line is the focus of all business, which is where good design can make a significant difference. The experiences created for customers, whether in a fast food chain, a Grand Hotel, an airport lounge, a shopping mall, a cinema or restaurant, are carefully managed. This applies also to workplace and leisure environments design.

As we live longer, our standard of living improves and our expectations inevitably rise. The middle classes of emerging economies have the money to spend and want to be invited to the party and are impatient for change. This is driving rapid development of new towns, railways, ports and infrastructure but we have to ask at what long-term cost? Our human condition craves change and progress and we are aware it is unstoppable. Striving to discover new and different things is part of our natural drive. We should not fight it but learn from the mistakes of the past, where forecasts for growth and demand have been over ambitious in certain areas. With a global recession like no other, affecting most countries in the world, we are now in a state of fear and sometimes panic.

Using design to bring people together and have better lives is possible, even if this may be a Utopian view. As the global population grows beyond seven billion people, there are more basic needs to provide. Food, water and shelter are still not available in some regions of the world but good design continues to help resolve this to some degree. Travelling to India on more than one occasion, I found it difficult to reconcile with the immediate and ubiquitous poverty, when there were well-catered, smart presentations taking place in plush hotels 10 minutes away. A huge programme of growth and development is in place, but the enormity of the task means the timeframe for any noticeable change is protracted. India is not the only country with this mission on its national agenda.

It is important to recognise that interior design has a responsibility to ensure that we are improving the quality of life for the masses as well as prolonging the earth's life rather than destroying it. Unfortunately, political and economic agendas are also part of the equation, that can steer the sustainability approach off course. However, there are a number of locations like Abu Dhabi, Australia and Singapore where they are taking the lead in green matters rather than just paying lip service to the ideas of protecting our future.

As an ambassador for British design, it has been exceptionally rewarding to meet different design communities and interact. I have also witnessed how much British design education and creativity is admired and respected around the world. On every trip, whether to Chicago, New Delhi, Paris, Toronto or Milan there was always a very positive reception. In Japan I encountered particularly high respect for designers from the UK that goes some way to explain Paul Smith's huge success in that region.

Working across several sectors has taught me a lot about the interior design business and the variations that exist, but ultimately the task is always the same: we begin with a vision of creating something unique, beautiful, relevant, something making an improvement on the existing. To have the opportunity to be part of someone's life or company for a brief period can be a challenge but also educating, rewarding and inspiring. The term "journey" may be clichéd, but it describes best the chain of events that defines the design process.

The essence of appealing internationally is to identify the soul of the design, whether it is a product or space. The international success of leading British designers such as Sebastian Conran, Tricia Guild, David Linley, Paul Smith or Lee Broom is their understanding of the local markets. More importantly, they share the creation of a message and identity and promote it with confidence, humour and personality.

The popularity of vintage, bespoke and heritage products and spaces is a contradiction to our need for the familiarity of brands and identities that we are bombarded with in everyday life. We have the ability to strike our own balance between these two competing worlds through personal selection. An eclectic mix, in varying degrees, is becoming more common and a truer reflection of who we are as people. The bland and impersonal, minimalist and highly polished style of the late 20th century is associated with false promises that we would share in the success of a highly developed world with big financial gains all round. Now that the bubble has well and truly burst, we find ourselves responding to a more human and intimate scale of ideas and solutions.

I believe that science and design will have a much closer relationship in the future than we may recognise today, as we currently exist under a heavy digital blanket. In order for the world to function well, it needs to use its limited resources with caution and discover and invent new technologies or materials, which are affordable and realistic for the future generation.

FOREWORD

BY KEES SPANJERS

Zaanen Spanjers Architects; Past President,
Dutch Association of Interior Architects (BNI)

Interiors are the architecture of the future. Design and architecture are no longer fashionable but are expected to provide specific answers to user demand and the need to improve our well-being. Health, safety and well-being have become important social themes, not least in the Western world where a shrinking and aging population corresponds with an increasing need for individual and small-scale design of the living environment, calling for particular attention to re-use and sustainable development. Well-designed interiors add value to the perception and quality of use of our immediate living environment, to our feeling of well-being and to the quality of life.

Interiors are the architecture of change. The life-cycle of a building knows many users and is subject to a continuous change of views. A building is never finished, giving every user the opportunity to attach their narrative to it. Interior architects/designers give shape to a sustainable renewal of buildings. While preserving the specific and sometimes unique architectural qualities, we provide and care for generation after generation to feel at home.

Interiors are the architecture of perception. One of the factors that determine the appreciation for our environment is time. Light and dark, as well as the changing of the seasons, have a defining effect on the perception of interior space. Fashion and trends play an important role as well. We are challenged by the new, but also nourish the known and well-acquainted. Pushing boundaries is a unique aspect of human nature, as is the need for meaning and a sense of security. Habituation is a special trait; much of what we encounter as strange and ugly at first sight will be valued over time. Aging, by contrast, is not a uniquely human condition. Materials age and wear. Sometimes that presents a new beauty, a patina we nourish or even try to imitate.

Interiors are the architecture of emotional culture. In a nice and stimulating environment people experience more commitment, more pleasure, satisfaction and success. People have a desire for association, expression, remembrance and beauty. They want to identify with their environment. This means that an environment ought to provide space for individuality and self-expression, which in turn offers new perspectives for improvisation, spontaneity, vision and imagination. Interactive encounters and ergonomic quality are key to accommodate socio-psychological aspects in a working environment. The "emotional house" may foster new models of efficiency and productivity. In public interiors as well, it is important to explore the functional potential of perceptional aspects, creating places that command desirable behaviour. People are easily influenced but want to be taken serious.

Interiors are the architecture of cultural history. Beyond their role as a utilitarian interface between user and building, interiors are the expression of our cultural identity and ambition. The decoration and design of our immediate environment is a time-honoured art. Intact historic interiors can tell us more about the culture, the fashions and habits of a certain place and time than in-depth scientific studies. However, intact historic interiors are even rarer than Old Masters paintings. Interiors form the user side of buildings and give meaning and value to them, but the user side is also vulnerable. Interiors are bearers of culture, but ever so often we remake them as they are overtaken by time.

Interiors are the architecture of responsibility. Designers take into account the consequences of their professional activity for the health, safety and well-being of all those who may reasonably be expected to use or enjoy the product of their work. This way of looking at design, going well beyond superficial styling and decoration, requires training, experience and an openness to life-long learning. It also needs a bent for research and development. But above all, it calls for a love for people.

May this book be of assistance to those designers.

IN BETWEEN

—

INTERIOR DESIGN BETWEEN ARCHITECTURE AND DESIGN

SYLVIA LEYDECKER

Pleasure in the job puts perfection in the work.
Aristotle

"Human-centred" is a term encountered regularly in the context of interior design because our spatial surroundings have such a fundamental influence on our lives. We are all aware of the value of spatial qualities, whether as a means of improving our sense of well-being in a space or for facilitating work processes. The architectural design of interiors influences our emotional sensibilities and in turn how we behave. It can communicate an attitude, provide an atmosphere of trust and safety, reduce anxiety, be relaxing, stimulating or alternatively reassuring. It influences our motivation to work, our sense of responsibility or disregard for a space, and it can be soothing or disquieting, spiriting or depressing. The design of spaces and their atmospheres affects the behaviour and well-being of *everyone* involved.

PUBLIC IMAGE

Interior design is generally perceived as lying between the poles of architecture and design. In the media and popular press, it is commonly portrayed as the furnishing of luxury residences, an image reinforced by the plethora of TV interior makeover shows. The role of interior architects and designers is often confused with being that of

"interior stylists" and, in an international context especially, they are perceived as being solely interior decorators. But interior design encompasses much more than that, and this is what differentiates professional interior designers from the clichéd image. Professionals will have completed a comprehensive programme of studies and work on a broad range of tasks that go far beyond that of luxury villas.

The field of interior design lies between those of other professions: on the one hand, there are architecture offices who work on the renovation and modernisation of existing buildings, traditionally a primary field of interior design; and on the other there are design agencies who create interiors as part of lucrative branding contracts. This situation, while problematic for the profession, also demonstrates that interior design is more in demand than ever.

The core aspect of interior design work is the design concept itself. Designs are usually characterised by different individual interpretations of the task: a personal style or signature. One and the same design task can embody differing degrees of creative and intellectual potential. In practice, professionals must adopt a standpoint that also defines how they see themselves and their own approach to work in their profession.

Interior designers have the skills and know-how to shape the quality of interiors for their future use, whether in a private house or for a large corporation. The spectrum of activities in the field of interior design is very broad and ranges from furniture design and product designs for industrial manufacture to designing in existing fabric.

So who is responsible for giving interior design a distinctive profile in the public arena? Who are the iconic interior designers of the day? Names that immediately spring to mind include designers such as Philippe Starck and Andrée Putman, or global design pop stars such as Karim Rashid or Marcel Wanders: the first is a universal genius at home in all genres from pasta to high-rise buildings, the second is the *grande dame* of interior design, and the last two are product designers who also work in the field of interior design. Further examples include offices, such as Concrete and Nendo or Kelly Hoppen or Shiro Kuramata, who create contemporary interiors, as well as Eileen Gray as a historic milestone and early protagonist of interior design. The number of "icons" in the field of interior design is modest in comparison to that of those in the field of architecture, which indicates that the interior design scene is not adequately represented in the public eye. While there are more than enough coffee-table books and popular maga-

zines, their general focus tends to be on interior decorating, and the featured interiors span the range from spaces designed by professional architects and interior designers to private houses designed by non-professionals, ranging from "Mr Big Shot's wife" to married couples with artistic ambitions. Glorified cushion arrangements for home living.

Compared with architects, interior designers are very much in the minority: good interior designers are rare and valuable. While the proportion of women within the profession is relatively high compared with other branches, especially during studies, this proportion decreases later when it becomes increasingly difficult for women to balance career and children. The resulting lack of professional female interior designers does not help to strengthen the image of the profession. Instead, the cliché of "Barbie the interior designer", which still prevails in some sectors, only reinforces the view of interior design as a kind of "pastime for women".

→ 17

A few more Beats Per Minute rather
than "less is more": taking a break
in one of the public cocoons of
the Cocoon Techno-Bar in Frankfurt,
a milestone of club interior design.
CocoonClub, Frankfurt am Main, Germany; 3deluxe

**The spotless white cruise
ship, launched by Lady Diana,
promises an elegant interior
design for an elegant clientele.**
MS Artania; CUBIK³

Swoosh: forward-looking dynamism expressed using clean white, free-flowing organic curves.
SYZYGY Office, Frankfurt am Main, Germany; 3deluxe

Run! The interior design for a corporate box is not to be underestimated, whether in a cricket ground or football stadium.
KPMG Corporate Box, Melbourne Cricket Ground, Australia; Artillery Architecture & Interior Design

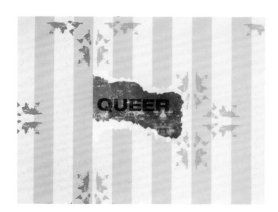

Queer: a small but telling detail.
HOSI Linz's Café Julius, Austria; Pudelskern

**Hollywood glamour meets Mick and Frank –
an ostentatious interior for a leading recording studio
and a corridor with a wow-factor.**
EastWest Studios, Los Angeles, California, USA; UBIK – Philippe Starck

Interior of a bungalow – the staircase is a sculptural composition of material, form and light.

Bungalow from 1960, Geluwe, Wervik, Belgium; Frank Sinnaeve, InteriorArchitect – Belgium

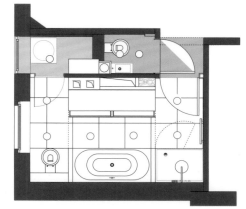

The bright, light-filled atmosphere of a private bathroom – pleasant and calming.

Apartment conversion and renovation, Frankfurt am Main, Germany; Innenarchitekturbüro Eva Lorey

PROFESSIONAL PROFILE

A further problem in this context is the naming dilemma: who may call himself or herself an interior designer, an interior architect, a planner or decorator? Various terms exist, all of which lack definition, with the result that few know who does what exactly. In some countries, such as in Germany, the chamber of architects strives to ensure quality standards in the profession and in turn provides consumer protection, but this is not the same elsewhere in the world. There are also national associations, but these too do not exist in all countries. The official designation is typically "interior designer" or "interior architect". Germany is one of the few countries where the title "interior architect" is protected, and interior architects are registered as a member of the chamber of architects once they fulfil the admission requirements and apply for registration, which consist of studies and a period of work in practice. In England, by contrast, an interior designer is not able to register as an architect, and as such interior designers are not officially recognised there. Among clients and the public, however, there is scant awareness of the title and whether or not it is protected. Following the EU-wide harmonisation of bachelor and master degree programmes, it is now often unclear whether a qualification allows a graduate to subsequently register as an interior architect or not.

One way or the other, interior architects and comparable interior designers around the world are professionals for the design and planning of interiors spaces, and their expertise is always the product of a well-grounded education. There are some notable exceptions that prove the rule: famous design personalities such as the Bauhaus-icon Walter Gropius, the minimalist John Pawson or the autodidact Tadao Ando have all gone on to be talented and successful architects with a recognisable signature despite the lack of an official qualification. However, true interior designers, who are committed with heart and soul to the profession, will undergo training. Without schooling, solutions can be arbitrary and based on personal taste. A schooled approach to tackling design problems achieves more lasting and successful results based on coherent and well-grounded design concepts. The thinking that precedes the actual design lays the groundwork for all that follows – it encompasses more than just the immediate parameters and includes a general consideration of the topic as a whole and of the specific design task.

Like architects, interior designers must adhere to a whole series of regulatory frameworks, guidelines and codes, whether they are DIN standards, health and safety guidelines for the workplace, energy efficiency directives or fire safety regulations. They prepare planning applications (and may have the unrestricted right of submitting them in some cases, such as in the German state of North Rhine-Westphalia) and are familiar with the planning, scheduling and supervision of works from construction to handover. They deal with construction details, such as damp-proofing, ceiling constructions or sections through service ducts, and are accustomed to working in a team alongside other professional disciplines and trades.

Today's interior designs are shaped by the interplay of economic, ecological, social, technological and, last but not least, aesthetic considerations. Here Aristotle's adage that "the whole is greater than the sum of the parts" applies: the key is to incorporate these different aspects and to find an optimal balance between them in the overall design concept. Nature follows the same principle. Reducing a design to individual components such as "the colour scheme", "a chair" or "the acoustics" will not result in a well-rounded and properly functioning system that serves its users. Every individual space is essentially a complex and multifunctional system.

Interior designers also play a key role as advisors to their clients, a process that begins during the design process. Whether the project concerned is commercial or private, the designer must take functional and emotional considerations into account. Intuition should likewise not be ignored, and ideas, brainstorming and challenging assumptions are all necessary parts of the design process to develop visions that from time to time become reality and will therefore be experienced.

In the design process, much is measured, analysed, observed, proven, simulated or calculated and designed on the basis of available evidence. The intention is to optimise a project as much as possible and to keep risks to a minimum. Without doubt, this approach is useful when testing a hypothetical assumption or applying research findings. But intuition and instinctive responses still play a greater role than many are willing to admit. For example, do we really need to measure the beneficial effect of daylight and contact with nature to know that it is good for us? Do we have to prove this to be able to make use of it? Or can we trust our own emotions and experience, after all these are just as much part of our natural and cultural evolution?

→ 20

The soul, that very essence of mankind,
evades logical explanation.
Max Planck

Strong colours in rooms that are used for short periods of time such as wardrobes or corridors. The girl's bright smile gives the vibrant interior a good mood – outstandingly normal.

Pusteblume-Zentrum, Cologne, Germany;
100% interior Sylvia Leydecker

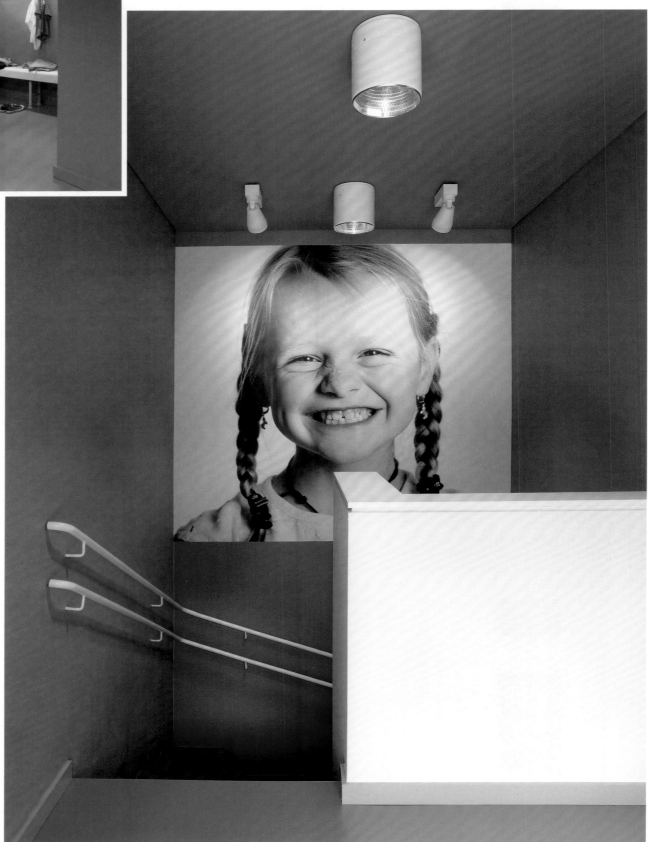

Movement is the captivating element in this pavilion in a flagship store in which the low red, fibreglass cubes appear to glide magically through the space.
Comme Des Garçons, Paris, France; Ab Rogers Design

INTERIOR DESIGN AS CORPORATE DESIGN

Spaces have the potential to communicate the character of a company. As soon as we enter a space, it creates a first impression, and this is something we can harness as part of a marketing strategy. Space becomes a powerful three-dimensional means of communication. By tailoring spaces to suit particular target groups, whether these are the future users or a group of potential investors, attractive interiors can contribute to corporate success.

It makes a big difference whether one is designing an office space for a public authority that will not change for ten years, a trade fair stand that will be dismantled five days later but may still leave a lasting impression of the company, or a shop that will be redesigned in three years' time. Trendy interiors have a comparatively short "half-life" and show their age much more quickly than a timeless design.

In private interiors, trends manifest themselves in the form of a style or look (oriental, Scandinavian, country cottage...) or the use of particular colours (apple green, crimson...) or materials (light maple wood, dark wenge wood, sand-blasted glass...). In the context of branding, however, it is the interiors that define trends because interiors, when used as a marketing instrument, make a corporate culture tangible in three dimensions.

Corporate design is often understood superficially to mean the two-dimensional design of a logo, business card, letterhead and website. What is lacking is a convincing attempt to translate this into three dimensions. Bland marketing text and spaces plastered with logos do not make authentic, unique corporate interiors. To successfully transform a corporate design concept from two dimensions into memorable three-dimensional brand experiences depends on components that are able to express and manifest the spirit of the company in the space, and thereby make it tangible. For this, marketing people develop concepts for interiors that are an integral part of the corporate identity and are skilfully interwoven with the story of the product or the company.

Form, materials, colour, light, textures, haptic experience, acoustics and even olfactory design – all of them traditional areas of interior design – help to characterise a corporate interior. While the world of cinema is busy developing 4D and 5D cinema experiences, every interior is in principle already a 4D or 5D space perceived with all the senses. For example, the materials used influence our haptic experience and in turn what we associate with a brand. Given the complexity of what constitutes good interior design, and the potential it has to affect us, failing to make use of this represents a lost opportunity to position a business or product. Through the interior design, it is possible to integrate key factors as perceived by the relevant target groups, to improve customer loyalty and to strengthen their relationship to a brand by making it tangible. An investment in interior design branding therefore pays off further down the line.

In most cases, such means focus primarily on improving the external visibility of a brand or company rather than on its internal potential, which benefits "only" the staff by motivating them and improving their sense of identification.

The use of corporate design and branded interiors can be seen at its best in the flagship stores of many international fashion labels, the office designs of pioneering agencies, the shop designs of mobile phone carriers as well as in the restaurant interiors of fast-food chains or the VIP lounges of major airlines. Companies such as a Coca-Cola, Lufthansa or Apple are trendsetters in their sectors and employ brand interiors to maximum effect. Corporate design, once the domain of large global players, has since been embraced by small- and medium-sized businesses, and today even local plumbers now have a letterhead, business card and website with matching vehicle livery. Corporate interiors, however, are still relatively rare, even among larger enterprises. The difference between a company's two-dimensional corporate presentation and the experience of its three-dimensional interiors is often striking. To be convincing, the 2D and 3D experience of a company must align and be as coherent as possible, and it should also embody the respective product or service. Companies that demonstrate a coherent and consistent approach are rare because the implementation is ultimately dependent on people – if a new head of marketing joins the company, his or her desire to leave their mark can torpedo a successful corporate identity strategy.

Branding, and accordingly branded interiors, play an especially important role in the fashion industry, whether for haute couture houses and their flagship stores, for instant guerrilla stores (set up by trendsetters such as Rei Kawakubo/Comme des Garçons) of the kind now emerging in metropolitan cities such as Berlin, for high-street chain stores or concept stores as well as for individual shops such as those by Paul Smith, which are each unique but recognisable. Hotel chains previously used to employ the same interior designs around the world. This was originally motivated by economies of scale, but also meant that the guest's experience inside the hotels differed only marginally, regardless of whether they were in New York, Berlin, New Delhi, Tokyo or Budapest. This triggered a counter-movement that aimed to tap into the genius loci, incorporating local characteristics into the interiors. Currently, certain unifying tendencies can again be observed, for example in the design of holiday resorts in Asia, which in themselves are very pleasant but follow similar patterns and therefore lack a specific sense of place.

Branded interiors are arenas of constant innovation, responding and adapting to changing market conditions and target groups, most recently for example with interactive applications. But as soon as everyone starts to follow the same trends, uniformity begins to displace variety. Interiors that are unconventional and have a character of their own are a good means of communicating and differentiating a brand's profile. Particularly effective are interiors that are different and have something unique about them but are also authentic, and therefore able to set new trends and generate new impulses. Uniqueness paired with a relevant interior design "history" is an increasingly powerful combination: the emphasis is on a strong profile as opposed to arbitrariness. The member hotels of the Design Hotels group, for example, differentiate themselves from mainstream hotels by offering a taste of lifestyle rather than just overnight accommodation, and budget hotels that employ effective branding have great development potential.

The design of branded interiors is therefore clearly marketing-driven and prioritises the "brand identity". Nevertheless, these interiors still need to help facilitate the workflow in the space and optimise the requisite processes. Given the shortage of skilled labour, greater attention is being given to providing an attractive environment for (potential) members of staff. Similarly, the opportunity for members of staff at all levels to be accorded a degree of status, whether a normal employee or high-flyer, is also desirable.

Property marketing also uses attractive interior design to create offers that appeal to a certain clientele. In many cases, the name of the architect is also a selling point (but rarely the interior designer, although the interiors are often what is shown). Factors that have a fundamental impact on the housing market, such as demographic change, are also reflected in the design of appropriate interiors, both to create demand as well as to increase the sale value.

Aside from when there is a good business argument, commercial interiors are only rarely people-focused. Work environments are mostly defined by functional considerations, such as the need to optimise processes and ease maintenance. The trick is to create an attractive environment that simultaneously motivates staff and represents the image of the company. Customers will accord even small companies greater competence when the premises they occupy are attractive and well-designed.

→ 29

The charm of an old warehouse lends this high-end restaurant a relaxed and authentic feeling. The graphic treatment of the surfaces of the cupboard doors seamlessly integrates the name of the restaurant and the door grip hole.
Noma Restaurant, Copenhagen, Denmark; 3XN architects

Reception area of the headquarters of a clinic operator: understated white and blue with enlivening elements such as an arcing plasterboard wall and a full-pile carpet. Quotes in the conference area underline the corporate design.
Sana Kliniken AG Headquarters, Ismaning, Germany; 100% interior Sylvia Leydecker

Cool and chilly: exposed concrete contrasts with coloured ice cream – convincingly executed in two and three dimensions.
Polka Gelato, London, England; Vonsung

The inspiring office as a brand characteristic in the London headquarters of the Internet giant – an atmosphere straight out of Star Trek.

Google Engineering Headquarters, London, England; Penson

**Animals at the doctors –
a simple and distinct
approach to corporate
design.**
Veterinary practice, Ratingen, Germany;
null2elf Dischek | Eitner GbR

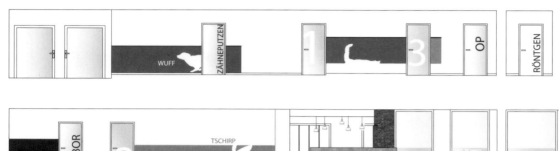

**A compelling, lifestyle-oriented
corporate design, accompanied
by an equally strong interior
design in black and white,
characterises this building
for a serviced office provider.**
Face To Face, Singapore; Ministry of Design MOD

Sir Raffles, head in the clouds: Singapore's colonial past mixed with modern chic forms the basis for the consistent corporate design of this boutique hotel.
The Club Hotel, Singapore;
Ministry of Design MOD

The conference room and cinema communicates the essence of the brand both cinematically and spatially.
Mercedes Benz Customer Centre,
Rastatt, Germany; spek Design

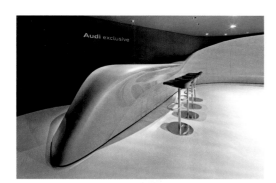

Smooth and sinuous flowing lines express the dynamism of the car manufacturer's corporate identity.
Audi Exclusive Lounge at the Geneva Auto Salon 2011, Geneva, Switzerland; Schmidhuber

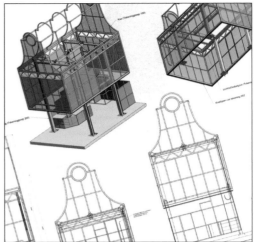

National clichés as brand elements – tulips, cheese and traditional buildings reinterpreted using contemporary means.
Schiphol Airport Lounge 3 / House of Tulips, Amsterdam, Holland; Tjep.

Beer branding translated to the interior of an airport bar.
Heineken Lounge, Newark Liberty
International Airport, New Jersey, USA; UXUS

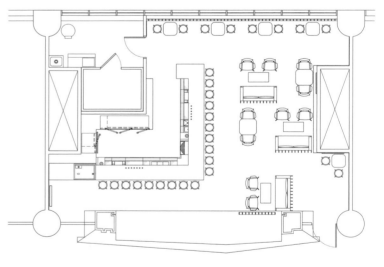

Digital made real: this concept store for an electronics firm aims to create a shopping experience using an interior concept that adheres to a global corporate design.
Sony Store, Los Angeles, California, USA;
Klein Dytham architecture

Splash: even utilitarian facilities such as car washes can benefit from brand design – here using echoes of 1950s America.
Clean Car, Berlin, Germany; Gisbert Pöppler

Social retail: on the "magazine street", brands meet people – analogue communication in a digital age.
Daikanyama T-Site, Tokyo, Japan;
Klein Dytham architecture

Destination brand: the interior design reflects the corporate livery and vocabulary of the international German airline.
Lufthansa Trademark Academy: Room for Innovations,
Seeheim, Germany; dan pearlman Markenarchitektur

The flowing forms and white surfaces of this residential loft in Manhattan combine the character of a gallery with a dramatic view.

Collector's Loft, New York City, New York, USA; UNStudio

Flowing forms characterise this restrained loft conversion in an old building.

Rounded Loft, Prague, Czech Republic; A1Architects

THE SOCIAL DIMENSION OF INTERIOR DESIGN

Commercially motivated branded interiors are comparatively superficial and showy. But aside from this, and also much more important ethically, interior design has a social responsibility and as such affords the capacity to influence society. The social component of interior design is a fundamental aspect. Good interior design does not have to be commercially driven or particularly showy; it can be self-motivated. An interior can also be still, modest and unassuming – a space that functions well, that is simply there and in which people feel comfortable. This quality should not be the exclusive reserve of an elite group who regard themselves as the guardians of good taste, simply by dint of having the financial means ("money creates taste" – Jenny Holzer). Regardless of earnings or background, everyone is entitled to enjoy a better quality of life through interiors in which they feel at ease. Good interior design, or for that matter taste, is not a question of wealth, gold tap fittings or designer status symbols such as Le Corbusier's Chaise Longue (which does not mean to say that these do not have their place). Inconspicuous mainstream design can be equally well suited as out-of-the-ordinary design, although the latter always runs the risk of dividing opinion.

"Human-centred" interior design aims to engender that much-cited sense of well-being, whether it be a feeling of safety and security in a hospital, a particular shopping experience, a sense of relaxation in a hotel, the perfect work environment in an office, or a feeling of leading a prestigious lifestyle. Adolf Loos accorded the interior a special status, arguing that the structure of a house plays a secondary role. The focus of his work was to create a warm and comfortable interior, although this cannot exist without the building structure. He drew a clear distinction between designing indoor and outdoor spaces: the reduction of his facade designs contrasts markedly with his designs for comfortable and often opulent interiors. He also allowed his clients the freedom to augment or complete the design after moving in, or by incorporating items of the client's furniture in the design from the outset.[1]

In the private realm, lifestyles are changing. The model of the nuclear family with a terraced house or a posh home in the suburbs is giving way to singles living in spacious penthouse apartments or factory lofts. Each of these different ways of living requires an appropriate interior design response: for example flexible hive structures or fine-grain cocoon structures in the centres of our metropolitan cities. In ideal circumstances, the interior design and the architecture work together in unison, or alternatively the user may wish to create a discrepancy – in either case, what is important is a standpoint that always considers how people will feel in that space when visiting it as well as when spending prolonged periods of time in it... whether they will enjoy whiling away time there or feel unpleasantly cooped up. Good interior design helps engender a sense of well-being, whatever the circumstances in life, and helps create quality of life so that people feel happy in the environment they are in.

→ 32

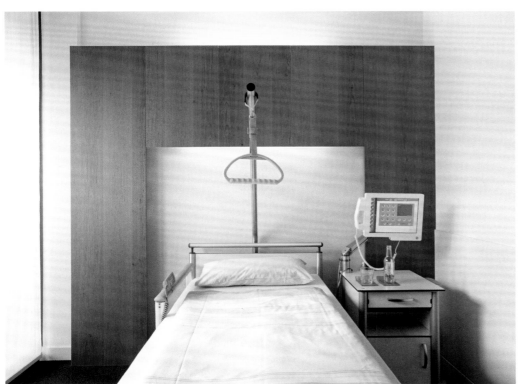

A pleasant atmosphere, comfort and high-quality materials support the process of recovery in hospital.
Sana Hospital, Bad Wildbad, Germany; 100% interior Sylvia Leydecker

Office spaces with a fun factor for a young design agency in the basement of a consecrated church.
Offices of the Upperkut Agency, Montreal, Canada; Jean de Lessard, Designer Créatif

Spot on: a powerful graphic effect in an unconventional office creates strong contrasts – light and dark, gold and black.
Office 00, Amsterdam, Holland; i29 interior architects

The attractive mirrored mosaic in the waiting room of a paediatrician's practice is better than a myriad of toys. It follows the contours of the wall and is also washable.
Practice for Paediatric Medicine and TCM, Drs. Schumann-Winckler-Schumann, Cologne, Germany; 100% interior Sylvia Leydecker

Cream: an elegant interior for older residents communicates a peaceful and comfortable atmosphere.
DKV Bremen Residence for the Elderly on the Contrescarpe, Bremen, Germany; Cossmann-Jacobitz Architekten – Uta Cossmann, two_Claudia de Bruyn

PRODUCT DESIGN

Interior designers also act from time to time as product designers in the context of interiors. What differentiates them from other product designers is that the products they design are always inseparably bound up with the interior and how it is used.

A successful interior design concept encompasses the entirety of the space – not just the floor plan and the surfaces that define it, such as the floor, walls and ceiling, but also the lighting and furniture, the colours and materials used. Interior designers therefore always have everything in mind from the design of the surrounding environment to that of the saltcellar, although only rarely are they responsible for all of this. Details that are out of keeping often interfere with the overall concept: clumsy decorations on reception desks, unsightly waste bins, homemade signage, paper serviettes with Easter decorations and condiment caddy, and last but not least a straggly Ficus benjamina – details that can quickly ruin the best interior design concept.

INTEGRATION

A fundamental part of developing a design concept for an interior is to bring together all the separate components into a coherent whole. The basis is a well-organised plan that is clear and works – that includes routes through the space and their relationship to the room's function, while also taking into account visual axes and views into the space. Atmospheres are created using materials, colour, light and forms. Colour, materials, light, furnishing, movement and directionality are interrelated and intertwined – removing one component changes the entire constellation and has a corresponding effect on the overall concept.

COLOUR

Colour defines spaces and has always been a favourite aesthetic means among interior designers. Ideally, colour is considered as an integral component of the design concept from the very beginning of the design process instead of being applied later in an arbitrary manner or as part of some predefined colour scheme. In the past, when the author was studying, architects only employed a very restricted palette of colours: the white of modernism, black, a "friendly" shade of anthracite and light grey! Fortunately, times have changed and colour is now commonly used for facades and interiors alike. Unfortunately, the use of colour often follows trends, and these run the risk of going out of fashion quickly.

MATERIAL

Materials have their own natural colouration, which can be used carefully to lend spaces a particular sensory atmosphere. The surfaces of woods such as Japanese birch, oriental rosewood, German oak, Canadian maple or African wenge create quite different atmospheres, as do different kinds of stone, for example Italian marble or rough-cloven slate. How the surface is treated also has an effect. Polished stone, sandblasted glass and waxed wood have a very different quality to bush-hammered stone, transparent glass and lacquered wood in terms of both their visual and haptic impression. Functional requirements must also be considered: non-slip floor surfaces are important not only in swimming baths to prevent accidents but also in restaurant kitchens or in the geriatric ward of a hospital. In societies where the population is aging, as it is in Japan and Europe, materials can be used to aid orientation for people suffering from different degrees of dementia.

Materials are not only an essential aspect of any interior; they are a joy to work with during the design process. The variety of materials and their possible combinations are practically endless. In interiors, we have a direct relationship to materials and can experience them physically as well as psychologically. The surface treatment and construction detailing determine how we perceive materials that are close by or that we can touch directly.

Actual materials of substance such as wood and stone still play the most important role. Imitation materials such as imitation wood or artificial stone have become much more widespread. These attempt to communicate a sense of quality with a lower-grade material that looks like the original. Designers, and therefore also interior designers, like to use innovative materials listed in materials databases. In the design world, the hype surrounding materials drives a continuing search for innovations made possible by new technologies. But traditional materials are still much in demand, and with them the skilled craftsmanship required to work them. Some materials databases take this into account. High-tech materials are often high-performance optimisations of existing materials – or else completely new materials. Early adopters among interior designers and clients are open to working with such materials as they often lead to new design possibilities. → 40

"All that is against nature cannot last in the long run."
Charles Darwin

Take a seat: for this set of chairs, the interior architect was both designer and craftsman.
Blütezeit Seating, Cologne, Germany; Karl Hussmann of Karl's Werkstatt

Japanese tradition, haiku, light and shadow, shoji proportions and wood – designed in Germany, handcrafted using innovative technology in Japan.
Lookalike Bench, Frankfurt am Main, Germany, and Asahikawa, Japan; DDC and Asahikawa Furniture Cooperative as patrons, Wolf Udo Wagner and Minoru Naghara as initiators, design by Sylvia Leydecker

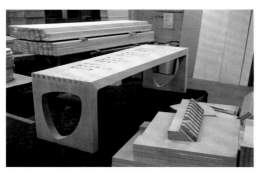

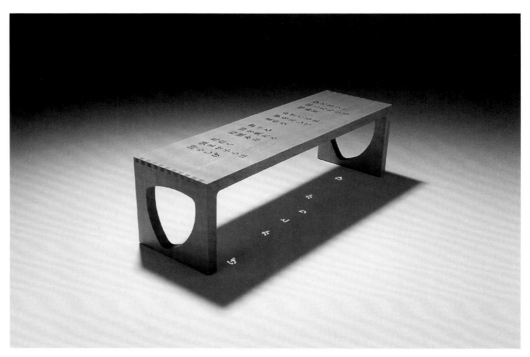

Flowing spaces with a few but quite different materials. The room cells are formed out of polyurethane foam with a polyurethane coating.
Beach house, Dutch coast; SAQ Architects

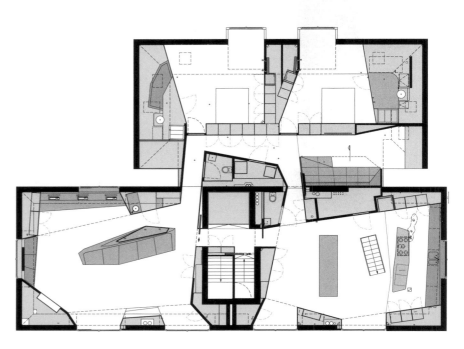

**Deluxe hospitality design
in a financial advisor's office –
warm grey tones, faceted
formal language and high-
quality finishes.**
Tebfin Office, Johannesburg, South Africa;
Source Interior Brand Architects

**Typographic: the club
in a former printworks
is decorated with giant
illuminated letters.**
BuckRogers Club, Fürstenfeldbruck,
Germany; camp Innenarchitektur.
Markenentwicklung

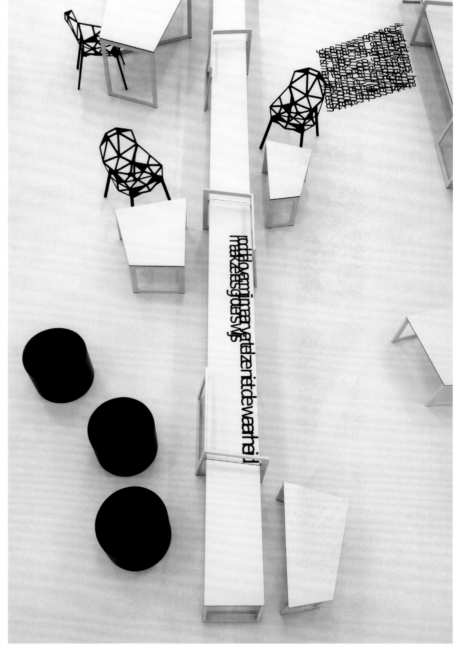

**Black and white:
poetry is used to
create identity in the
form of a graphical
patterning and
carpeting in a state
school building.**
School 03, Amsterdam, Holland;
i29 interior architects

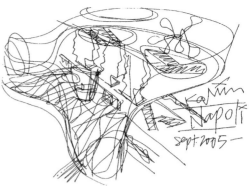

An Italian metro station forms a counterpart to the historical environment – digital forms and colours dominate while mirrors dematerialise boundaries.
Metronapoli – Università Station, Naples, Italy; Karim Rashid

An elegant, minimalist staircase in a renovated old farmhouse leads upwards, its lightweight sculptural form accentuated by the use of invisible supports and materials such as marble and glass.
Casalgrande Padana, Conversion of an old farmhouse, Casalgrande, Reggio Emilia, Italy; Kengo Kuma & Associates

An altar space using just two materials – concrete and oak – and one colour: white.
Altar in the Lutherkirche, Düsseldorf, Germany; Lepel & Lepel

Clarity: the view from the stage of the former food hall affords a panorama of the colourful library in its entirety.
SchulStadtbücherei, Arnsberg, Germany; Keggenhoff | Partner

The graphic treatment of the walls of this corridor in a health centre saves it from becoming sterile and faceless.
EWK Spandau Medical Centre, Berlin, Germany;
r2_innenarchitektur und design

Peeling: a simple shop design enlivened by a play of layers: one side is black, the other white.
DURAS Nagashima, Kuwana, Japan;
Sinato – Chikara Ohno

VALUES

The current changing attitude towards the authenticity of materials is particularly interesting. The scale at which the appearance of materials is being imitated is quite amazing. Elementary and well-loved materials such as wood and concrete are now available as laminate, PVC or even tile imitations which look deceptively realistic and are sometimes even preferred over the actual material. They are less expensive, easier to clean and maintain, and their visual quality is more consistent than that of the real thing. For the same reasons, these imitations even come with a fake patina, which in real life would normally appear over time. The imitation of materials has a long tradition – one need only recall the technique of painted faux marbling – but the available technology is now ever more refined. Not all that long ago, the quality of PVC wood imitations was very poor, but now the visual appearance is surprisingly realistic. The artificial products cannot, however, replicate other properties of the original such as the haptic quality. In the past, imitations were regarded as a "cheap copy", as inferior to the real thing, but today the imitation is not always a poor copy. For certain requirements the imitation might even be the better solution. Tiling that looks like wood may be a higher-grade material than a comparable, perhaps inferior wood product, and it also offers additional properties that may be desirable. The quality of the material should therefore be considered independently of the authenticity of the material.

Which product to use is a question of standpoint. For many, the qualities and patina of an authentic material are undesirable because they make it look worn and uncared for. At the same time the imitations are given an artificial impression of having aged, which seems absurd. The visible process of aging, which is part of the charm of a real material such as wood or metal, is not present in the same way in the imitation. The replica material looks static, lifeless and also predictable. In Japanese culture, which has a tradition of clear and simple interiors, the play of light and shadow and of natural phenomena is held in high regard, as is the quality of patina, which is appreciated as a specific aesthetic quality (wabi-sabi). For example, the value accorded to a copper vessel increases with the time it requires to acquire a patina. The instant patina of an artificially produced surface simply does not compare to the charm and aura of the natural patina.

In this respect, real materials will perhaps after all be accorded the appreciation they are due. For this there has to be an appreciation of their beauty and quality; think of the smooth waxed surface of a flat-planed piece of wood. This is where craftsmanship plays a role. Industrial manufacturing and mass production cannot achieve the same level of perfection that a craftsman invests in an individual piece. Adolf Loos, in his day, was a proponent of efficient building, not just in the design of the floor plan but also through *Raumplan*, through thinking in terms of volume.

For him ornamentation was as an economic extravagance. Today individual character is mass-produced. Modular building systems, the choice from a selection of colours and decorative surface treatments as well as a variety of possible combinations create the impression of individual choice, but ultimately it remains cloned mass customisation. Discerning interior design goes a step further, creating individual and unrepeatable interiors designed specifically to fit the respective context and based on overall concepts that are unique to each and every situation.

As a response to the dilemma of mass production and perfect clean interiors, a renewed fascination with patina and traces of wear and tear has arisen as seen in "shabby chic" and "rough luxe" as well as in traditional craftsmanship, and DIY is likewise being hyped. Vintage and retro are once again popular, and in the fashion world, for example, go hand in hand with streetstyle. People now appreciate the traces of use, traditional craft techniques, high-quality short-runs or custom-made items, either for their outstanding quality and excellent workmanship or conversely for their hand-made look and the love that has gone into making them: an example from the do-it-yourself scene is urban knitting. Soul and authenticity coupled with the history of a building are skilfully juxtaposed to create a contemporary interior. For many this is true luxury as it responds to real human needs and evokes genuine emotions.

Manual work is held in such high regard because it requires the skill of craftsmanship, the ability to work exactly and in accordance with the material's properties, which in turn is based on intimate knowledge of the material. Quality and the details of good workmanship go hand in hand. One need only think of ornamental decorations and the meaningful arrangement of individual components in space, as seen in Indian carvings or Arabic calligraphy, which in many cases are sumptuous, ostentatious works of great splendour. Traditional craftsmanship also satisfies basic emotional needs and heightens our appreciation of values from the past. But this on its own cannot offer us a model for the future. Interior design that is forward-looking always encompasses something new and represents some form of progress. A mixed approach can be seen in the combination of art and architecture and the collaboration of engineers and architects at art schools like the Cranbrook Academy of Art near Detroit or the Bauhaus. Such progressive teaching models, which combine approaches from art and architecture, have brought forth numerous famous protagonists of architecture and design.

This principle applies similarly for interdisciplinary collaborations between creatives and industry and science. Here interdisciplinary teams work together to find market applications for new, pioneering technologies. At present, examples of this approach are few and far between, but interior design that aims to be forward-looking will need to work from this basis. Creative verve, inquisitive research, explosive discovery, stimulating interdisciplinary and fun-driven collaborations, thinking out of the box paired with a sense of realism can provide new impulses for the field of interior design. But progress and development also means taking a step into the unknown and requires a readiness to take risks. And although the digitalisation of our world continues unrelentingly, electronic spaces – virtual light and virtual materials – can never replace the real world in its enormous complexity; however perfect the copy may be, it can only ever be a replica. → 42

A sense of time: this private apartment exudes the charm of times past.
Apartment at Maybachufer, Berlin, Germany; Gisbert Pöppler

TRENDS

Jumping someone else's train...
Robert Smith

Predictions for future trends can be useful when, for example, they tell us about user behaviour. Oscar Niemeyer said that we have the task "to create today the past of tomorrow".[2] But the danger is that we design today for the world of tomorrow, and then when it is built – it is from yesterday. This is a further reason why it can be useful to look ahead from the present day.

There are countless trends that are more or less short-lived. Wellness is one trend that has since developed into a thriving industry around the world. A soothing gingko tea in a spa will be served in a very different interior environment to that where black tea is served as a teabag. In all aspects of design for the elderly and Universal Design, whether in the care sector in nursing homes and serviced apartments or in housing for the elderly, good interior design is a must. The healthcare sector profits from demographic developments all over the world, whether it be for the provision of basic care needs or the comprehensive support of well-heeled private patients in hospitals.

In the workplace, changing communication patterns brought about by information technology, the increasing flexibility of work processes, and the trend towards greater transparency and shallow business hierarchies have given rise to so-called nomadic offices and open workspaces. Hot on the heels of this trend follows the problem of acoustics. The deficits of such spaces, which are a factor of the space maximisation of such interiors, need to be compensated for through the acoustics. While much attention is devoted to the visual appearance as well as other factors, such as making it easy to clean, the acoustics are often neglected or the acoustic potential is not exploited. Relevant data for the acoustics is required in order to create pleasant soundscapes (virtual acoustic spaces); put another way the quality of the input data of the acoustic surfaces is crucial for virtual sound design simulations.

While 3D visualisation systems do not yet offer corresponding virtual acoustic simulations, noise absorption factors and noise reflections are still not considered adequately in the design of spaces. This results in spaces with poor acoustic conditions – in schools, in conference rooms or restaurants for example – and high noise levels in offices, entrance lobbies and corridors, which in turn can have a harmful effect on our health and well-being.

Environmentally conscious interior design is about much more than "prettifying" spaces, as the cradle-to-cradle visionary Michael Braungart[3] has provocatively termed the work of designers. While companies certainly like to market an eco-friendly image to demonstrate their credibility and awareness of customer needs, superficial greenwashing has become so widespread that people have grown wise to it. In many cases, one can observe an understandable desire for a natural look, using natural colours and materials made of renewable raw materials. But in practice, interior design is much more complex. In an age in which sustainability and environmental consciousness are of increasing importance, green interiors are much in demand, as evidenced by LEED, BREEAM and DGNB. The ecological certification of interior fitouts is still relatively uncommon and only rarely implemented, mostly because their cost is disproportionately high in comparison to the cost of the building works. But this should be seen in the context of more than just the initial investment. The running costs such as life-cycle costs and facility management also need to be considered. Possible approaches range from the avoidance of hard-to-separate composite materials to better recyclability strategies or cradle-to-cradle concepts. Ever more products are coming onto the market to cater to this need: modular systems, flexible and reconfigurable furniture that can be moved around on wheels, coloured textiles and so on. Despite this, the majority of offices continue to be inoffensive and innocuous interiors furnished with grey carpets, white walls and black swivel chairs "for decisionmakers" – more often than not the green future is not quite as revolutionary and innovative in reality. Unless, that is, interior designers are involved: in such cases the client is generally more aware of how interiors can enhance the image of a company, of their potential to improve work processes and staff motivation, and it shows. → 49

Strong contrasts and strong colours – a symbiosis that nevertheless manages to be harmonious.
Bar le Lounge,
Ste-Julie, Québec,
Canada;
Jean de Lessard,
Designer Créatif

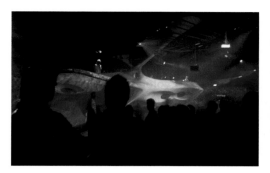

DJing and VJing: a symbiosis of sound and light in the legendary Cocoon Club – an interior design that has yet to be equalled.
CocoonClub, Frankfurt am Main, Germany; 3deluxe

Bar and restaurant – the flexible spatial concept of the latter has the atmosphere of a spacious trattoria but can also accommodate an intimate family gathering.
MAZZO, Amsterdam, Holland; Concrete Architectural Associates

Shelter: this "relax box" offers a protective enclosure within the entrance lobby of a health education centre.
ROC Health & Care, Apeldoorn, Holland; Tjep.

The redesigned restaurant in the iconic Barbican Centre in London fits perfectly into the existing surroundings while also offering something for the soul.

Barbican Food Hall, London, England; SHH

Eye-catching: this optician presents glasses as precious objects in small display cases – white and sculptural, with a hint of green.
FreudenHaus Optik, Munich, Germany; tools off.architecture

Points of view – depending on where you stand, you see either an abstract jumble of lines or an architectural drawing of the interior behind the walls of this stairwell in a 1970s building.
Anna, Basel, Switzerland; ZMIK

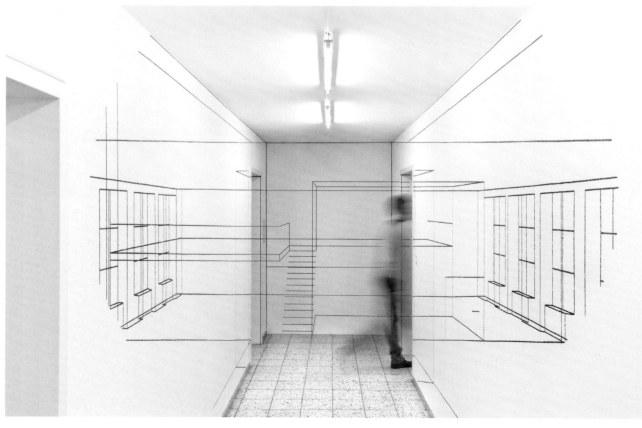

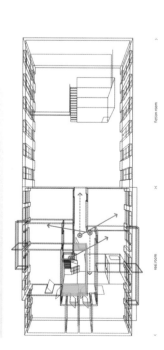

**Transport design and dining –
a harmonious blend of modern
design and traditional British food,
and not a trace of pub nostalgia.**
Canteen, London, England;
Universal Design Studio

**A room for entertaining:
a light-filled room for lots
of guests in a private house.**
Private residence, Ypres, Belgium;
Pieter Vanrenterghem Interior Architecture

**The monochrome and rigorously
symmetrical layout of this high-end
fashion store is illuminated by a
star-shaped pattern of neon lights.**
Shine Leighton Center, Hong Kong, China;
NC Design & Architecture Limited

**House in a typical Tokyo
neighbourhood – compact
and comfortable, the
contrasting decorative end
wall unites the entire space.**
Sasao House, Tokyo, Japan;
Klein Dytham architecture

In addition to acoustics, a further aspect of the ecological quality of interiors is the indoor air climate. Indoor air quality and the reduction of harmful emissions is a topic that features increasingly on the conference circuit. In new buildings, sick building syndrome is now recognised as a problem. Substances such as formaldehyde, alkenes and VOCs in general have differing degrees of toxicity; benzene, for example, has been proven to be carcinogenic. Building materials should be selected that have general building control approval. Products and materials that are completely odourless and free of pollutants are already possible from a production point of view; they are just more expensive. Interior design must consider olfactory criteria, both in terms of the subjective perception of building users as well as their health.

Another interesting problem in the context of green building, particularly in Europe, is the public subsidisation of insulation measures for existing buildings to improve their energy efficiency. As with corporate identities, the identity of cities is also manifested in part through their energy-efficiency credentials. At the same time, the appearance of buildings and ensembles is defined substantially by their facades, and the eradication of their aesthetic qualities as a result of insulation measures therefore also impacts on the quality of life in cities. Interior design therefore has a responsible role to play in the renovation of existing buildings because it can affect a building's appearance. Sustainability in interior design cannot be reduced to energy balance calculations alone but must also take aesthetic qualities, which are equally long-lasting, into consideration – and that means choosing appropriate insulation strategies.

A further overarching trend is the availability of living environments for different lifestyles: whether minimalist, Bauhaus-inspired, classicist, romantic, high-tech or eclectic, all these styles can be seen in the manufacturer's set designs. Consumers never cease to be fascinated by the retro-style – a mixture of glamour, olde worlde and rustic chic. Interior design can cater for many different lifestyle environments from minimalism to horror vacui baroque.

Finally, one should not forget that attention can shift to new topics simply because they present an opportunity to earn money, for example through conferences, consulting services, licensing or the sale of new products. In principle, however, the consideration of all these aspects – from acoustics to communication to emissions – is what constitutes the complexity of good interior design that neglects neither one nor the other aspect.

"I have never thought... that man's freedom consists in his being able to do whatever he wills, but that he should not... be forced to do what is against his will."

Jean-Jacques Rousseau

INTERIOR DESIGN IS A REFLECTION OF THE ERA

Lifestyle is a phenomenon that has always existed and the desire to portray it did not first emerge in the modern age. Interiors communicate the lifestyle of the inhabitant to the rest of the world; they project emotions into space and stimulate motivations and desires. Authentic interiors that are an appropriate expression of our time and reflect the age we live in, differ from those of the past. Authenticity is here the key: authentic spaces communicate credibility, while artificial pretensions (as seen, for example, in the field of the so-called "creative office") reveal themselves as such in stylistic uncertainty and confusion. Interior design is for people, and designers need to be aware of essential human needs and how to cater to them.

The popularity of psychoanalysis in the post-war period is manifested, for example, in the name given to the Womb Chair designed for Knoll. Scandinavian design and its formal language are still very much in demand. Many current chair designs look like copies of moulded chairs from past decades. Designs from 50 years ago are still felt to be modern today. The same goes for architecture and the so-called Bauhaus style, which has been around for almost a hundred years. Clearly something is wrong here.

Progressive design requires a suitably enlightened client who is willing and courageous enough to be responsible for putting forward-looking designs into practice. Successful projects are ultimately the product of a collaboration between interior designer and client. The better the combination, and the chemistry between them, the better the end result. A prominent example of one such successful collaboration is the work of the designer Philippe Starck and the hotelier Ian Schrager, who, over an extended period, jointly realised a series of innovative and pioneering hotel concepts.

The use of smart technologies and materials is an expression of our time. The machine age has passed, the mass consumption and mass production of serially prefabricated parts has become normality, and we are now heading for new shores. While we are only beginning to make use of smarter and cleverer materials, the first steps have already been taken. A part of this is the integration of new and old building fabric, especially in Europe. Interior design today, as well as in the past, has always rejected standard formulas in favour of specific, tailor-made solutions. New buildings and the design of their interiors are, by contrast, able to accommodate progressive concepts from the very beginning. Ignoring this in the early concept phases represents a missed opportunity. Visionary architecture needs equally visionary interior design that does not simply adhere to tried-and-tested principles, but continues to develop and to push forward the boundaries. → 52

The interior of this Japanese residence is characterised by the subtle interplay of materials, traditional shoji proportions and nature.
Kitanokaze; Nakayama Architects

Small made big: by playing with proportions and using soft colours, this interior shifts our perspective and sense of perception to that of a child.
Baby Café, Tokyo, Japan; Nendo

In this conversion of a 1980s house, enlarging the openings allows space to flow freely, while the subtle pigmented colouring of the walls gives them a powder-like appearance.
Villa, Neuss, Germany; Silvia Pappa – Innenarchitekten

Craftsmanship at its finest: every detail of the interior of this 70 m long luxury yacht has been tailor-made to the highest quality.
Numptia Super Yacht;
Achille Salvagni Architetti

BUILDING TYPES

Numerous different areas of work are relevant for interior design: from private houses, trade fair stands, office interiors or healthcare facilities to schools, hotels or the sensitive conversion of historic buildings.

As Louis Sullivan postulated in his credo "form follows function", aesthetics are inseparably bound up with function. Formation processes in nature are always influenced by functional requirements and for the most part, people find them "beautiful". There is a seamless transition between the rational and emotional aspects of a design, which translates in space to the correspondence between emotional well-being and smooth working processes. The functional and technical aspects of interiors for the elderly, for example, which are attracting greater interest as society ages as a whole, focus on requirements such as barrier-free access, process optimisation, energy efficiency, fire safety, cost effectiveness, hygiene, accident prevention, incontinence, multimorbidity, dementia, etc. At the same time, the olden days are of relevance in interiors for dementia sufferers, because traditional reminders of how one once lived refer to the individual biographies of the residents, helping them to feel more at home. Good interior design, like biographical therapy, does not look solely to the past but looks firmly to the future from the present. This can mean taking account of future developments in care concepts that may give rise to different ways of staff organization, as well as current developments in science and technology that help to improve work processes. In this respect, flexible spaces are sustainable in the true sense of the word. This applies equally to office interiors, hotels and other interior spaces.

Healthcare encompasses a wide range of interiors from the traditional doctor's surgery and medical care centre to wards in hospitals or rehabilitation centres to care homes and hospices. On the one hand, healthcare interiors should optimise processes and workflow and fulfil hygiene requirements, and on the other they must give patients and their relatives a sense of security, trust and reassurance as well as serve as an attractive environment for staff.

Commercial trade fair stands, on the other hand, serve typically as an advertisement for a company, and must vie for attention with other stands in the immediate vicinity. They need to serve as a magnet for the envisaged target group, display the products or services effectively, should be easy to assemble and disassemble, and in many cases be re-usable and modular. They should contain spaces for presentation as well as communication, and sometimes also for refreshments and comestibles. The production of trade fair stands is a fast-moving business that requires commitment and the willingness to work under constant pressure. There are many players involved and the field is hotly contested by a variety of competitors.

Restaurants and hotels are a favourite field of work for interior design offices because high-quality interior design is known to represent a competitive advantage. Guests should feel – and want to feel – attracted to the interior. The interior design plays an essential role in creating a sense of hospitality and is indispensable for good hotel and restaurant experiences – whether for a luxury burger bar or low-budget city hotel or an exclusive star restaurant, cocktail bar or a grand hotel.

A further interesting area of work for interior designers is shop design; here interior designers are most often commissioned to design attractive, individual and therefore authentic shop interiors. Shop design is both about communicating a brand identity as well as an efficient interior and works hand in hand with traditional shopfitting. The key parameter is the turnover and profit per square metre both in retail shops as well as department stores. But retailers are increasingly becoming cross-channel players who operate several parallel distribution channels at once – physical stores, online shops and mail-order print catalogues. The shopping world is therefore in a state of flux.

The work of interior architects for private clients often begins with simple lifestyle consulting and can range from showroom apartments for housing associations to private villas in the high-end luxury segment. Loft conversions and tips on "how to maximise space in a small hallway" are also part of the work of interior designers. Solutions for everyday needs are meaningful and important to people, and are a more realistic reflection of what goes on outside the pages of glossy magazines. This is not the place for prize-winning design experiments but for down-to-earth, practical solutions. Having acted as a resident expert for two live German radio call-in shows on the topics of "What to do with an empty room when the children leave home" and "Redesigning the home", I have experienced first-hand what it means to help solve often quite banal and everyday problems.

The concept of an exhibition is a holistic affair in which both the venue as well as the didactic concept of the exhibition plays a role. In addition, routes through the exhibition, security aspects and conservation requirements such as illumination and air humidity levels also need to be carefully considered. In museums, theatres and cinemas, large numbers of people come together to be entertained, which entails incorporating a whole series of necessary security and safety considerations into the overall design concept for the interior.

Over the last decades, wellness has developed internationally into a vast market, generating a need for spaces with an especially soothing atmosphere. Recreational interiors, such as swimming pools but also yachts and private aircraft, can be significantly enhanced through interior design, but such tasks typically require specialist knowledge generally learned in practice and not during studies, for example in the use of specific materials or construction methods.

A final area of interior design is the design of reception areas and lounges. These are noteworthy because this is where the first impressions influencing the overall experience are made. In principle, this also applies to corridors and paths through buildings, although as secondary circulation spaces these are not always given the attention they deserve. The opposite applies to reception areas, which interior designers are often commissioned to design because these spaces are the first point of contact, even when other related spatial situations are sometimes neglected.

The breadth of topics touched upon in this introduction to interior design will be further elaborated in the following chapters. Interior design is for people, and represents a complex system with a fascinating ability to stimulate and be reinvented over and over again in new ways for the benefit of its users. Spaces are omnipresent and affect everyone who resides in them. The conscious design of interiors – with or without the help of interior designers, but better with – represents an opportunity that should be grasped as a "common sense" approach to how we use space rather than as a means of their exclusive treatment.

1 Adolf Loos, "von einem armen reichen Manne" (Poor little rich man), *Neues Wiener Tagblatt*, 26/04/1900.

2 *The Curves of Time – The Memoirs of Oscar Niemeyer* (London: Phaidon Press, 2000/2007/2010), p. 129.

3 Lecture at the Interior Designers Convention of the German North-Rhine Westphalian Chamber of Architects during the interzum fair 2011.

Bar design with club character.
The Club Hotel, Singapore;
Ministry of Design MOD

Live on stage: the lighting concept, glass and mirrors turn this bedroom into a private stage.
Alessandro Bergamo House, Oderzo, Italy;
Simone Micheli Architetto

The sales area of the bakery has an almost industrial character while the seating niche offers a cosy atmosphere in which to enjoy bread rolls and coffee.
Treiber Bakery, Leinfelden-Echterdingen (left) and Bernhausen (right), Germany; RAISERLOPES

Play of light: strips of light in the floors, walls and ceiling of the cinema deconstruct the surfaces of the cinema's interior.
W Hotel, London, England; Concrete Architectural Associates

Carefully directed light and a subtle formal language create a calm and pleasant atmosphere – and prove that white does not have to be sterile.
OLIVOMARE Restaurant, London, England;
Architetto Pierluigi Piu

Chairs climbing up the walls...
Private residence, Toronto, Canada; Jennifer Worts

Trade fair stands – such as this two-storey stand – are also a part of the interior designer's repertoire.
Siemens trade fair stand for the Interkama 2007, Hannover Messe; Germany; bahlsconcepts

Down-to-earth: a clearly structured office environment with integral lounges for informal communication.
Aareon AG office, Mainz, Germany; andernach und partner

Golden stones: the riverbed stones in the staircase for this apartment house on the Goltsteinstrasse make reference to the location's genius loci – it was once an engineering works on the banks of the Rhine.
GoltsteinForum Cologne, Garbe Group, Germany; 100% interior Sylvia Leydecker

A house in a house: this pop-up bar in the middle of the Tent London design fair employs a simple black and white colour scheme, seats like large inverted beakers and a curtain that is cut-off at the just the right (shoulder) height – intriguing from outside and comfortable to be in.
Tent design fair, London, England; Vonsung

The showrooms of this kitchen appliance manufacturer communicate the company's own culture, using ingredients such as materials and formal language.
Gaggenau Showroom, Amsterdam, Holland; eins:33 GmbH

The unconventional branding of a mail-order pharmacy is clearly communicated in this high-street store.
DocMorris Pharmacy, Limburg, Germany; Klaus Bürger Architektur

This store design for a perfume chain is based on expert retail know-how and seamlessly incorporates the corporate design.
Douglas: Luxury & Elegance in Düsseldorf, Germany; Schwitzke & Partner

The coloured t-shirts and brand-oriented photography are shown off to maximum effect in the minimal interiors of this international clothing chain.
American Apparel, Berlin, Germany; Philipp Mainzer Office for Architecture and Design

The maker of a dark-coloured lemonade mingles the company's global corporate design with the Mexican bird-gods that adorn its training facilities.
Espacio C Mixcoac, Mexico City, Mexico; ROW Studio

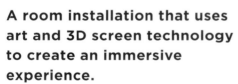

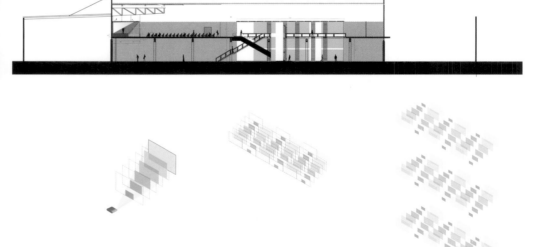

A room installation that uses art and 3D screen technology to create an immersive experience.
Panasonic Convention, Munich, Germany;
Atelier Brückner GmbH

Japanese craftsmanship meets modern design in this 36th-storey bar which makes particular use of light and shadow.
MIXX Bar & Lounge, Tokyo, Japan; Curiosity

Stylish and luxurious hotel space – a traditional field for interior design offices.
Hilton Frankfurt Airport Hotel, Frankfurt am Main, Germany; JOI-Design

Minimalism is not here: hotel spaces that transform into a design adventure playground.
Hotel Überfluss, Bremen, Germany;
Concrete Architectural Associates

DEVELOPING A DISCIPLINE: INTERIOR DESIGN EDUCATION AND RESEARCH

JOANNE CYS

Interior design has a relatively short history and it is generally accepted that it is still developing as a discipline, a professional practice and a field of research. The role and contribution of specialised interior design education has evolved, and is evolving, in parallel with the maturation of the discipline. Education historically served to legitimise and professionalise interior design practice by distinguishing qualified practitioners from "untrained" amateurs, namely the interior decorators who had pioneered the practice in the United Kingdom and North America during the late ninetee 19th and early 20th centuries. This chapter will focus upon the context, relevance and contribution of interior design education: originally as professional training; then as study content required to meet standards of graduate capability (in some regions manifest as for programme accreditation and knowledge required for examination for certification to practice or use of title); and increasingly as research contributing to both the theoretical knowledge of the discipline and the practice of the profession.

Traditional texts included in curricula for interior design students have largely portrayed interior design history as a history of interior spaces, regardless of the profession of the author.[1] Within the last decade another history has emerged. Influenced by feminist theory, it reveals the practice, motivations, limitations and opportunities of the individuals who founded the profession, as opposed to the conventional presentation of a chronology of interiors designed mostly, but not always, by architects.

Pioneer practitioners of the late 19th and early 20th centuries had no formal qualifications in the specific field that was to become their profession, a field initially called interior decoration and now known globally as interior design and, in some regions, as interior architecture. They professed (and published) their expertise as innate good taste and style. As Stanley Abercrombie points out: "Near the beginning of the century... Elsie de Wolfe could declare herself a professional simply by having some cards engraved, announcing her availability as a designer: there were no standards."[2] Yet there is evidence that many participated in activities to gain knowledge and skills to influence and extend their creative practice. Although not formal learning, activities such as travel, writing and publication, visual art appreciation and association with others that afforded opportunities for skill and knowledge development were indeed educative. In the USA, journalist Ruby Ross Wood instructed herself as the ghostwriter for Elsie de Wolfe's *The House in Good Taste* (1913) and later produced her own interior decorating text;[3] Frances Elkins accompanied her brother, architect David Adler, when he travelled abroad to study at the École des Beaux-Arts;[4] and Eleanor McMillen undertook courses in business and art history.[5] UK designer Eileen Gray enrolled in drawing courses at schools in London and Paris and sought lacquer lessons from a Japanese master.[6] In Australia, Marion Hall Best made use of her acquaintance with a professor at Sydney University to attend architecture lectures.[7] Others, such as Syrie Maughan in the UK undertook on-the-job training in Fortnum & Mason's antique department.[8] Pioneers such as Candice Wheeler and Eleanor McMillen publicly espoused the importance of education and actively promoted it through published articles as an attainment that distinguished professionals from amateurs.[9] It was in this context of desire for professional acknowledgement that formal interior design programmes were consolidated in design schools in many regions around the world during the 1930s, 1940s and 1950s, simultaneous with the ascension of national professional associations and the publication of interior design journals.

Many contributors to the creation of significant works in interior design's brief history, however, have been educated in something other than interior design. Penny Sparke's *A Century of Design: Design Pioneers of the Twentieth Century*[10] describes the majority of influential creators of important interiors as "architect-designers" or as "figures in architecture and design", yet of the 82 individuals she profiles, only Finnish designer Antti Nurmesniemi is credited with an interior design qualification.[11] Possibly the best known of all British interior designers, David Hicks studied at London's Central School of Art and Design, where he undertook a broad curriculum during the 1950s.[12] Hicks reflected on his education: "Qualifications are important, but even more vital is any period of relative freedom that can be spent exploring alternatives to the full…During this process of exploration, I realized that I would never reach the top in any of the fields I had chosen to study: theatre design, painting, book illustration or typography. What I did discover was a profound and lasting interest in the way people live."[13]

The complexity of the connection (or lack of connection) between academic qualification and the field of professional practice continues today. When asked to nominate the leading interior designers of recent times, interior design students across the globe are likely to offer names such as Philippe Stark, Petra Blaisse, Eva Jiřičná, Mark Newson, Zaha Hadid, Andrée Putman and Thomas Heatherwick. Of this example group of globally renowned designers, only Philippe Stark undertook formal interior design education. "Stark was registered as a student of furniture and interior design at the Camondo School in Paris in 1968 but, it seems, was seldom present at classes."[14] This condition has caused some interior design

educators around the world to carefully consider their academic practice and the positioning of their interior design programmes. As Joo Yun Kim identifies, "…interior design is actually a place where any other designers from other fields, such as architects, industrial designers, can easily approach and work in… Am I a person who educates students to become designers similar to architects but not architects?"[15] For some commentators such as Suzie Attiwill, the questions of professional identity (who creates interiors) and professional territory (what interior design is) are not the most critical factors for the profession and education. She suggests that it is in the greater interests of the discipline to "…pose questions in relation to practice – asking 'how' as distinct from 'what is interior design?' or 'who is an interior designer?'"[16] This presents another role for interior design education, to not only provide skill and training for professional practice, but to contribute to a disciplinary body of knowledge and a field of research. This is evidence of a maturing of thinking about interior design research: its role in the education of future interior designers, its position within the global academy and its contribution to the continuing development of a body of knowledge for this relatively new discipline.

In his review of the literature of women in interior design history, John Turpin proposes that the lack of scholarship dedicated to interior design history is due to the fact that most academics in the discipline do not possess an advanced research degree. It should also be acknowledged that a high proportion of interior design academics do not hold professional qualifications in the field and therefore their research interests are likely to be focused elsewhere. There is also evidence of confusion, or ignorance, regarding interior design within other academic disciplines. In the introductory chapter for their edited issue of *The Journal of Architecture* Barbara Penner and Charles Rice explain that the articles in the journal explore the domestic interior through a cultural perspective and "… define a new field of inquiry into the interior, one that is of particular relevance to historians, theorists and architects concerned with the positioning of domesticity within contemporary culture".[17] The value of this research to interior designers is not recognised here. Lucinda Havenhand recounts another example whereby the call for papers for an Association of Collegiate Schools of Architecture conference invited contributions from a range of allied and associated fields, but not from interior design.[18]

John Turpin takes a fundamental and grounding position when he reminds us that "First and foremost, the future of interior design lies in its students. Their perceptions of the world are, for the most part, based on the information they receive during their education."[19] For the future of the profession, it is critical for interior design education to find motivation for development beyond what has been described as "Interior designers'… near-paranoiac need to define 'this is what we do'".[20]

Instead of continuing academic and professional emulation of architecture, Havenhand encourages interior design to accept its "marginalized" position and learn from Karen Franck's "Women's Ways of Knowing" to identify the valuable approaches such a perspective can provide for interior design education and practice. She urges interior design to "… acknowledge its marginality… [to]… provide a starting place for change, innovation and the successful establishment of an autonomous and distinct identity for it. In this light… interior design can be seen as having the potential for being a truly transgressive, creative, and transforming activity with a unique role to play in design practice and education."[21]

Scholars Ellen Klingenberg, Andrew Stone and Suzie Attiwill perceive the benefits of participation in a discipline, an area of study or a field of research that neither directly results from, nor is the generator of, interior design practice. Describing the approach to interiors education at the Faculty of Design at Oslo National Academy of the Arts, Klingenberg positions interior architecture as an entire field of study rather than as discreet entities of academia and practice. She observes that, historically, what interior designers do as a practice has set the standard for interior design education and argues that it is now necessary to "…describe the difference between field and profession, so that the field of interior architecture can be described as something in itself, a field for research and development, regardless of the profession".[22] In acknowledging that much interior design knowledge is silent, being undocumented, unwritten and unpublished, Klingenberg[23] calls for the development and dissemination of a kind of theory for the discipline that is generated by, and applicable to, both academia and practice alike. Stone also identifies gains that may result from an approach to interior design distanced from professional practice. Within the context of tertiary design education in the United Kingdom, he asserts that education needs to provide future interior designers with the ability to "… reflect seriously and confidently on their subject… to distance themselves from industry demands in order to invest in the subject critically and creatively".[24] Stone proposes that there is opportunity and need for education to address the relevance of practice in less commercial realms such as "… speculative practice… social responsibility… technological innovation… [and]… spatial experimentation…".[25] Participation and skill development in methods of speculative and experimental practice is a whole of career investment. Attiwill also views interior design education as an ongoing experience, something that does not end upon entry to the profession. She provides moderation with her proposal "to counter-pose the expectation of the profession of graduates with the expectation of graduates of the profession".[26]

Other commentators, however, connect interior design research more closely with the profession. US academics Denise Guerin and Jo Ann Asher Thompson argue that universal acceptance of the value of interior design can result from (Master's level) education that "… must prepare future practitioners to implement evidence-based design criteria into the design process and thus improve the quality of the designed environment".[27] Guerin and Thompson maintain that educators must teach interior design students the value of research[28] and that through their proposed Master's level education model, "… Interior Design students will be trained to be good consumers of research" to ensure that the spaces they design in practice "… enhance the health, safety and welfare of clients and all users of interior spaces".[29] Although there is acknowledgement of the need for a "partnership"[30] between design educators and design practitioners, Guerin and Thompson's view of research is fundamentally as a service to practice.

Caren Martin and Denise Guerin[31] formalised the study *The Interior Design Profession's Body of Knowledge (IDBOK)* with an extensive literature search of publications within, and related to, interior design. The listing is predominantly comprised of quantitative scientific and behavioural research publications that justify the public importance of interior design which is a regulated and protected profession in some states of the US. Earlier writing by Guerin and Martin[32] describes their approach to defining the body of knowledge through "… a review of documents from professional interior designers' representative stages of the career cycle, that is, education, experience, examination, and regulation".[33] As David Wang and Ali Ilhan claim,[34] this suggests that there is no body of knowledge for interior design other than that which is directly related to, or filtered through, practice.

An example from Europe demonstrates a balance between a system of academic accreditation and encouragement for research leadership and exploration in the field. The European Council of Interior Architects (ECIA) has established the Charter of Interior Architecture Education, a recognition programme for accredited institutions across the European Union. As a system of formal accreditation, the programme acknowledges the role of interior education to not only prepare students for practice, but also to lead the profession in new directions through research.

The work of Tiiu Poldma, an academic within the North American interior design paradigm that Guerin and Dickinson also occupy, represents another shift toward a broader perspective of the discipline. Poldma identifies a goal of research "… to move a profession forward and give it tools that are transferrable into other domains. This forward movement gives a profession the means to develop towards a discipline".[35] Poldma explains that academic research can "… forge new knowledge and innovation through the study of both process and practice… As an emergent discipline interior design must respond to new ways of thinking and doing that consider… multiple cultural, economic, and political contexts".[36] Poldma goes on to identify issues of human ethics, democratisation of space and historical narrative that should influence interior design as a discipline.

As a counter to contemporary interior design practice (and education) that she sees as driven largely by aesthetic solutions and practical concepts, Poldma makes the following demand: "If we consider thinking and doing in interior design to be understanding the intimate aspects of people in their interior environment, then interior design research should include developing knowledge about interior spaces as the dynamic backdrop of human activity. In this type of thinking, we might consider that space is not just a physical area but also a dynamic place where needs change constantly and where one might see different components that change with the needs. Or we might also consider how people behave within the environment, or what perceptions they have of their surroundings given their background, age or social status."[37]

Poldma's position would align with many interior design students' reason to enter the profession, and this is what the discipline must continue to advance. Interior design has evolved significantly in a short period of time. Perhaps the key contribution of interior design academic endeavour has been the expansion of the understanding of interior design education as training for practice and of research as information gathering for, and justification of, decisions in practice. It is a position that recognises the contribution of education not only to practice, but to the development of the discipline as a whole.

1 See for example Pile, John, *A History of Interior Design* (London: Lawrence King, 2005).

2 Abercrombie, Stanley, *A Century of Interior Design 1900 – 2000* (New York: Rizzoli, 2003), p. 7.

3 Massey, Anne, *Interior Design of the 20th Century* (London: Thames and Hudson, 1990), p. 130.

4 Kirkham, Pat and Sparke, Penny, "A Woman's Place…?" in Kirkham, Pat (Ed.), *Women Designers in the USA, 1900 – 2000: Diversity and Difference* (New Haven: Yale University Press, 2000), p. 309.

5 Massey (1990), p. 129.

6 Constant, Caroline, *Eileen Gray* (London: Phaidon Press, 2000), pp. 8 – 11.

7 Quinn, Catriona, "Marion Hall Best's Early Career", in Bogle, Michael (Ed.), *Designing Australia: Readings in the History of Design* (Annandale, NSW: Pluto Press, 2002), p. 66.

8 Massey (1990) p. 131.

9 Massey (1990) p. 125.

10 Sparke, Penny, *A Century of Design: Design Pioneers of the Twentieth Century* (Heuppauge, NY: Barron's Educational Series, 1998).

11 Sparke (1998), p. 206.

12 Hicks, Ashley, *David Hicks: Designer* (London: Scriptum Editions, 2003), p. 18.

13 Hicks, David, *Style and Design* (London: Viking Press, 1987), p. 10.

14 Sparke (1998), p. 247.

15 Joo Yun Kim, "Interior Architecture: the State of the Art", in *Interior Design: the State of the Art* (Singapore: IFI, 2006), p. 28.

16 Attiwill, Suzie, "What's in a Canon?" in Gigli, John *et al.* (Eds.), *Thinking Inside the Box: a reader in interiors for the 21st century* (London: Middlesex University Press, 2007), p. 65.

17 Penner, Barbara and Rice, Charles, "Constructing the Interior – Introduction", *The Journal of Architecture*, vol. 9 (Autumn 2004), p. 272.

18 Havenhand, Lucinda, "A View From the Margin: Interior Design," *Design Issues*, vol. 20, no. 4 (Autumn 2004), p. 34.

19 Turpin, John, "The History of Women in Interior Design: A Review of Literature", *Journal of Interior Design,* vol. 33, no. 1 (2007), p. 2 and 6.

20 Stone, Andrew, "The Underestimation of the Interior", in Gigli *et al.* (2007), p. 227.

21 Havenhand (2004), p. 42.

22 Klingenberg, Ellen, "Interspace," in *Design Competence* (Oslo: KHiO Faculty of Design, 2005).

23 Klingenberg (2005), p. 5.

24 Stone (2007), p. 236.

25 *Ibid.*

26 Attiwill, Suzie "Moderator Comments", in Caan, S. and Powell, B. (Eds.), *Thinking Into The Future: IFI Roundtable Conference* (New York: IFI, 2007), p. 136.

27 Guerin, Denise and Thompson, Jo Ann Asher, "Interior Design Education in the 21st Century: An Educational Transformation," *Journal of Interior Design*, vol. 30, no. 1 (2004), p. 1.

28 Guerin and Thompson (2004), p. 1.

29 Guerin and Thompson (2004), p. 6.

30 Guerin and Thompson (2004), p. 1.

31 Martin, Caren and Guerin, Denise (2005), *The Interior Design Profession's Body of Knowledge*, http://knowedgecentre.iida.org, accessed on 6.02.12.

32 Guerin, Denise and Martin, Caren, "The Career Cycle Approach to Defining the Interior Design Profession's Body of Knowledge", *Journal of Interior Design*, vol. 30, no. 2 (2004), p. 8.

33 Guerin and Martin (2004), p. 1.

34 Wang, David and Ilhan, Ali, "Holding Creativity Together: A Sociological Theory of the Design Professions", *Design Issues*, vol. 25, no. 1 (2009), p. 11.

35 Poldma, Tiiu, "Interior Design at a Crossroads: Embracing Specificity through Process, Research, and Knowledge",*Journal of Interior Design*, vol. 33, no. 3 (2008), p. xv.

36 Poldma (2008), p. vii – viii.

37 Poldma (2008), p. xiv.

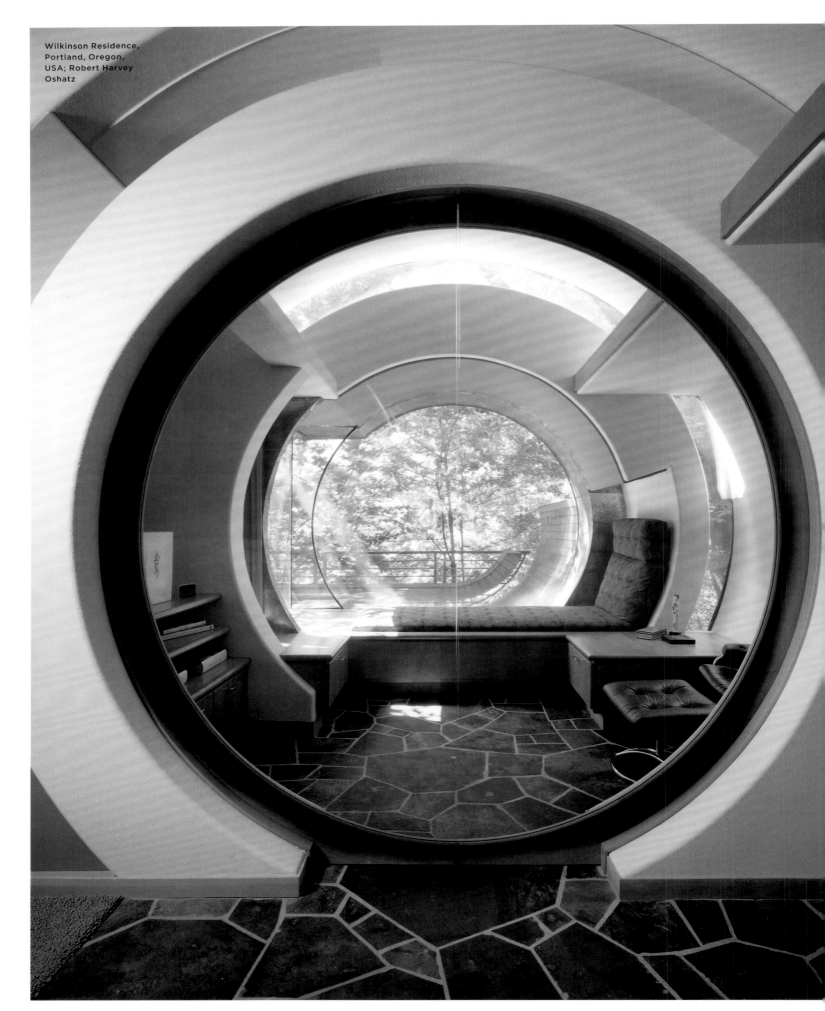

Wilkinson Residence,
Portland, Oregon,
USA; Robert Harvey
Oshatz

SUSTAINABILITY: INDUSTRY STANDARDS AND INNOVATION

LILIANE WONG

SUSTAINABILITY THROUGH INDUSTRY STANDARDS

Within the building sector today, it is universally accepted that buildings contribute in a significant manner to climate change through both consumption and emissions. In the EU, buildings account for 40 % of its annual energy consumption and 36 % of its CO_2 emissions.[1] Similarly, the American building sector consumes nearly half (49 %) of all energy produced in the USA and is responsible for 46 % of its CO_2 emissions.[2] The fact that "buildings are the major source of global demand for energy and materials that produce by-product greenhouse gases (GHG)"[3] has generated initiatives worldwide to reverse this trend by reducing and maintaining a global average temperature of less than 2° C above pre-industrial levels. The building sector constitutes the single largest economic and environmental opportunity for a collective reduction of GHG levels.

The European 2020 Strategy and the American 2030 Challenge aim to achieve 20 % energy savings as initial steps toward long-term energy and climate change goals. These goals may be met through the adoption of sustainable practices that promote integrated whole-building planning, design, construction and operation, innovative design with minimal environmental impact, building management with a reduced life-cycle impact on the environment and even on-site production of renewable energy. Such practice extends well beyond the building profession to management, education, development, business and real estate. While sustainable practice has been in use for some time, especially in Europe, it is relatively uncharted as a global endeavour. Environmental assessment methodologies, in the form of rating systems, have emerged in order to provide some measurement of the efficacy of such practice. There are over 600 such rating systems worldwide today and they fluctuate in scope, from one to the next, in measuring the different aspects of sustainability – social, environmental and economical.

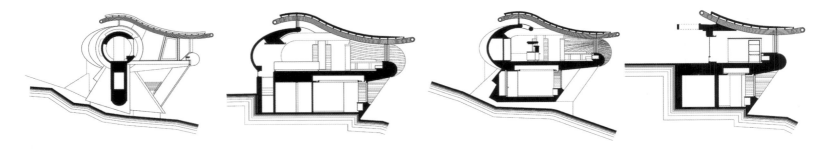

Focused: "This house evades the mechanics of the camera... One must actually stroll through the house to grasp its complexities and its connection to the exterior." (The architect)
Wilkinson Residence, Portland, Oregon, USA;
Robert Harvey Oshatz

The building has 6 Star Green Star – Office Design v2 certification from the Green Building Council of Australia and is regarded as a benchmark of sustainable architecture.
ANZ Centre, Melbourne, Australia; HASSELL

RATING SYSTEMS

Green rating systems are tools that "examine the performance or expected performance of a 'whole building' and translate that examination into an overall assessment... for comparison against other buildings".[4] The development of these systems began in the UK with the introduction of BREEAM (Building Research Establishment's Environmental Assessment Method) in 1990. This was followed in succession by the French system HQE (Haute Qualité Environnementale) in 1992, the Hong Kong BEAM (Building Environmental Assessment Method) and the international GBTool (now SBTool) of the iiSBE (International Initiative for a Sustainable Built Environment) in 1996, the USA LEED (Leadership in Energy and Environmental Design) and the Canadian Green Globes in 2000, the Japanese CASBEE (Comprehensive Assessment System for Built Environment Efficiency) in 2001 and the Australian Green Star in 2002.[5]

These form the basis of many other similar systems around the world including Switzerland's Minergie, Germany's DGNB System (German Sustainable Building Council), Portugal's LiderA, Singapore's BCA Green Mark (Building and Construction Authority), and Taiwan's EEWH (Ecology, Energy Saving, Waste Reduction and Health). Many countries have also adopted rating systems through their membership and chapter in green building councils and organisations such as the World Green Building Council. Today, BREEAM and LEED have emerged globally as the two most recognised and used systems.

The character of the outdoor areas is continued into the interior of this office for a furniture manufacturer.
Samas Office Furniture Headquarters, Worms, Germany; 100% interior Sylvia Leydecker

Most rating systems consist of a suite of tools that assess a building through its construction type and space use. Construction type differentiates between new and existing construction with further distinctions, in some systems, of core and shell, commercial interiors and limited construction/operations and maintenance. Space use categories include retail, healthcare, education, commercial, industrial, domestic and community development. The systems universally address issues of global and local environments, internal environment, design assessment, operation of the building and its management. Some systems also have the capability for assessing the management, operation and maintenance of a building at any post-occupancy period. Rating categories are further separated into land use, water use, energy and the atmosphere, transport, materials, indoor environmental quality and, in some cases, innovation. Within a system of designated points, an assessment of the whole project is premised on the total points earned from each of the categories. Most systems weigh the points equally with the sum total leading to a rating of the building. The ratings differ from system to system, with star ratings from 1 to 6 for Green Star, bronze/silver/gold/platinum for LEED and pass/good/very good/excellent/outstanding for BREEAM.

There are many similarities in the general organisation of rating systems – each with the primary purpose of measuring the sustainability of the built environment. These tools ultimately serve an extensive circle that surrounds the primary user group of built environment professionals and includes developers, building management, members of the real estate sector, manufacturers of materials and products, code officials, organisations for the protection of the environment, sectors of the health profession and even building tenants. While some rating systems were developed in conjunction with government-related agencies (Green Globe, BREEAM), many rating systems were developed by private, non-profit organisations. The major rating systems set strict standards for practice and contrast with "green" building codes that establish minimum requirements for sustainable practice. The rating systems are voluntary and not generally integrated with governmental building regulations, although in some countries, rating systems are adopted and enforced as building regulation. In the UK where BREEAM was developed by the Building Research Establishment (BRE), at the time a government-funded research body, local governments have begun to require compliance with BREEAM as part of their planning policies. Wales and Northern Ireland have both adopted sections of the BREEAM system into their local codes. In Wales, as of July 2008, for example, all healthcare buildings must achieve a Very Good to Excellent BREEAM assessment. In England, all new school projects must achieve a Very Good rating as a condition of funding.

Interior design, as an individual discipline, is not addressed as a separate category within most rating systems. Where differentiations are made between new construction and existing buildings, interior design issues are addressed in the latter category. In many cases, the systems address indoor issues, typically termed "Indoor Environmental Quality" (IEQ), which include aspects of building performance that impact the health and well-being of the occupants. This category includes safety and security, hygiene, indoor air quality and ventilation, thermal comfort, lighting, acoustics and building amenities.

The rating systems that specifically address interior design are few and include Green Globes, Green Star and LEED. The Green Globes rating system includes the tool Fit-Up, which is both a guide and an assessment protocol for commercial interiors. Issues of Indoor Environment, Project Management, Energy, Emissions, Effluents & Other Impacts, Resources-systems Options and Materials and Water are addressed through an interactive, online questionnaire. While third-party verification is possible, Green Globes generates an online report based on a completed questionnaire. The Green Star system offers the category Office Interiors in Australia, South Africa and New Zealand. This category is designed for owners, tenants and interior designers to assess the impact of office tenancy fitout, both during the design phase as well as in post-construction. Issues include access to natural light, waste management, energy conservation, materials manufacture and use. This tool is accessible to all users, but a project can only claim such certification if used by GBCA (Green Building Council of Australia) certified individuals. LEED Commercial Interiors similarly provides a green benchmark for tenancy and high-performance interiors. Its rating categories are Sustainable Sites, Water Efficiency, Energy and Atmosphere, Materials and Resources, IEQ, Innovation in Design and Regional Priority. LEED Commercial Interiors is designed for complementary use with LEED Core and Shell, as a specific rating system for developers, owners and tenants.

Tech-Nature: a facade perforated with braille dots gives this unusual pharmacy a lively and inspiring lighting effect – laboratory and nature in coexistence.
Placebo Pharmacy, Athens, Greece;
Klab Architecture – Konstantinos Labrinopoulos

Pop-up hotel project for a TV programme showcasing the creative use of recyclable materials.
Recycling – Artistic room concept for a hotel, Cologne, Germany; Raumkleid – Anke Preywisch, os2 designgroup – Oliver Schübbe

EVALUATION

As evidenced by the proliferation of green ratings systems around the world since their introduction in 1990, the impact of these systems is potentially far-reaching. At a minimum, these tools have raised the awareness of environmental issues and encouraged sustainable practice in the built environment at all levels of participation from policy to planning, from design to construction, from resource to product and from real estate to tenancy. For building professionals, these complex rating systems provide a practicable structure and framework for measurement and assessment. Often these systems complement building codes and regulations and, in many cases, they exceed them. For governments, they can and do serve, in the instance of BREEAM and policies of Wales and Northern Ireland, as a link to governmental energy policies. For individuals – from building managers to tenants – they provide a method of evaluating and improving maintenance and operation of buildings that reduce their impact on the environment. This overall level of awareness should not be underestimated.

As a global endeavour, green rating systems have made significant progress in the two decades since the introduction of BREEAM in the UK. The positive impact of the systems as a worldwide catalyst for understanding sustainable practice cannot be disputed, but there are shortcomings in implementation and execution. As these systems gain wider general acceptance, common concerns have surfaced that are specific to some systems and generic to most. These concerns pertain to efficacy, consistency and cost – each a crucial aspect – and, if unresolved, could undermine the future possibilities of the system as a whole.

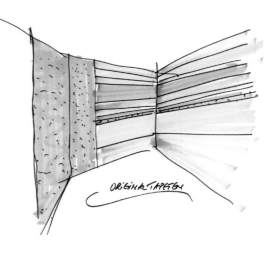

The most common concern questions the premise of the ratings structure, one that is based upon a pre-occupancy condition. Designs envisioned for optimal pre-occupancy conditions are seldom translated verbatim to construction and realisation for many reasons including budget. Decisions made late in the design process, including value engineering at the completion of the design phase, contribute to the construction of a project that differs from the designed one. In this sense, the rated performance does not hold a clear relationship to the actual consumption and environmental performance of a building in a post-occupancy state. Interior design parameters that address the comfort of the occupant – temperature, ventilation, lighting, air quality – are crucial to the overall assessment of performance but are not, in fact, regulated in actual use. There are many ways to resolve this lack of definitive connection between anticipated and actual performance. The involvement of a buildings operator in the design and construction phases or the creation of the position of Environmental Performance Manager for building management are some possibilities. BREEAM addresses this concern by its recent requirement of a Post-Construction Review. For their ultimate rating of Outstanding, a BREEAM In Use certification is required within the first three years of occupancy.

Space maximisation: flexible curtains give this tiny hotel room an intimate character.
CitizenM Hotel, Glasgow, Scotland; Concrete Architectural Associates

Hanging garden: sustainability is also the theme of this contact lens shop in Omotesando.
Magic Store, Tokyo, Japan; Torafu Architects

A study of French HQE-certified buildings indicated that certified buildings, in fact, performed better than non-certified buildings, but not as well as forecasted in the certification process.[6] This is consistent with findings around the world. Such findings, however, have not affected public perceptions of certified buildings. Real-estate market studies in the USA indicate that "green" office buildings demand higher rent, hold a higher rate of occupancy and have a higher resale value than "non-green" buildings of a similar nature.[7] Such perception questions the rating systems' use of points as an indication of success. There is conjecture that design professionals are more interested in the acquisition of points and owners with the economic benefits and prestige of certification than with effective sustainable design. The term "LEED brain" has been coined to describe "what happens when the potential PR benefits of certification begin driving the design process".[8] Such conjectures damage the reputation of the systems and their potential for influencing energy policies in the built environment.

The development of a universal rating system is a distant ideal. The regional variations of climate constitute one important factor among many that explains why the systems differ dramatically from criteria to scores. A comparison of assessment criteria for twelve different rating systems used in the UK, Asia, Europe, US and Australia that focused on fifteen key issues including energy, CO_2, Indoor Environmental Quality, land use, renewable technologies, transport, waste and water indicated that none of them used the same list of criteria for assessment.[9] In a study published by BRE, the findings indicated that there was no equivalent for BREEAM's rating of Excellent. A rating of Very Good in BREEAM was found to be equal to Platinum and Six Stars, the highest scores respectively in LEED and Green Star, while there was no such equivalent in CASBEE.[10] This lack of consistency and parity between systems does not allow for a universal standard of comparison.

The cost aspect of building certification raises the issue of economic divide. While data demonstrates that the ultimate cost of a certified building is not significantly higher than that of an uncertified one, many additional costs exist in the assessment process. These so-called "soft" costs include the use of the rating system and materials, project registration fees, fees associated with certification and design team fees. Indirect costs also include the cost of time for a certification process that can take from a week to two months, fees for membership with Green Building Councils and costs of education and testing for certifying design professionals. In the USA, recent costs associated with LEED certification that included registration, document submission, AP document gathering and design team documentation ranged from 22,000 USD to 100,000 USD.[11]

The green rating systems have made significant progress in quantifying the impact of building on the environment. Cynics, though, point to the low number of buildings certified over a period of 20 years: 200,000 through BREEAM and 9000+ through LEED. The dissemination of such quantification methodologies alone, however, is an enormous benefit. It is important, too, to recognise that no environmental assessment system is perfect. By virtue of its quantification, the system does not have the capacity to address aspects of the built environment outside this intentionally limited view. It is a tool for measurement, not for design.

Water as a luxury resource is the theme of this azure blue pool in a hotel in a medieval building.
Hotel Zenden, Maastricht, Holland;
Wiel Arets Architects

SUSTAINABILITY THROUGH INNOVATION

One proposed solution for the reduction of greenhouse gases (GHG) is to attain fossil fuel reduction standards through implementing innovative design strategies.[12] Despite its unquantifiable characteristics, the importance of design innovation in sustainable strategies for the built environment is recognised in some of the major rating systems. BEAM, BREEAM and LEED each address the subject of innovation as extracurricular; an achievement beyond the methods of established best practice. Innovation is rewarded with bonus points. BEAM does not provide a prescribed path for innovation; rather it allows a client to submit such proposals for evaluation and consideration. Projects assessed through BREEAM can receive bonus points either by exceeding established best practice criteria or through a proposal requesting assessment for innovation. LEED assessment criteria include specific descriptions for earning ten possible bonus points that permit a project to score 110 %. Six out of these ten bonus points are allocated for Innovation and may be earned through any combination of three paths: achieving significant and measurable performance not addressed in LEED, achieving exemplary performance by exceeding LEED criteria or attempting a pilot credit. This approach to ecology in the built environment addresses the demands of a changed and rapid world through strategies that embrace the intangible characteristics of flexibility, adaptability and multifunctionality.

Exposed concrete with soft moss inhabiting its cracks, blown up in scale to create a dramatic graphical pattern.
Orto – Living Covering; IVANKA Concrete Design

BUILDING SMALL AND THE INFLUENCE OF ECONOMY AND ECOLOGY

At the close of the first decade of the 21st century, many industrialised countries are marked by post-industrial decline. Europe and the USA, in particular, are troubled with economic recession in what is now termed the Global Financial Crisis. In such a state, scarcity of resources, both natural and financial, is a key issue facing design today. When approached primarily through the lens of products, sustainability in design practice is often viewed as economically disadvantageous due to perceived additional costs.

Once the purview of the value engineer, reductions of project scope and scale have become a recognised approach to sustainable practice. Smaller projects typically cost less to build and maintain, consume less energy in construction and use and emit less CO_2, ultimately resulting in a reduced carbon footprint. A diminution of size does not necessarily equate to fewer programmatic requirements and functions. Rather, building "small" is accompanied by the design challenge to accommodate more within a lesser footprint.

Small structures must be flexible to perform the same programmatic roles as larger ones. Flexibility in the floor plan is historically linked to the 18th-century invention of coke smelting and its subsequent impact on the history of modern architecture. The resultant mass production of iron led to the evolution of the steel industry in the mid-19th century, a benchmark that brought about an independence from load-bearing methods. The introduction of steel framing forever changed the definition of the room. Previously restricted by the limited structural spans of load-bearing members, rooms were now freed from such constraints. With the general acceptance of steel framing in construction, the classic floor plan of the late 19th century, with its enfilade of formal rooms, gave way to the new open plan in which many functions could coexist in one undefined space. The implication of this change on the modern floor plan is noted in Le Corbusier's untitled 1925 manifesto *Architecture Vivante* as one of the "five points of architecture" and further illustrated in his Domino House diagram.[13] Almost a century later, this freedom and flexibility is at the heart of the challenge to build small.

Into the box: in this youth hostel, pinewood and greenery establish a direct connection with nature.
"Haus Untersberg" Youth Hostel, Berchtesgaden, Germany; LAVA – Laboratory for Visionary Architecture

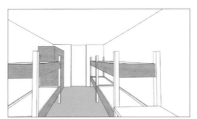
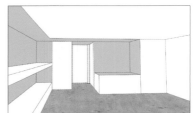

Completed in 1972, the Nagakin Capsule Tower in Toyko is the quintessential precedent for both compact and environmentally respectful design. The project consists of two towers, each housing 140 prefabricated "capsules". Each capsule was designed with built-in furniture, a bathroom unit, built-in appliances as well as a TV and audio system to accommodate the needs of a single occupant. (Multiple occupants or families could be accommodated through the connection of multiple capsules.) Responding to Tokyo's perennial shortage of space, both commercial and domestic, this project was intended for use as homes or offices. The success of the 58 m² (621 sq ft) compact floor plan in meeting so many programmatic needs is due to the flexibility of the space itself. In contrast to the traditional floor plan in which spaces were dedicated to individual functions, a single space simultaneously accommodated many functions.

Flexible use: curtain open, curtain closed.

"Blaue Fabrik" office interior, Thalwil, Switzerland; ateliersv Innenarchitektur

Embracing small is a visible trend today, both in residential and commercial projects. In residential design, modern-day successors to the compact apartments of Nagakin Towers reflect a reversal from the McMansions – oversized suburban houses that are incongruous in scale and aesthetic to their surrounds. Most compact houses today are defined by the efficiency and flexibility of an open floor plan. A well-orchestrated design meets programmatic needs through such a multifunctional attitude. The Micro Compact Home m-ch, a 7 m² (76 sq ft) project, developed by researchers and designers in London and at the Technical University in Munich, exemplifies this approach. A cube measuring 266 cm x 266 cm x 266 cm / 8 ft 8.7 in, the m-ch is designed for and adapted to the dimensions of the human figure in essential domiciliary activities. Designed especially for students and vacationers, it features two double beds, storage, a sliding table to seat up to five, a bathroom and a fully equipped kitchen. A low-e version of the m-ch is powered by photovoltaic solar cells and a wind generator. When no longer required, the m-ch is designed for recycle and disposal in which the materials can be re-used for another home. In an eco-analysis from materials, construction, manufacture, delivery to final disposal, the low-e home is potentially zero CO_2 emissions.[14]

While net zero energy is the ultimate goal of many compact residential projects today, there is also a focus on making a smaller impact on the environment through a "smarter" lifestyle, one with fewer encumbrances. This is challenging in a consumer-driven society, but sculp(IT), a four-storey office/residence in Antwerp, embraces this notion of "less is more". Sited on a narrow 2.4 m / 7 ft 10 in lot, each storey houses a different function: office, kitchen, bedroom and bathroom. In contrast to the Micro Compact Home, where multiple functions coexist in a single compact space, each miniscule floor plan accommodates requisite functions through a spartan approach of minimalism.

Narrow sites with very little space require out-of-the-ordinary interior design solutions.

Narrowest Apartment in Antwerp,
Antwerp, Belgium; sculp(IT)

Water, air and nature: sustainability versus environmental pollution is an issue around the world – also in China as seen here in the visitor centre for the Qinhu Wetland National Park.
Visitor Centre in Qinhu Wetland National Park, Jiangsu, China; TRIAD

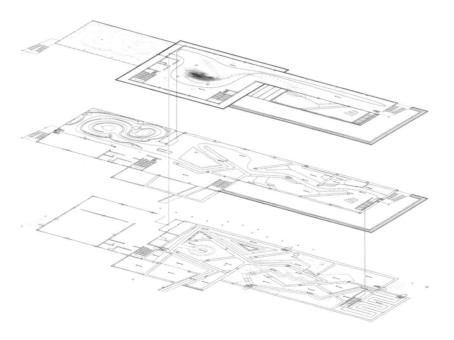

CASE STUDY: FOUR SMALL PROJECTS, NEW YORK, USA

In the design of commercial interiors, the recent economic climate has imposed the dual constraints of small spaces and tight budgets. For some architects and designers, these constraints become opportunities. Three restaurant projects in Manhattan by the New York firm LTL Architects are exemplary in illustrating the use of tight spatial constraints as a point of departure for design and innovation: the Ini Ani Coffee Shop is 33 m² / 350 sq ft, Dash Dogs is 20 m² / 220 sq ft and the Tides Restaurant is 39 m² / 420 sq ft.

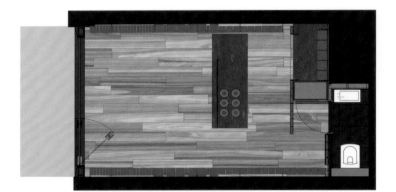

One long counter stretches the length of the hot dog restaurant ...
DASH Dogs, New York City, New York, USA;
LTL Architects

A limited palette of materials and minimal furnishings give this small room a pleasant feel.
INI ANI Coffee Shop, New York City, New York, USA;
LTL Architects

... while here the walls are a storage space and design feature in one.
XOCOLATTI, New York City,
New York, USA; de-spec

"Rather than avoiding these obstacles through formal or logistical gymnastics, the tactic of catalyzing constraints generates an impassioned inquiry into the unavoidable limits of architectural production."[15] Viewed as opportunities for "generative solutions", these projects accept predetermined restrictions and shift the focus of design intervention elsewhere. The restrictions here included both a dimensionally limited envelope and economically driven requirements for the greatest capacity of seats, circulation and service space. In each case, the floor plans are organised simply so as to maximise programmatic requirements: the Tides Restaurant with a line of tables and built-in banquettes; the Ini Ani Coffee Shop with spare seating arrangements that differentiate the varied activities of the café lounge; in Dash Dogs, a single linear counter, strategically placed to direct the client traffic from door to order window to pickup and exit.

The design investigations instead focus on the interior skin, wall, floor and ceiling surfaces not required for programmatic functions. As a canvas for innovation, these planes are addressed as homogeneous internal membranes rather than as opportunities for the application of various treatments. At the Ini Ani Coffee Shop, two separate "surface treatment volumes" are created – one of corrugated cardboard strips, compressed in a steel cage, and the other of plaster, cast with plastic coffee-cup lids. In a single open space, these volumes serve to differentiate the lounge area with its self-absorbed WiFi clientele and the service counter with its bustle of take-out customers. At Dash Dogs, where the client space is only half as wide as its depth, an internal membrane is inserted to create order, both physical and visual, in a high-volume retail setting. The membrane, a band of steel strips, runs continuously from a sloping ceiling to the sloping floor, referencing the mechanical "people mover". At the Tides Restaurant, an inner volume is created on the ceiling of an undulating topographical landscape of sea grasses, constructed from bamboo skewers. Optical film on the glass entry doors distorts the diners' views, contributing further to the sensibility of shifting surfaces.

Xocolatti, a chocolatier in SoHo, Manhattan, NY, illustrates a similar approach to flexibility within a retail setting. In a 14 m² / 150 sq ft rectangular storefront, an inner membrane is created from walls of stacked green signature chocolate boxes. These walls of boxes – some closed and some open to display the sweets – simultaneously function as wallpaper, display, storage and kinetic art. As the boxes of chocolates are sold, the wall pattern mutates, forming a history of the day's sales.

In embracing the notion of "small", architects and designers search for increasingly complex and inventive solutions for the design of the compact structure. Inherently sustainable through size, small structures are not necessarily valued only for this efficiency. In 2010, the Victoria and Albert Museum invited seven international architects to design and build small full-scale structures in the museum, resulting in the exhibit "1:1 – Architects Build Small Spaces". As a celebration of small space, the exhibition investigated "small-scale structures and how they can define and enhance notions of everyday experience and personal space".[16]

MODULAR MEANS

The energy efficiency of m-ch and other compact homes on the market today is due, in great part, to modular construction and prefabrication. Modularity as a method is one that successfully addresses wasteful processes in design and construction. Today's compact houses are primarily modular. As in the Nagakin capsules, also fabricated off-site and hoisted in place, they are factory-fabricated and shipped to an intended site. The ecology of being small is coupled with the benefits of prefabrication – reduction of materials waste, reduction of construction waste, minimal structural foundations and lower embodied energy – all of which contributes to a smaller carbon footprint and a lower impact on the environment.

Modular construction is most often used in new residential applications. The benefits of modular construction are now extending to existing buildings as modular retrofit. In large and repetitive institutional projects, the use of modular units in retrofit is both economically and ecologically beneficial. In a systems upgrade project for a college dormitory, bathroom pods were fabricated off-site and hoisted through the windows. This method of replacement realised an enormous reduction of construction waste and time. On an individual scale, modular retrofit kits such as the Modular In-Home Office are used to create a room within a room. With the goal of minimising heating costs in home offices, the kit provides an innovative low-tech solution to zoned heating. Utilising the concept of the common greenhouse, the kit consists of wood frames, covered with an insulating wrap material, that serve as walls of an in-home office space. This kit is configured through creative geometry to an existing window. With the window serving as a source of heat and ventilation, a separate mechanical zone is created within the home, naturally heating only a single targeted location.

IMPERMANENCE

Since the start of the global financial crisis, empty storefronts are common sights in cities around the world. In a diminished real estate market, a trend has emerged toward impermanent enterprises. Both temporary and mobile stores are now widespread in commercial retail. They offer various opportunities for the retailer to test a market without serious financial commitments of rent, to sell a product without construction/build-out costs, to give an online retail company a brief physical presence or to gain visibility in prime locations for a short duration. For landlords, it is an opportunity to generate rental income and to increase visibility in otherwise unpopulated properties. Temporary structures are well suited for retail, a design type with an inherently brief lifespan. The more brief duration of the temporary structures contributes economically and materially to a reduction in the energy expended for both construction and maintenance.

Temporary stores have gained immense popularity recently, earning the nickname of "pop-up retail". The concept of the temporary store is not a new one. Retail establishments of seasonal products historically operated only in the applicable months; a Christmas store, for example, operated for the fours weeks of the season. Predicated on supply and demand, this concept adapted for the general retail market as the economy declined. In the first half of 2011, pop-up retail businesses in the USA increased 14 % from the previous year.[17]

The temporary nature of pop-up retail stores often implies a limitation of budget. Such financial restrictions have inspired creative and novel uses of common materials, fabrication and detailing. Used in multiples, the common document archive box serves as pattern, texture and colour for a pop-up menswear store. Detailed in stretched and overlapped layers from ceiling to floor to shelving, 154 pairs of stockings create a cave-like landscape of textile stalactites and stalagmites for a three-day pop-up promotion of a clothing collection. The London temporary bookstore, Foldaway Bookshop, optimises the structural capabilities of cardboard through stacking, folding and pleating operations that create walls, shelving and furniture. At the conclusion of its tenancy, the bookstore was entirely recycled.

The enthusiasm for pop-up stores has caused a trickle-up effect with the trend permeating the high-end retail market. Recent pop-up stores feature products of designers such as Kate Spade and Prada. Designer pop-up retail stores, in contrast, are not driven by economics. Rather, the temporary nature is exploited for its exclusivity and serves as a new form of marketing. For example, the Prada pop-up in Paris was designed at significant expense to resemble the Pont Mirabeau bridge. As branding tools for exclusivity, these projects do not share the budgetary constraints of the original pop-up retail. This trend has instead resulted in new opportunities for architects and designers, as retailers aim to promote products from coffee to neckties. Typically small in scale, these projects, with full financial support, have become extravagant exercises and unique experiments for design strategies that push the envelope of flexibility.

80,000 bamboo skewers in a small space focus attention on materials and texture – poetic and beautiful.
TIDES Restaurant; New York City, New York, USA; LTL Architects

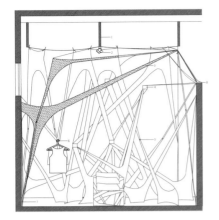

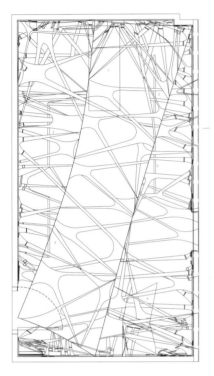

Through the sparing but creative use of cheap materials, this boutique has been transformed into a work of sculpture.
Temporary concept store for the Arnsdorf Opticks collection, Melbourne, Australia; Edwards Moore

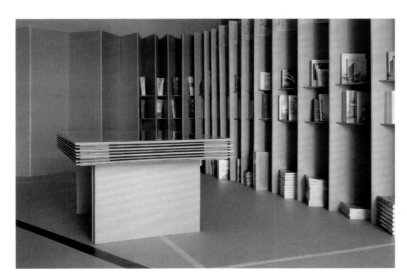

Out of the box: modular construction – efficient and practical.
RIBA Foldaway Bookshop, London, England; Campaign, Claire Curtice Publicists

CASE STUDY: ILLY CAFFÈ

The recent history of the retailer Illy illustrates this new type of pop-up. A series of temporary stores in the USA and in Europe were commissioned to promote Illy Caffè, an Italian gourmet espresso coffee. In partnership with the Fondazione La Biennale di Venezia, Illy enjoys a promotional presence each year through the construction of a temporary signature café. At the 52nd Venice Biennale in 2007, this temporary structure featured a café fashioned from a shipping container that opened, with the push of a button, to reveal a fully furnished space with a kitchen, dining room, bathroom, bedroom, living room and library. Entirely fashioned from recyclable materials, this project exemplified the designer's belief in the adaptability of space and materials.

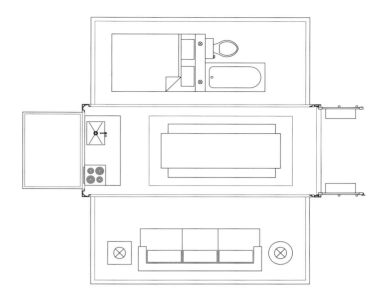

A shipping container with completely recyclable furnishings unfolds at the press of a button into a pop-up café.
Push Button House – Illy Caffè,
Venice Biennale 2007, Italy; Adam Kalkin

A flexible system consisting of 200 cubes of different dimensions offers an infinitely adaptable approach to defining space.

Illy Shop, Milan, Italy; Caterina Tiazzoldi with Illy Art Direction

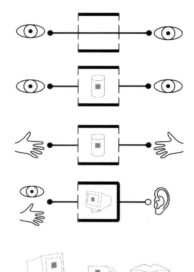

By contrast, the Illy pop-up store in Milan, in operation during the Christmas season, was an opportunity to use generative geometries as a vehicle for designing reconfigurable space. A single cube (45 cm x 45 cm / 17.7 x 17.7 in), modulated through combinatory logic, yielded 3,000 configurations with variations of the cube's physical properties of depth, thickness, opacity and length. At the Milan store, 200 of these variations were used for functions specific to the display of coffee products and espresso machines. The adaptability of the cube to different conditions – size of product, accessibility of product, numbers of products to be displayed, quantity of light required – allows the cubes to be reconfigured at another location.

The mobile or portable structure is a unique type of compact space with semi-permanent characteristics. Mobile structures have traditionally been, and continue to be, used as toilet facilities and food sellers. The economics of mobility, lower operational costs and the ability to serve a larger population, are highly conducive for other programmes such as libraries, police stations or even hotel rooms. The use of portable structures for serving one or more communities is ecologically resourceful and cost-effective, especially where municipal budgets have been severely diminished in the economic downturn. The design of these compact structures, unlike the pop-up stores, is additionally challenging due to the demands of specific programme functions. In these instances, innovation is often found in the ability to extend the limits of the ordinary. In the need to establish an omnipresence within the city, the Hannover Mobile Police Station enhanced its visibility through the introduction of floor-height openings, thereby visually extending the 8 m² / 83 sq ft space. The 4 m² / 41.5 sq ft Sleepbox, a mobile hotel room to serve one to three persons, demonstrates the opposite approach in creating a sleeping space in a public setting. The openings, placed high within the space and supplied with automatic blackout features, offer privacy for the weary traveller. The eco-friendly Robi, a mobile library serving the Heilbronn area of Germany, maximises the atmosphere of the narrow space through the use of transparent acrylic shelving.

CASE STUDY: TOOLBOX, TURIN, ITALY

Toolbox, a project for a business incubator in Turin, acknowledges the existence of the new generation of workers with different needs and locations and at different times of the day. In a new approach to the workplace, the project builds upon the coexistence of such users and the ability to adapt the space to their varying needs. By maximising space use, the waste generated through overlap and redundancy is eliminated. The programme comprises two distinct parts: co-working workstations in an open space and enclosed rooms that contain common functional services (kitchen, meeting rooms, mailboxes, bar, etc.). Drawing upon principles of topological hybridisation, the design focuses on the ability to constantly and efficiently reconfigure space to the needs of the various users. It does so on different levels. First, through an automated centralised system, the design provides different organisational structures for different users based on individually defined needs. The system controls access, lighting, sound, and services such as telephones and printers. Each user customises a badge that establishes his or her own specific profile of space needs. The automated system allows or denies access to functions and spaces – variations include colour, acoustic materials, reflective surfaces, floor treatments, etc. – according to this profile. "By varying the accessibility and use of the functions hosted in the space, such as co-working areas, meeting rooms, kitchen, patio, parking, it is possible to achieve an endless modality of use of the same space."[18]

The interior design of the space itself also provides visual manifestation of this adaptive ability. The reception area is designed with 400 white cubes that serve as a visual map of the different functions of the office. Using a parametric device, the depth of each cube is manipulated to connect it with a specific programmatic function. The design of Toolbox illustrates an innovative method of achieving sustainability that focuses on adaptation rather than on material wastes and consumption.

THE PERFORMATIVE: FLEXIBILITY TO MULTIFUNCTIONALITY

Life in the 21st century is a set of rapid and complex negotiations in a world of connected networks. This connectivity allows infinite permutations in our ordinary choices, all of which constitutes one's daily existence. Such negotiations require an ability to function, simultaneously, at many levels. The smartphone, used for communication but also for photography, filmmaking, entertainment, reference, commerce, music, archiving or recording, is emblematic of this defining characteristic of life today. Multifunctionality, the heir to flexibility and adaptability, is a paradigm for the 21st century. Buildings and spaces are required to do no less.

By adapting and varying the accessibility and use of functions hosted in the space, it is possible to achieve an endless modality of use.
Toolbox Torino Office Lab, Turin, Italy;
Caterina Tiazzoldi / Nuova Ordentra

87

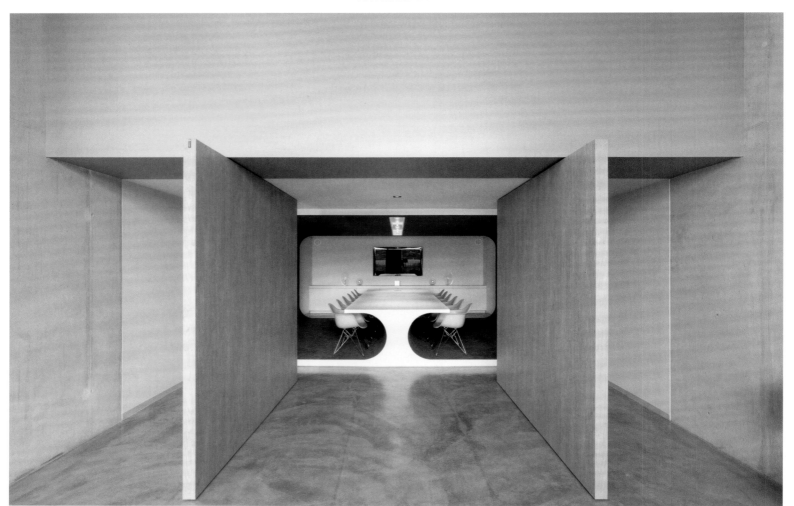

**Open and closed: flexible
wall planes define space.**
Post Panic, Amsterdam,
Holland; Maurice Mentjens

A space with many functions can also be described as "performative" – a term defining design that extends itself from the static.[19] With the anticipation of serving more than one purpose, the economy of performative space has important implications for issues of the environment. Each space has the potential for increased output without additional expenditure of energy.

Completed in 1998, OMA's residential project, Maison à Bordeaux, is exemplary in demonstrating this performative quality in architecture. Designed for a client with a physical handicap, the concept of a hydraulic elevator inspired the use of a moving platform to connect and transform different spatial volumes of the house. Fully furnished, the moving platform seamlessly assimilates into each level as part of each room. The moving platform is one room performing many different functions; it serves as circulation, library, kitchen and bedroom. Giving new meaning to Le Corbusier's "machine for living", this performative characteristic set forth in Bordeaux has since inspired many projects.

Dual- and multi-use approaches have many possible applications in design. David Adjaye's IDEA Store in Whitehall, a concept for a series of aging and underused libraries in London, demonstrates the effectiveness of this approach applied to planning and development. Merging the institutional needs of the city to attend to an underserved population through its library system with the un-met educational needs of that same population, the first IDEA Store successfully fused the programme of library and community education centre. Two programmes, from unrelated building types, benefit from an unusual juxtaposition and an enhanced proximity. Premised upon the existence of similarities in certain shared spaces and users, this example of dual use achieves enormous efficiency with the construction of a single building instead of two. In eliminating duplications and redundancies, the programmes have also benefitted from a new and dynamic interaction between the two user groups.

Fold and slide: the function of rooms can be adapted to the desired use.
Friggebod Holiday Home, Göteborg, Sweden; b-k-i / brandherm + krumrey interior architecture

Sit, stand, recline – a prototype for a multifunctional Panton-esque space-saving piece of furniture.

turnOn experimental vision for living,
überall & nirgends; AllesWirdGut

The boundaries between wall and object, between space and furniture, between engineering and interiors offer potential venues for other applications of multi-use in the built environment. Invented in 1900, the Murphy bed, a bed that folds up into a wall, is an early precedent for such a blurring of boundaries between wall and object that embodies the spirit of dual use. It is a precedent that has successors in various project types. The architectural projects and furniture designs of Eileen Gray uniformly employ a multifunctional approach. The interior surfaces – wall, floors and ceilings – and objects, especially in E.1027, share an elastic relationship, mirroring human nature and the desire to perform more than one task at a given time: a wall in the bedroom conceals a writing desk; cupboard drawers pivot to serve the needs of two different rooms; a hinged, metal seat transforms into a ladder; a false ceiling conceals storage units and folding steps for access. These designs expand on those boundaries, enhancing them with dynamic interpretations. This work has resonated through the years and remains the inspiration for projects today. Interior walls and furniture, for example, have fused with entirely different outcomes and styles at the Nokia Office in Silicon Valley and the Norwegian Wild Reindeer Centre. In both cases, this dual use approach results in spatial dynamism that expands the space through the performative action of the wall.

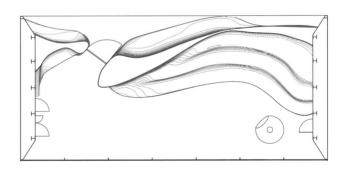

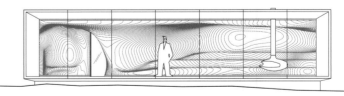

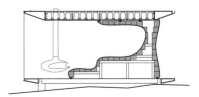

Landscape and interior meld into one – no reason to step outside...
Norwegian Wild Reindeer Centre Pavilion, Hjerkinn, Dovre, Norway; Snøhetta Oslo

The exploration of the boundaries between related design fields has also yielded additional sites for multi-use. Product design is the point of departure for the development of objects in the interior that transform to define space and serve as furniture. Mobile Fold-Out Home Office, a box-like product, serves as today's version of the historic secretaire. Stick figure-type graphics stenciled onto the surface reveal the many drawers and surfaces that transform the object to a fully functioning workstation. Loftbox, an unassuming rectangular volume, unfolds to serve as a small but fully furnished living room. In its unfolding, the divide between product and space is eliminated. Similarly, the field of graphic design, with its use of new digital printing capabilities, has enabled the rapid transformations of an interior space through the use of mutable wall treatments.

The digital phenomenon has also created new boundaries of time and place. Without a need for physical presence in the workplace, working at home or dialing in from a different time zone allow one to cross these boundaries many times in a single 24-hour day. Modern life requires a negotiation of such boundaries and virtual lines of existence, often with little differentiation between living and working and between night and day. Spaces for living have expanded in scope to accommodate these new demands. A multifunctional approach is especially effective in expanding the potential of such space. Superimposed upon already flexible space, such characteristics culminate in super qualities that can exponentially extend the spatial promise of the same footprint. Two projects in Asia illustrate the hyper-potential of small space through multiple physical overlays of space upon space, use upon use. The Domestic Transformer, a three decade-long renovation, is a 32 m² / 344 sq ft Hong Kong apartment project. Using a vocabulary of moving walls, sliding panels, fold-down furniture, suspended overhead units, shifting tracks, hydraulic platforms and pneumatic surfaces, the space transforms, as required, in constant kinesis from public space to intimate space and from day to night, yielding 24 possible configurations from a single space.

Suitcase House Hotel, an experimental development near the Great Wall of China, further pushes the limits of reconfigurable space. The house, a 44 m x 5 m / 144 ft 4 in x 16 ft 5 in rectangle, blurs the division between inside and outside, intimacy and exhibitionism, meditation and revelry. Using similar techniques inspired by the manoeuvres and architectural hardware used in the Domestic Transformer, an open floor plan with typical residential functions for two occupants has the potential to accommodate a music chamber, a library and fourteen guests in seven possible guest rooms. The design considers the different space needs of a 24-hour cycle and employs multifunctional devices to overlap these functions for maximum efficiency.

The concept of the wooden box is applied to all areas, even the bathroom.
Suitcase House, Beijing, China; EDGE Design Institute Ltd.

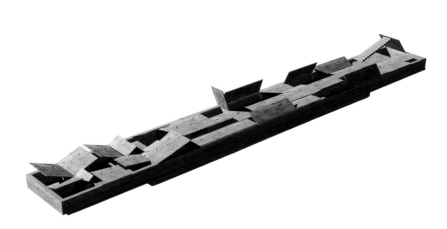

Technological advancements have also enhanced these investigations with new computational tools that extend the limits of structural and digital geometric analysis. Two-dimensional material is transformed into three dimensions with economic efficiency through the new possibilities of fabrication in the work of designers Bek, Martí and Zamorano. A project for a pavilion, showcased at the spoga Design Exhibition, is an expandable room formed from a two-dimensional sheet of plywood. Enabled by a parametric computational tool, a geometric pattern cut into the plywood made possible the creation of a double curvature, transforming two-dimensional sheet material into habitable space. Similarly, an intricate three-dimensional lace ceiling is created using CNC fabrication. Installed in a 16th-century building in Malta, this techno-lace, a tribute to the local craft of lacemaking, creates a space within a space through the use of digital geometry.

This pavilion made of precision-cut sheet material is modular and can be extended to fit different room sizes with zero material wastage.
Expandable Surface Pavilion, spoga+gafa 2011, Cologne, Germany; Pablo Zamorano, Nacho Martí, Jacob Bek

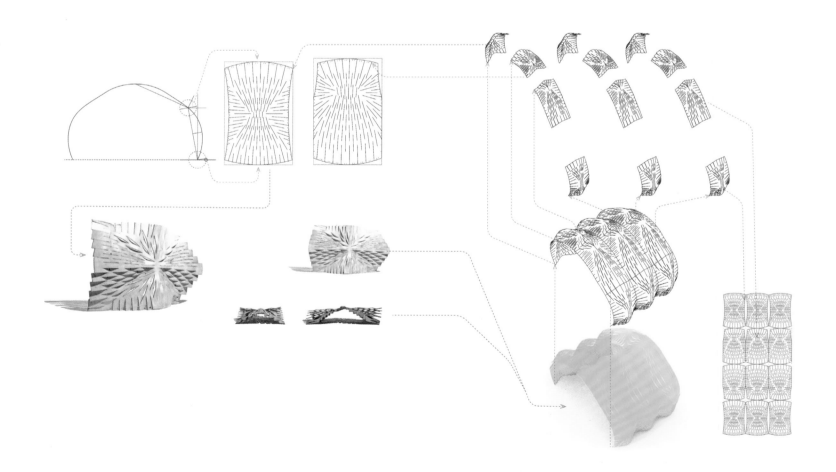

Cross-fertilisation with electronics has yielded some of the most dramatic developments that thrust the performative role of space to new expectations. Applications are no longer directed only toward issues of spatial function but include a range from the emotive to medical diagnosis and from surveillance to energy production. BotoxLamp and Slow Furl are, respectively, light and textile applications within the interior that respond to human presence. They have the ability to capture and also to make tangible the human experience within its interior environment. Using networked LEDs within aluminium sheets, Botox-Lamp detects, reacts to and interacts with humans through various states of inertia and alertness. The lamps flash and pulse to the presence of an inhabitant. Presented in 2011 at DMY Berlin, BotoxLamp is part of a trilogy of interactive installations. Similarly, Slow Furl is a large-scale textile installation that reacts and shifts slowly as it detects the presence of inhabitants. Pioneers of robotic membranes, the designers experiment with embedding informational technology and digital systems within responsive textile systems that move, open, close and flow to the actions of the occupant of the space. The implications of such works on the future of interior space are immense.

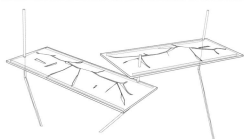

Light, geometry and space: precision-cut using a plasma laser, the folded sheet aluminium lamp is back-lit with energy-efficient LEDs.
BotoxLamp, Berlin, Germany; The Principals – Drew Seskunas, SAQ Architects, Zumtobel

A simple, practical and charming kitchenette – just my cup of tea!
Eine Küche / Keine Küche (Kitchen / No Kitchen), kitchenette in a cupboard in a loft apartment, Leipzig, Germany; Steinert & Bitterling

ADAPTIVE RE-USE

The practice of interior design is one that takes place in many different settings, from tenant fitout within new core-and-shell construction to the re-use of a building, or part of one, with a complex structure and history. The practice of adaptive re-use is routinely defined as transforming an unused or underused building into one that serves a new use. Within such a framework, every interior design project is, in essence, also a project of adaptive re-use. As a field of practice, adaptive re-use "is rich and varied and its importance includes not only the re-use of existing structures but also the re-use of materials, transformative interventions, continuation of cultural phenomena through built infrastructure, connections across the fabric of time and space, and preservation of memory – all of which result in densely woven narratives of the built environment".[20] While the rating systems for assessing sustainability using industry standards cannot measure the effectiveness of such practice, the opportunities for ecological good through design innovation are immeasurably vast. If indeed "the greenest building is one that is already built", such innovation in interior design is already inherently sustainable.

1   "Electronic Energy Performance of Buildings Directive", http://training.eebd.org.

2   http://architecture2030.org/the_problem/buildings_problem_why.

3   http://architecture2030.org/2030_challenge/the_2030_challenge.

4   Fowler, K.M. and Rauch, E.M.,"Sustainable Building Rating Systems", completed by the Pacific Northwest National Laboratory for the U.S. Department of Energy by Batelle, July 2006, p. 1.

5   The year the system was initiated is not necessarily the same as the year it was available for public use.

6   Carassus, Jean, "Are 'Green' Office Buildings Keeping their Promises? Actual performance, real estate value and 'HQE Exploitation' certification", commissioned by the Centre Scientifique et Technique du Bâtiment and Certivéa, 2011, p. 11.

7   Ibid., p. 18.

8   Schendler, Auden and Udall, Randy, "LEED is Broken – Let's Fix it", iGreenBuild.com, The Voice of Sustainable Design & Construction, 9 August 2005, p. 3.

9   King Sturge, "European Property Sustainability Matters retrofitting buildings and places", 2009.

10   Saunders, Thomas, "A Discussion Document Comparing International Environmental Assessment Methods for Buildings", BRE, 2008.

11   Burrows, Victoria Kate and Starrs, Melanie, "BREEAM vs. LEED – a white paper", Inbuilt Ltd., February 2010.

12   http://architecture2030.org/2030_challenge/the_2030_challenge.

13   Eliel, Carol S., L'Esprit Nouveau: Purism in Paris 1918-1925 (Los Angeles County Museum of Art in association with Harry N. Abrams, Inc, 2001), p. 14-15.

14   www. microcompacthome.com.

15   Lewis, Paul, Tsurumaki, Mark and Lewis, David J., Opportunistic Architecture (Princeton, NY: Princeton Architectural Press, 2008)

16   Thomas, Abraham, "V&A Curator of Designs and curator of the exhibition '1:1 - Architects Build Small Spaces' at the V & A", dezeen magazine, 15 June 2010.

17   Kaplan, David, "A permanent trend of pop-up shops", Houston Chronicle, 11 December 2011.

18   Benamor Duarte, Eduardo and Tiazzoldi, Caterina, "Toolbox", Int|AR Journal of Interventions and Adaptive Reuse, vol. 2, 2010, p. 48.

19   Cohen, Preston Scott, "Dexterous Architecture", Harvard Design Magazine, Fall/Winter 2008-09, p. 66.

20   Berger, Markus, Hermann, Heinrich and Wong, Liliane, eds., "Editorial", Int|AR Journal of Interventions and Adaptive Reuse, vol. 1, 2009.

YOU HAVE TO BE INSPIRED… FASHION, MUSIC, ART AND SCIENCE AS DESIGN INSPIRATION

MARINA-ELENA WACHS

WHAT DOES DESIGN/ DESIGNING MEAN AND WHAT DO WE UNDERSTAND BY QUALITIES?

Discussing design qualities in interior architecture requires that we first need to ask what we understand by design and quality in the context of space. For the most part, it is clear that the design of a space is determined by the functions and the activities taking place within it, and that this must follow a "human-centred process". But interior design is not solely a product of reason. In addition to functional and pragmatic considerations, there is emotion and narration as well as something we find agreeable but hard to identify that gives space a quality that enriches our lives – something that makes us feel comfortable in the space or reinforces our sense of self and consequently evokes a feeling of belonging.

When comparing the terms interior design and interior architecture, we need to ask ourselves: "What do we mean when we speak of architectural quality? … Quality architecture to me is when a building manages to move me. …

How do people design things with such a beautiful, natural presence, things that move me every single time?"[1] For Peter Zumthor, architectural quality is expressed through "atmospheres". What at first sounds deceptively simple has preoccupied philosophers for many thousands of years, and the field of architecture and aesthetics for several hundreds of years. Over the past few decades it has also found its way into the field of design and in particular of interior architecture: the ability with the help of a particular atmosphere to generate and elaborate a space, to complement an underlying mood with softer and louder elements in the right rhythm and at the perfect moment to build up to a crescendo at the climax of creativity.

If an interior is to be designed for music, then once again it is the functions, room programme or surrounding functions in the context of its environment that determine the brief for the design. Only rarely does a transdisciplinary approach, an abstract natural form or the sound of a note of a particular instrument serve as inspiration for the first sketch of the building's interior design, although this is sometimes the case for the exterior of buildings for music.

Are such approaches to designing – those that are infused with feelings, creative freedom and chaotic and hard-to-

Inspired by the forests of fairy tales, this poetic white landscape in a gallery is made entirely of paper with peepholes for visitors.
Wald aus Wald, Hong Kong, China; Takashi Kuribayashi

elaborate inspirations – really only possible in the comparative freedom of studies, or are they the sole reserve of star architects and interior designers? Or do we need to give greater room to philosophical and ethical values – in addition, of course, to resource-friendly sustainable approaches to design and the respective functional concerns?

Besides "the resource of ideas", a further aspect is important in terms of the design qualities of interior and "exterior" design, or architecture (by which interior architecture is gradually being subsumed). "In the supermarket of vanities", as the philosopher and philosophy professor Hannes Böhringer has called it, the question is how much personal distance there is to designing for society. Böhringer writes: "For this reason, to philosophise means to follow nature, to live according to nature, and art means to imitate nature. One need rarely invent something new when nature provides us with models that we need only imitate: burrows, nests, canopies of leaves for example in architecture. In fact, one need no longer build at all as burrows, nests and canopies of leaves already exist. For this reason, building is not as important as 'living', as being a 'global citizen', as living in the world.... Why then do so few people live according to nature?" asks Hannes Böhringer in his essay "The Absence of Architecture. Mies and Modernism", before offering a philosophical answer of his own: "Greed and possession, answered Seneca, and Rousseau nodded in agreement." [2]

The word "greed" can encompass the notion of sustainability and reduction when the inspiration leads to the creation of a classic design, a design that is timeless in postmodern space, and as such can be converted into a model. To continue Böhringer's philosophical approach, the question remains as to how these "global citizens" live in interiors today – and with what corresponding possessions? Our knowledge of the finiteness of resources, the need to make sparing use of manufactured goods, the unforeseen technological possibilities, a high degree of mobility and of flexibility in the way we manage and perceive time – it is these aspects that, alongside the tangible functions, define the parameters of interior design on which the design of the "atmospheric qualities" of interiors must focus.

Visitors enter into another world inspired by nomads and the orient in this nightclub in Amsterdam.
Nomads Restaurant, Amsterdam, Holland;
Concrete Architectural Associates

Inspired by the roaring twenties – gramophone and vintage wave hairstyles.
Leila Restaurant, Dubai, UAE;
Bachir Nader – Interior Architect

INSPIRATION: BETWEEN EMOTION AND FUNCTION

"An apple and a pear elevated to imposing monumentality – this is how the Frankfurt painter Justus Juncker presents the fruit in his two still lifes from the year 1765.… Depicted against a dark background and illuminated by a bright ray of light, the apple and pear exude a magical presence. Masterly painted in a manner evocative of the Dutch painters of the 16th and 17th centuries, Juncker reproduces the different materials and surfaces, showing the traces of aging on the stone pedestals on which the over-ripe fruit rest, along with the fleeting shadows of the insects that feed on the fruit and their fragile bodies." The view that the art historian Max Hollein relates in the catalogue *The Magic of Things – Still Life Painting 1500-1800*[3] is not typical of art historical texts. It is a directed, many-layered description of the way of reading the work of art, which represents nature in a certain way according to the ideas of the artist in the 18th century. What Hollein describes here, and makes palpable for the reader, is its narrative value.

Image, narration and readability are equally important concepts for the spaces in which we live. An interior is often an image of the ideas, desires and values of its residents, which are manifested in the arrangement of rooms, in the choice of objects, ensembles and combinations they contain and in the use of form, colour, material, surface, light and other details of the interior's architecture, which together communicate an overall concept. It is not just a first impression of the atmosphere that is being portrayed here and instinctively directed, and that shapes inspiration too. Interior architecture is also a platform that serves to interpret the details of the interior design as an overall view of the person, or people, who live(s) in it – and who chose that particular interior design.

We read the things in direct relation to the people in their private realm: the original work of art by Pablo Picasso or "the" Corbusier recliner that contrasts with a wooden footstool found in a workshop speak to us as a social commentary; the contrast, itself emblematic of modernism, is understood as an expression of personality and social position. What served as inspiration in this case: the work of art or the image of contemporary living?

A private space may be inspired by an item of furniture, or by a painting, a particular wall texture or covering, a restored historical mural, or the dominant elements of the space itself, such as high ceilings, large glazed surfaces, its quality of light… all these are possible inspirational elements that influence or characterise the quality of the space because they (help to) shape it.

The inspirations, such as the choice of elements, and how they have been portrayed to best effect under the prevailing circumstances in a person's private space present an image of the individual, their personal taste and emotional character in a way that the design elements of a semi-public space, such as a hotel lobby, or a public space, such as a concert hall, never can. These need to accommodate many individuals, to provide an appropriate setting in terms of the style and period in which people feel "at home" for the short time during which they are there. The intention here is that people respond positively to the space, through the objects in it, the arrangement of the space, the quality of light and so on which – in combination or individually, and without additional help from other details – strike a chord with the visitor.

For the visitor, individual design objects, lighting elements, sculptural works of art or particular surface qualities serve as highlights that provide visual orientation and can also be inspiring – and the designer's inspiration in turn inspires the "user" of the space: *you have to be inspired…*

YOU HAVE TO BE INSPIRED… BY MUSIC

In the discipline of music, one can fill spaces with a carpet of sound, or the timbre and resonance of a voice. But can a room itself have a timbre? Can an interior be given a carpet of sound that has a soft and velvety tone, or that reflects the sound of a viola playing pianissimo and awakens associations with wine-red velour? Some people are able to make a direct synaesthetic connection between sensory sensations and a corresponding conceptual or three-dimensional design quality. In the world of theatre, this mechanism is of central importance, inspiring and giving shape to the production. The design seeks to capture, to interpret the freedom of thought by means of verbal or emotional association but always ultimately returns to function: the function of creating an atmospheric quality for the interior.

Music is a very good example of how emotions can be captured, and the same principle applies equally to the design of interiors. People are able to feel and sense abstract ideas, and these are not solely expressed verbally but also in material form. Nicole Brüggmann, describes the inspiration for her design for a temporary interior for the Classic Lounge in the Museum of History in Hanover in 2010 as follows: "I associate classical music with sensuality and emotions.… My design draws on the characteristics of classical music and makes them accessible in a virtual form."[4] Here the focus of the design is its synaesthetic quality, which needs to be made visible, tangible and multi-dimensional in the design of the interior.

This ability to make connections between different senses is something we can all do, and is a skill that can be trained to a greater or lesser degree through practice, as described by the psychologist Elsbeth Stern in her elaborations on research into human intelligence.[5]

YOU HAVE TO BE INSPIRED... BY ART

In the search for inspiration(s), the term "uniqueness" features often in today's design processes. At the Contract-World Expo in 2011, the Finnish architect Teemu Kurkela presented his country with the question, "What makes us unique?" So what is it that makes us unique, what makes him and his office unique, what is unique about the qualities of creative design from Finland? Uniqueness is sought after as an antidote to cheap uniformity, as a means of attracting interest in a difficult economic climate and, of course, as a means of increasing turnover. Many companies introduce more strongly differentiated luxury brands and premium labels in an attempt to raise their profile, using this quality of uniqueness.

To this end, companies are constructing atmospheres and communicating them with the help of narratives. This can be seen clearly in shop-in-shop concepts, such as that of Montblanc and other manufacturers of high-quality writing implements, which use precision-made showcases and light installations to create a particular shopping experience. Expressly unique atmospheres can be created with the help of unique products, for example furniture that has a particular patina: Maarten Van Severen's design for a table for the manufacturer Vitra illustrates a trend towards more authenticity by giving its surface an artificial patina to lend it an impression of age, and with it an air of uniqueness, as if it has a history of its own to tell.

When I describe an object using a word in French, it "sounds" different to how it does in its native language. This foreignness is initially perceived as being exciting – it has a tonality communicated in this case through the French language. It would be interesting to investigate how the creation of atmospheres varies internationally, i.e. whether people of different nationalities – German, French or English for example – experience or perceive atmospheres differently as a product of their linguistic and cognitive background.

The power of style is, one could say, ingrained in the genetic material of French craftsmanship: interior designers such as Christian Liaigre produce work that has a particular linguistic design quality, work that upholds design codes for interior design that are reflected both in the history of craftsmanship as well as in the natural and cultural design tradition of the land, the value of which in the case of France is supported and cultivated by the state and other institutions. An association like the Comité Colbert, founded in 1954 to represent manufacturers such as Les Gobelins, the royal crystal and glass producers and others on the international market, and therefore to strengthen the reputation of *la grande nation*, would not go amiss in other countries as they increasingly seek to differentiate themselves from others in the context of increasing globalisation. Then as now, the Comité Colbert is a patronage for style savants.

It underlines the power of style in matters of synergetic or synaesthetic impression.

The narrative and the unsettling potential of art can create a secretive atmosphere. In this context, the design instrument of abstraction should also be mentioned. It can be found in art both in sculptures such as Picasso's *Bull's Head* (*Tête de taureau*, 1942) – an assemblage of the saddle and handlebars of a bicycle – as well as in the design and seating object *Mezzadro* (1957) by Achille and Pier Giacomo Castiglioni. In the context of an increasingly uniform market place that arose in part out of the idea of a globally understandable design language, which is today thankfully being called into question, we should concentrate more on our particular cultural qualities, on what makes us different. This we can achieve with a little abstract thinking: the sketch by the Finnish architect Teemu Kurkela and the Lavazza espresso cup made of cookie dough illustrate how the use of inspiration works with objects, which ultimately all have to take a concrete form.

As part of their design studies, students are often set tasks that examine transdisciplinary creative concepts. A typical task involves the students using an edible Lavazza coffee cup as inspiration for designing a pavilion. With only a few materials, perhaps clay in place of concrete and some kind of renewable, semi-permanent material to be developed later, the students form an enclosure – initially rough and ready using a paper model, then using a model made with the edible Lavazza cup, which is then modified, formed, joined together and shaped for the design of the pavilion. Art, or an artefact, can therefore serve as inspiration, through an unreal moment of associative design interaction, and be used as a motif in abstract form for innovation in the realm of interior design.

Another entirely different use of art is as part of the design of a space in a manner familiar from boardrooms where large-format oil paintings are used as dominant eye-catchers. Here art is used as a design element of a space. As an expression of a standpoint, or a declaration thereof, such a use of art often resembles a display of power, a way of cultivating a space by providing strategic focus. When works of art dominate a space, they contribute to the quality of a space within the context of its readability: what is the room owner trying to tell us? Why has my friend decided to hang this particular work of art? Is it something he or she likes, was it just a good investment, or does it happen to be in fashion? Or was it actually the product of a flash of inspiration – an idea of how art can contribute to the space – that motivated the decision?

A particularly fascinating manifestation of the art of spatial appearance could be seen in the installation *appearing rooms* created by the artist Jeppe Hein for Lichtparcours 2010 in Braunschweig: formed out of rows of water jets illuminated by floor-mounted lights, the walls of the installation spouted vertically out of the ground. At short intervals, new temporary constellations of spaces would be created: much like in an open-plan office, the position of walls changed, creating rooms of new sizes with differing subdivisions. The spectacle was especially magical in the evening and at dusk when people occupied the installation for short periods, jumping from room to room more than walking around it. The fleeting presence of the walls and their semi-transparent, slightly fuzzy appearance was quite enthralling, and yet also quite evidently a folly. This kind of flexible, fleeting moment in which elements temporarily structure a space is something that office-furnishing systems can provide. In this case, art was probably not the motivation for such systems, but rather the need to respond to changing production processes and workflows gave rise to such functionality, which in turn influenced its design. → 110

Real fake: nothing appears to be real in this complete illusion.
Baccarat, Paris, France; UBIK – Philippe Starck

inflation_deflation: interactive plastic bags are the only protagonists, inflated and deflated behind the scenes by micro-controllers and ventilators.
One Hundred and Eight, Berlin, Germany; Nils Völker

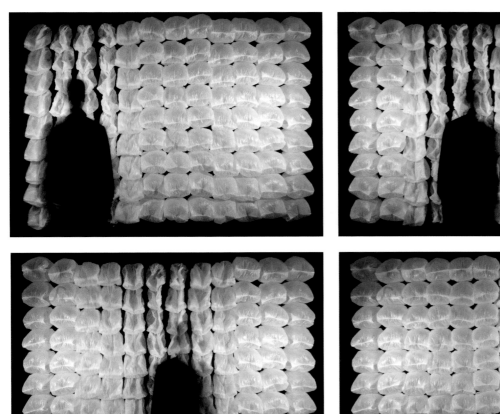
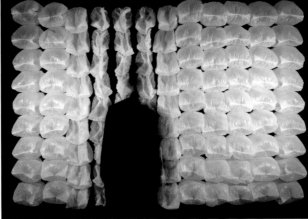
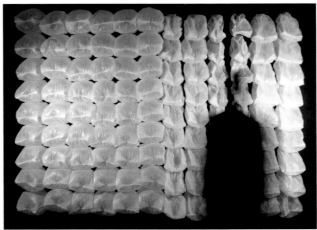

Dots cover the entire room, turning it into an endless continuum.
Dots Obsession; Yayoi Kusama

"One in a million" – this is how the artist sees herself, inspired by her motto "polka dots all over".
Portrait of the artist Yayoi Kusama

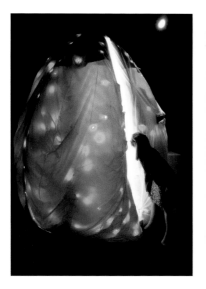 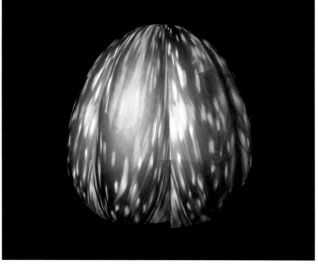 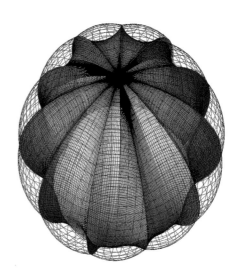

Inspired by nature – Smart Skin, an adaptive system as a protective envelope.
"corpform", Weil am Rhein, Germany;
Marco Hemmerling

Product of Lebanon: inspired by rotating wine caskets, the room becomes a decorative wine store that connects the other floors.
Braai, Beirut, Lebanon;
Bachir Nader – Interior Architect

Orient, ornamentation and mosaic.
Juliet Supper Club, New York City,
New York, USA; bluarch

Inspiration: cocoa in gold and chocolate brown.

"Chocoladium", Special Exhibition in the Universum Science Center, Bremen, Germany; GFG Gruppe für Gestaltung

The call of the mountain: the former industrial building is transformed into a contemporary interpretation of the traditional alpine interior.

Elemänt Restaurant, Langenthal, Germany; barmade ag

Temporary installation in Chinatown in New York – a topology based on four forms and five sides, made of insulation board and mirrors illuminated in pink.
Turning Pink W, New York City, New York, USA; Leong Leong

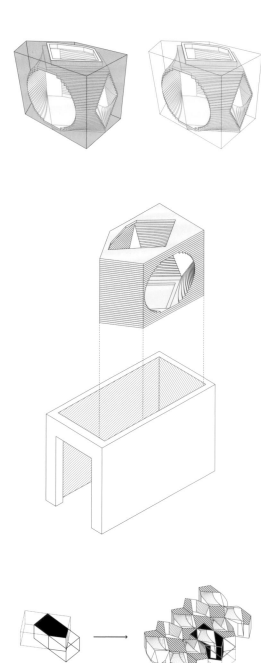

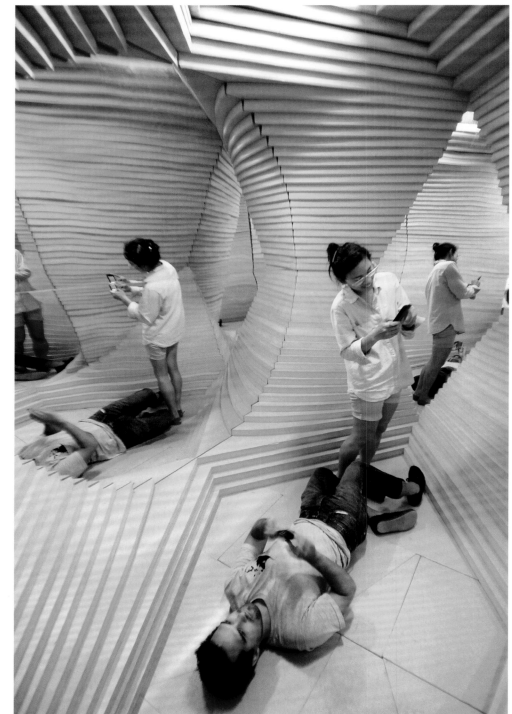

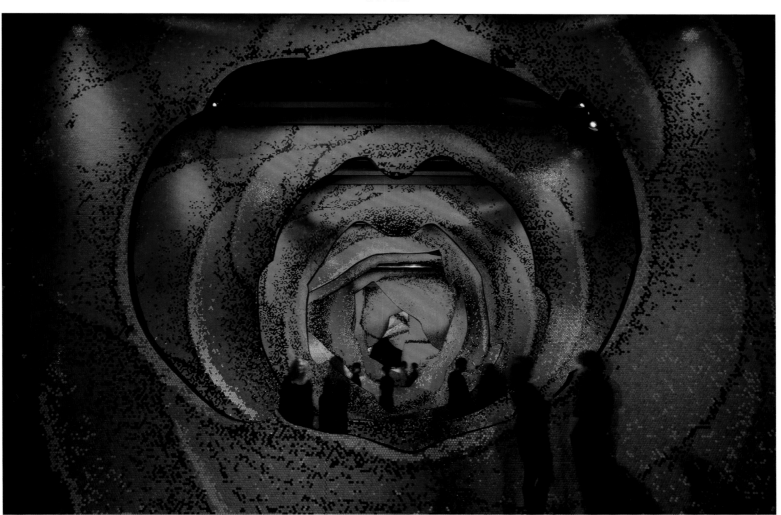

If you like red and love roses – in this walk-in rose, one loses one's sense of space and becomes part of the story.
"Il Fiore di Novembre" Exhibiton at the Triennale Design Museum, Milan, Italy; Studio Fabio Novembre

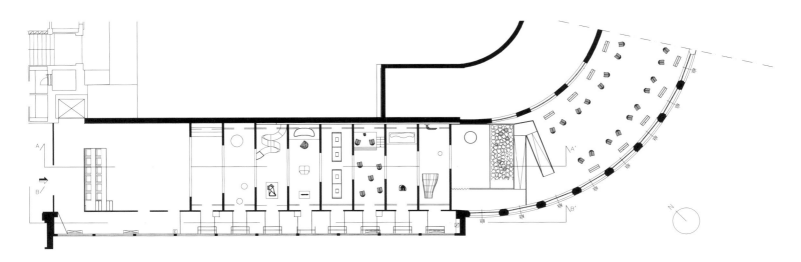

YOU HAVE TO BE INSPIRED... BY FASHION

When people are asked to name designers at the intersection of interior architecture and fashion design, Hussein Chalayan or Philippe Starck are often the first to come to mind. Back in the 1990s, Starck designed a tube dress made of jersey that could be worn as a miniskirt or as a maxiskirt and could also be used as a tent. Even extreme cases such as overalls or coats that can be turned into tent coverings with an interior that can be inhabited and therefore designed – whether predesigned or flexibly adaptable – are measured in terms of their spatial quality once they have been "converted".

At the same time we think of pioneers working at the frontiers of fashion such as Comme des Garçons: at the end of the 1990s in particular, the company produced man-made skins that distilled elements of a foreign realm and the new by employing the method of deconstruction from art: constructive elements were deconstructed and put back together in a new context. The methods of deconstruction was first elaborated in the philosophy of Jacques Derrida before making its way into architectural theory and practice in the work of Bernard Tschumi and others. Today it is a familiar aspect of fashion (Martin Margiela, Martine Sitbon among others). The model, or the process, is founded on the principle of taking parts of conventional objects, for example pieces of furniture, and integrating these in new furniture, or combining old and new furniture in unusual ways and means: a construction of the deconstructed.

Cultural heritage as a source of inspiration is not restricted solely to recycling, converting and reconfiguring pieces of our heritage. It can also be an opportunity to learn from tradition, to rediscover the value of traditional crafts and to use traces of the past as bearers of identity for inspiring new interiors: by way of example, a wall covering made of horsehair in the dining room of an old villa or fragments of a former kitchen and bath mosaic that are re-used on the ceiling of an entrance hall.

A further transdisciplinary cross-over between fashion design and interior architecture is the use of metaphors or terms that describe trends and stylistic movements: the "Belle Epoque", in 2011 a trend in fashion as well as in interior design, describes the return to stylistic elements from the good old days of finery. It characterises a longing expressed in fine materials such as silk, velvet and embroidery and a cut that is suitably luxurious.

This yearning for traditional, noble values also finds its expression in a renewed enthusiasm for patterning walls! "Retro Couture in Interior Design" borrows, for example, from the technique of grisaille from the 18th century for the patterns and drawings on wallpaper.

Similarly, a yearning for motifs from nature is expressed, for example, in the strong colours and patterns of wallpapers that brighten and enliven the mood of today's knowledge society as it goes through a time of economic uncertainty. This delight in colour and patterns in interior design expresses a sense of *joie de vivre*, of youthful spirit and a sensibility towards nature and culture, especially when we draw on traditional patterns, references and ornamentation.

The influence of design qualities from fashion as inspiration for interior architecture can also be seen in the reappropriation of cultural values. The use of old technical achievements does not preclude the notion of "back to the roots", of a return to traditional methods, which are often felt to be timeless and classic, and therefore precious and unique.

Synergies between the design qualities of fashion and of interior architecture are, of course, also to be found in the clothing sector. Clothing implies some kind of function, for example in the area of protective clothing. The technologies of applied textiles, such as textile filter materials that neutralise smells and pollutants, are making their way into the field of interior architecture, for example this year as textiles for hospitals and clinics.

Inspiration for the "second skin" of fashion can be derived from photographic images of architectural facades that are then applied as digital patterns for clothing and fashion – and vice versa. The work of the young designer Judy Zhang from London, with The *Versus Concept* (TVC), demonstrated in 2011 how fashion and architecture enter into a symbiosis, ultimately becoming part of the interior design. The interplay of analogue and digital images and construction methods could become a model for interior design in a manner similar to how inspiration and construction influence one another in the realm of bionics.

The current work of the Dutch product designer Mieke Meijer illustrates a model for how architecture can serve as inspiration for product design: she traces the precisely constructed forms and history of historically important architectural monuments and transforms them later into furniture, such as in her series entitled "Industrial Archaeology".[6]

The use of legacies from the past for built elements in space, or for elements in fashion, refers to a current trend towards reintegrating our history into our future. "Recruiting the cultural heritage" is how I would summarise this use of our cultural heritage, which can serve as a lasting source of inspiration for design as much as the model of natural systems described below.
→114

Undulating: inspired by street style, the overlapping white cables draw attention to the ceiling, creating a vivid contrast.
Shine Fashion Walk, Hong Kong, China;
NC Design & Architecture Limited, Laboratory
for Explorative Architecture & Design Ltd.

Wooded parkland and the urban jungle inspired this maze-like garden of garments for visitors to wander through.
Garment Garden, Messe Frankfurt 2006, Germany;
J. Mayer H. Architects

A bar interior inspired by zebras and by op art – impressive, particularly given the low budget.
Zebar, Shanghai, China; 3GATTI

The ornamental figure used on the walls of this gynaecological practice is inspired by the "flower of life". The free-flowing organic shapes of the floor inlays can be a racetrack or a duck pond depending on how the children interact with it.

Gynaecological practice, Maria-Hilf Hospital, Brilon, Germany; 100% interior Sylvia Leydecker

What's that we see growing?
A playful interpretation of greenery.

"Garden of Things", Museum of Arts and Crafts, Hamburg, Germany; dan pearlman Markenarchitektur

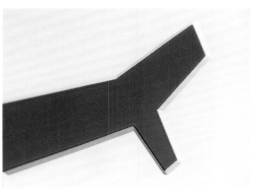

Fish, waves and coral create a distinct and fitting background for this restaurant.
OLIVOMARE Restaurant, London, England;
Architetto Pierluigi Piu

Organic forms that draw inspiration from coral and from bones alike: a scaled-up walk-in experience.

nonLin/Lin Pavilion – FRAC Centre, Orléans, France;
MARC FORNES / THEVERYMAN

YOU HAVE TO BE INSPIRED... BY SCIENCE

When considering how scientific and technical aspects serve as inspiration for interior architecture, we need to take a closer look at what space is. How do we understand space today, and how do we want to "live in it as global citizens", to refer back to the beginning of this chapter? One answer may be that we want to live naturally, sustainably and comfortably while being simultaneously mobile. With the help of such properties, we can draw up criteria: for an item of furniture, for example, this might mean that it should be easy to clean, easy to use and durable, that it must be produced sustainably and under fair conditions – whether it is destined for use in the home, in a doctor's practice or in an office or hotel. At the same time, these properties also indicate how it will be used in a furnishing concept, through its functionality, its style and its arrangement in the given context, i.e. in relation to the spatial conditions such as light, the size and height of the space as well as paths leading through the space.

Ultimately all these considerations come down to how we wish to lead our lives – that we want to lead a good, healthy way of life in spaces that have been consciously designed, that are functional, safe and sustainable and consequently benefit the atmosphere in which we live. The associative inspiration that from the very beginning informed the interior design concept is therefore a very crucial part of the design planning and its later realisation.

The general idea that we aim to incorporate into a design – whether it be inspired by bionics or analogies with natural forms – expresses a closeness to nature and to healthy living. The design for the Fondation Cartier in Paris by Jean Nouvel under the then president François Mitterand was particularly far-sighted in this respect. Here the outside areas of the building – both the natural surroundings and the social activities outside – are brought into the interior of the building using a cleverly designed glass facade. Since then a number of different approaches to integrating nature directly into the building have arisen. Jacques Ferrier Architectures, for example, designed the French Pavilion at the Shanghai Expo in 2010 to incorporate nature, training it in the form of vines to run in and through the building, and using it to create spaces for recreation as well as to refresh the quality of the air.

Fresh and healthy air will in future play an essential role for the design of interiors. The indoor air climate is dependent not only on the presence of nature in a space, but also on technical installations that control air flow rates, temperature, the acoustics and levels of illumination. In the fine arts, there is the idealised notion of arcadia, as portrayed in the "Le Jardin Anglais" wallpaper, an idea that Jacques Ferrier transformed into three dimensions in 2011. Here an idealised view of nature – with an almost archaic quality – serves as inspiration for the design. → 119

ICD / ITKE Research
Pavilion 2011,
Stuttgart, Germany;
University of Stuttgart

Bionic life as inspiration: the model for the morphology of the modular construction of this pavilion made of 6.5 mm thick plywood is the structure of a sea urchin.
ICD / ITKE Research Pavilion 2011, Stuttgart, Germany; University of Stuttgart

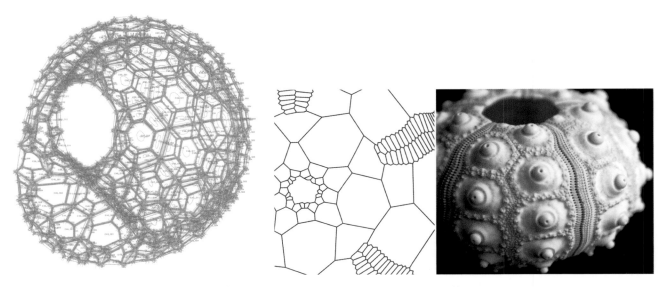

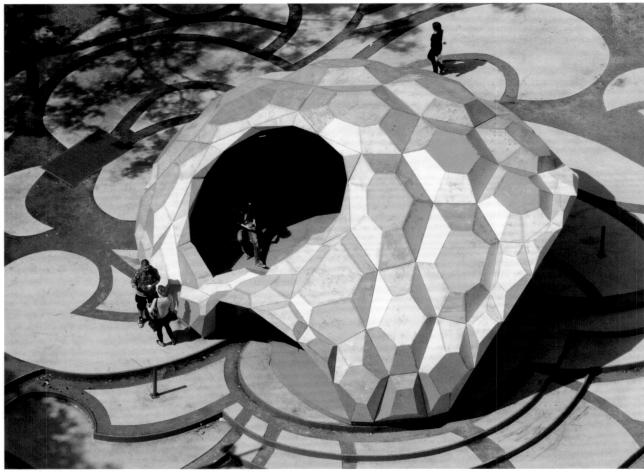

The temporary "snowscape" of this boutique was cut by hand out of polystyrene and contrasts dramatically with the wares on sale.
Dig, New York City, New York, USA; Snarkitecture

Dig, New York City,
New York, USA;
Snarkitecture

Another equally fascinating source of inspiration from the sciences are natural (building) materials: the natural materiality of a wall surface made of earth, for example, also helps to create an optimised indoor room climate by regulating the air temperature and humidity and improving the quality of life in living areas. Such approaches draw on traditional living environments and building methods, inspiring on the one hand a retro-movement and on the other contemporary approaches to sustainable building. Inspired by the properties of the material, Jacob Buse designed an earthen seat in 2010 in which the surface is fashioned entirely out of earth without any other artificial substance sealing the surface.

The principle of drawing analogies from nature, or more precisely the mechanisms of nature, can be seen in a project by the design student Ilka Bernhard in 2011: SOLution is an example of how bionics can contribute to the design of spaces by making use of the natural energy of our solar system. A photovoltaic or solar plant located discreetly outside the building channels energy into the interior of the house that is in turn used for electricity and water heating. Systems integrated into the interior architecture will increasingly exploit the technological possibilities, and what they produce, rendering them visible in the design: in the SOLution project, polychromatic, organically produced pigments, which are already available, are used to create a synthesis of interior and exterior space, catering to an increased need for islands in the city in which one can relax outdoors even when the weather is bad. The result is a new kind of conservatory inspired by natural energy systems that makes the principle of energy gain visible. A good overview of current examples for a "healthy (natural) way of living" in interior design can be found in the publication Sustainable Textile Design.[7]

Another kind of inspiration derived from natural systems and analogies with nature is one that creates space out of two dimensions. The principle here is one of folding where building elements fold together, unfold or fold into themselves. From the viewpoint of bionics as well as in terms of formal construction, the strategy of folding remains as popular as ever, not just due to its space-saving potential but also because its aesthetic appearance continues to hold fascination. From pleated skirts to the folds of the skin of the Gina concept car by BMW, or folding mechanisms in architecture – all these examples draw inspiration from folding systems that can be found in nature, such as in the wings of a ladybird.

The catalogue Skin + Bones – Parallel Practices in Fashion and Architecture[8] offers stimulating inspiration for a transdisciplinary comparison of fashion and architecture – and interior design – and their formal principles, and in turn for developing new creations. Transdisciplinary crossovers, the underlying creative themes, the parameters of building construction as well as socio-political considerations are detailed in a way that is especially stimulating for the development of design qualities that can serve to inspire architecture and interior design. These are the things that help us experience the "beauty and natural presence" of designed atmospheres with all our senses.

Further Reading:

Bahamón, Alejandro and Pérez, Patricia, Mineral Architecture – Analogies between the mineral world and contemporary architecture (Badalora: Parramón Ediciones, 2008).

Kemp, Wolfgang, Architektur analysieren (Munich: Schirmer und Mosel, 2009).

Wachs, Marina-Elena, Material Mind – Neue Materialien in Design, Kunst und Architektur, (Hamburg: Dr Kovac Verlag, 2008).

Wiedemann, Julius (Ed.), Product Design in the Sustainable Era (Cologne: TASCHEN, 2010).

Marina-Elena Wachs (BS, 12.12.2011)

1   Zumthor, Peter, Atmospheres (Basel, Boston, Berlin: Birkhäuser, 2006), p. 11.

2   Böhringer, Hannes, Enger Spielraum – Über Bauen und Vorbauen (Munich: Wilhelm Fink Verlag), p. 77.

3   Hollein, Max, Foreword of the German edition of the catalogue: Sander, Jochen and Städel Museum Frankfurt am Main (Eds.), Die Magie der Dinge – Stilllebenmalerei 1500-1800 (Ostfildern: Hatje Cantz, 2008), p. 9.

4   Brüggmann, Nicole, Press text accompanying the Classic Lounge in the Museum of History in Hanover, 2010.

5   See Stern, Elsbeth, "Intelligenz, Wissen, Transfer und der Umgang mit Zeichensystemen", in: Stern, Elsbeth and Guthke, Jürgen (Eds.), Perspektiven der Intelligenzforschung (Lengerich: Pabst, 2001), p. 163 ff, and p. 170 f. in particular.

6   See FORM, no. 238 (May/June 2011), p. 78 ff.

7   Wachs, Marina-Elena and Bendt, Ellen (Eds.), Sustainable Textile Design/Nachhaltiges Textiles Design (Hamburg: Schaff Verlag, 2013).

8   The Museum of Contemporary Art, Los Angeles (Ed.), Skin + Bones: Parallel Practices in Fashion and Architecture (New York: Thames & Hudson, 2006).

QUALITY OF LIFE

MICHAEL CATOIR

QUALITY – THE QUIET REVOLUTION

Visual quality is certainly one of the most important qualities in our everyday lives. Our whole experience is visual and we are constantly being bombarded with visual impressions. The quality of these is as varied and diverse as the impressions themselves, and new aspects are appearing every day. A flood of forms, lines, symbols, images, texts and textures befalls us from the moment we open our eyes in the morning. Amazingly, our eyes and heads are still able to manoeuvre us through this complex jungle, despite the sensory overload, and provide us with the parameters we need to be able to make decisions. In a fraction of a second, we can see that a chair will be uncomfortable without having sat on it. Similarly, a poorly designed door handle already produces an unpleasant sensation in one's hand just by looking at it, an impression that is reinforced when we use it. By contrast, a sculpture by Anish Kapoor evokes a desire to touch it (although we are usually not allowed to).

In such processes, the eye is many times faster than the mind – or to be more precise, than our intellectual response –, and it is not rare for our minds to play tricks on us. The Eames Plastic Side Chair, for example, has had such phenomenal commercial success that it has advanced to become a cult object; in the process one forgets just how uncomfortable it actually is, an experience I endured for years in our kitchen until I placed a sheepskin on it to protect my skinny rear. Ludwig Mies van der Rohe's Barcelona Chair is another candidate with great looks but poor comfort. But the master of deception is the Louis Ghost Chair: through its combination of historically inspired form and gleaming lightness and transparency, Philippe Starck's armchair is so attractive that it is able to make us forget all the disadvantages of a plastic chair.

But the eye can also be deceived by all manner of different parameters. It is hard to believe that the dome of St. Peter's Cathedral is over 100 metres high at its apex, such is its form and rich decoration. We have to refer to our travel guide for confirmation. The same principle also works at the other end of the scale: a small room when suitably decorated can look larger than it really is. This phenomenon can be seen in guest toilets around the world, and also in the Hôtel Costes: the rooms, in typical Parisian fashion, are often tiny, but Jacques Garcia has succeeded in decorating them so nicely that one entirely forgets the size of the room. A really beautiful example of the optical extension of space through the use of decoration is the Convent of San Marco in Florence: Fra Angelico painted wonderful frescoes on the walls of the cells, thereby skilfully reducing the sense of confinement.

But ultimately, the eye and mind have developed a relatively reliable system of values by which to perceive and understand the quality of things. For example, despite all

Coffee aroma – books aplenty, parquet flooring and mocha brown leather turned on its side!
D'espresso, New York City, New York, USA; Nema Workshop

the efforts of industry to make artificial versions of natural materials, our eyes and mind are still not always convinced. Artificial materials of this kind must be applied with skill and care for us to accept them: the weak point is often how they are employed or worked. For example, manufacturers have succeeded in making very good laminates with real wood veneer, but they are often given away by the treatment of their edges. Imitation stone tiling by Gres suffers the same problem. More convincing in terms of looks are materials that are coloured right through, such as colour core laminate, artificial stone or Corian, but these rather good imitations still lack the haptic feel of the original. To properly exploit the qualities of artificial materials to create a convincing object requires an almost holistic design concept. Ettore Sottsass, for example, succeeded in combining original forms and colours to create objects in which the weak point of the materials – their artificiality – was turned into its virtue. That, however, was an individual phenomenon. More often than not, many artificial materials are employed because they are cheaper and more hardwearing, and this can be seen especially in commercial projects. As a consequence, we associate in our minds that laminate flooring, for example, is a sub-standard product.

Visual quality plays a decisive role in how we evaluate our surroundings. Everyone is aware of this, and tries therefore to exploit this for their own aims. Unfortunately, in some cases, instead of visual quality one is presented with a visual impression of quality, and although this may work

to a certain degree, the eye sooner or later uncovers most deceptions – or else sees itself corroborated by the quality the visual impression has communicated.

Why is it that when we enter a Christian Liaigre or Promemoria store we feel part of an atmosphere of elegant luxury while when we visit a large furniture outlet, we just feel like we are in an expensive furniture shop? The answer lies in the multitude of perfectly crafted details that industrial production cannot replicate, in the spacious arrangement of the store and in the intimate lighting, all of which tell us that what we see are not mass-produced goods where "exclusive quality" is only to be found written on the label. → 126

The huntsman's greeting: a cosy corner in the centre of Paris.
Apartment, Paris, France;
Studio Catoir

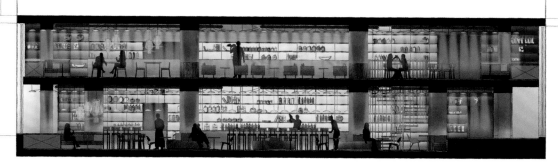

Country life with city chic: the restaurant of an international lifestyle hotel chain with the charm of grandma's preserves shelf.
Spice Market, London, England;
Concrete Architectural Associates

A patient's room with the atmosphere of a hotel creates a sense of comfort and hastens the speed of recovery.
Private Patient's Hospital Room of the Future, Medical Lounge, Berlin, Germany;
100% interior Sylvia Leydecker

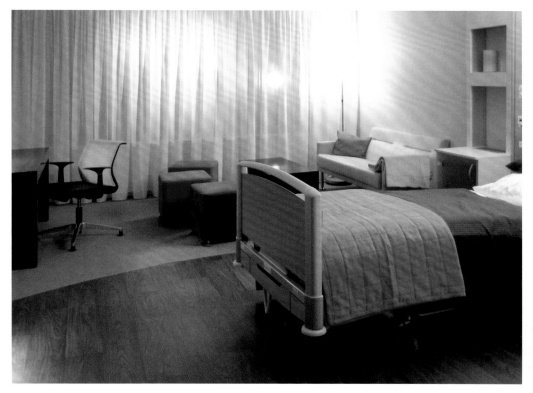

A cooker, a couple of pots and pans and a handful of kitchen utensils – that's all one needs to enjoy cooking. The accessories have been carefully chosen to fit into the overall concept.
Apartment, Paris, France; Studio Catoir

But there are also good examples at the other end of the scale that demonstrate what can be achieved with a limited budget. McCafé, for example, has managed to shed the cheap-as-cheap-can-be image of McDonald's, and in many of its establishments one can now enjoy a good caffè in pleasant surroundings. By skilfully combining laminate surfaces with classic pieces of furniture by Jean Prouvé (for example in McCafé in the rue du Renard in Paris), the fast-food chain has managed to liberate itself from the wash-down, vandal-proof aura of the 1980s.

The continuing uncertainty among consumers about the origin of products, caused in part by globalisation, has also sharpened our senses. The question of quality is therefore as relevant as ever. Creating visual impressions is a valid means of sending signals, attracting attention, creating harmony and so on, but quality is what creates real trust. This is what the tandem of visual impression and quality needs to achieve: to reassure consumers that what they see is not a pretence.

The re-editions of Jean-Michel Frank's furniture by Hermès and Écart, for example, are of such exquisite beauty and perfection that they have rightfully been lauded in the press. The craftsmanship is exceptional and shows what is possible when quality is the motor of an idea. Well-kept classic cars exude a similar fascination: every screw, every seam, the wonderfully crafted coachwork and the thick layer of paint are a delight to set eyes on. Even those who are not car enthusiasts can see the fascination in the craftsmanship of a *Gesamtkunstwerk* of this kind.

It is precisely this quality that the client should strive for. An interior that has been developed with such love and attention is a true oasis of peace, fascination and inspiration. Pierre-Alexis Dumas, *directeur artistique* of Hermès describes the home as a sheltered place to which one can retire in order to relax and to recharge one's batteries before venturing out again into the world outside.[1] This is the quality one needs to capture for the private areas or quiet zones in hotels, airport lounges or clubs. This quality is already evident in the graphic quality of the layout. A plan that looks harmonious on paper will be harmonious when realised in three dimensions because the eye sees the symmetry and relationships that create the sense of order and calm. The articulation of the details, the well-matched materials and qualities, the use of light, acoustics and air quality – the eye and mind take note of all these things, communicating to the viewer the care and attention to detail invested in the room, signalling that nothing has been left to chance, that the designer knew exactly what he wanted. One immediately feels reassured, and can begin to enjoy the harmony of the room. The style of the room plays only a secondary role. In the moment in which the eye registers what constitutes the space, the mind begins to examine it intellectually, to delight in it, regardless of whether it is in the style of John Pawson or Alberto Pinto. Of course, that does not mean it can be boring – the eye searches for new stimulation and new themes and the mind delights in each new moment of surprise.

Such moments of surprise are often created through the use of decoration, but this is altogether a particularly thorny issue. This is where the most serious stylistic clashes or lapses in quality occur. The worst mistake is not to deal with the issue at all. At the very least, measures should be taken to reduce, as far as possible, the impact of a potential defect. Andrée Putman, for example, forbade the placement of plants in any of her projects, using only a white orchid as floral decoration. Jil Sander had the surfaces of the windowsills in her offices slant so that members of staff could not place things on them or use them to display personal items. But the desire to add decoration is very common and this should be catered for in the design: as such, one should not shy away from it!

Decoration is unquestionably a part of every interior. It should therefore be an integral part of the design: even unbelievably expensive works of art can look out of place if not chosen and arranged with care and sensitivity. Masters of interior design such as Christian Liaigre or Alberto Pinto call themselves *décorateurs* and create perfect, complete works of art. Damien Hirst delights in creating decorative artworks for hotels and other institutions and even Jean Nouvel decorates his architecture with coloured ceilings.

Colour and colour combinations are popular ways of decorating spaces. Even in Switzerland, where concrete, glass and right angles predominate, large surfaces of bright colour can happily evoke a quirky nostalgia for the 1970s (for example in the supermarkets of the Migros chain). Luis Barragán was a master of colour who translated the spirit of South America into wonderful colour schemes. Today, architects such as Ricardo Legorreta or Sauerbruch Hutton create works of great beauty that owe a debt of inspiration to Barragán. In these examples, colour is able to communicate a fresh and positive emotional impression without being overtly contemporary. The use of colour is, however, not always straightforward. Not every client is receptive to the idea, or courageous enough. In public or semi-public projects such as hotels, trade fair architecture or foyers, decision-making committees have been known to feel so unsure of themselves that a prize-winning artist has had to be consulted before painting a wall red. At the same time, others are over-zealous in their use of colour in an attempt to make themselves noticed above the general competition for attention, which in turn further fuels the uncertainty of decision makers. Moroso, for example, is now designing trade fair stands and products that are so overladen with decoration that one can no longer see the wood for the trees. The celebrity designer of interiors Marcel Wanders drowns his projects with a degree of ornament-overkill that borders on the obscene. Visuality sells, but only in the right dosage! →128

A floating living room – comfort and relaxation aboard a luxury yacht interior.

Salperton IV; Adam Lay Studio

Float: the contemplative atmosphere creates a peaceful place for relaxation.

Gallery apartment with pool, Trudering, Germany; Anne Batisweiler

THE QUALITY OF SPACE: ORDER, FREEDOM, STRUCTURE AND PATHWAYS

One of the foundations for the quality of a space is unquestionably its layout. Here there are two camps: those who favour order and those who favour freedom. Well-ordered layouts are characterised by symmetry, alignment, axes and geometry. There are many diverse examples of this type, which has existed since man put one stone on top of the other, and in most architecture offices this is the standard approach to room layouts. An orderly layout may seem boring on paper, but if well executed and with skilful styling, it can achieve very good results. Masters of well-ordered layouts, such as Le Corbusier and Mies van der Rohe, constructed every wall and every item of furniture according to mathematical rules and built some quite fascinating sculptures using this approach. Andrée Putman always worked with geometric and well-ordered layouts and used them to create wonderful projects without the slightest hint of monotony. Orderly layouts are in many cases the best approach to create calm, spacious and elegant spaces while allowing a good degree of freedom for styling. Geometry and order can help to unite disparate functions and, due to their timeless quality, are generally received favourably. But caution should be exercised when the sense of order becomes too dogmatic. While many of the minimal projects that take these ordering principles to extremes are without doubt very photogenic, they are a nightmare to live in or use on a daily basis. As a result, it is not uncommon for these kinds of projects to subsequently be made "more friendly", causing the precarious balance of the *Gesamtkunstwerk* to fall apart as a consequence of the often absurd stylistic constellations that can then arise.

Free-form layouts take, as it were, the reverse approach. As a counterpoint to the timeless appearance of ordered layouts, it has become somehow trendy to design free-form layouts, and, as before, there are both good and bad examples of this approach. Free-form layouts are more tolerant of mistakes and imperfections than ordered layouts, and are therefore often used for precisely this reason. It is, of course, an illusion to believe that when a layout is as "crea-tif" as possible, it will be good. The "Big Bang" of free-form layouts is Future Systems' design for the Selfridges Department Store in Birmingham: a project in which island-like areas are freely arranged over several storeys, and which promises a very special shopping experience. As this concept has as yet not been replicated elsewhere in the world, one can assume that it is not as practical as hoped in everyday use. A very successful project in this category of layout is the Camélia Restaurant in the Mandarin Oriental Hotel on rue Saint-Honoré in Paris by Jouin Manku, which is a wonderfully flowery project with flowing forms and perfectly executed craftsmanship. It delights the eye with many surprising details without detracting from the overall originality of the idea.

Placed in a category often forgotten and given too little attention are layouts that have successively grown: floor plans of old apartments, hotels or office buildings that over the years have been altered by their users and now have what amounts to a second skin bearing the traces of its past life. Layouts in this category are able to accommodate all sorts of inconsistencies and to explain them away as part of the place's character. An absolute masterpiece in this category is the Palazzo Fortuny in Venice. Like many old palazzi, it is a wonderful building steeped in patina, red brick and wonderful details. But what is most exciting about it is the succession of universes on the different storeys. Originally a house and atelier for Mariano Fortuny, the palazzo now serves as a museum and exhibition venue. Visitors wander through the different rooms, before being confronted with the concerted power and distinctive beauty of the life and work of Mariano Fortuny in a room on the first floor. The walls are a vast patchwork of different layers covered with the famous Fortuny textiles, and one has the impression of being in an oversized jewellery box. In every corner of the room there are anecdotes from the rich life of Mariano Fortuny – a prototype of his lamps here, a huge wooden model of a stage set there; the sketches, patterns and paintings all meld into the fascinating universe of an exorbitant snowball.

Here one can see that it is very difficult to replicate the particular interplay of harmony and tension in such successively developed floor plans. Philippe Starck likes to use excerpts of such layouts in his projects, and has succeeded in realising them to great effect. →132

Fake door: doors spiced with a pinch of humour are the theme of this shop design.
INDULGI, Kyoto, Japan; Nendo

This residence for the elderly offers a suitably tasteful living environment for well-off residents.
Residence for the Elderly, Les Jardins d'Alysea,
Roeser, Luxembourg; JOI-Design

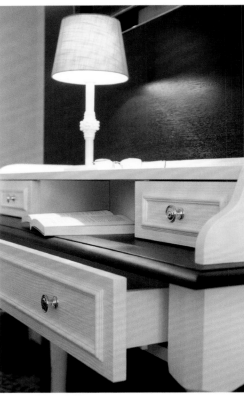

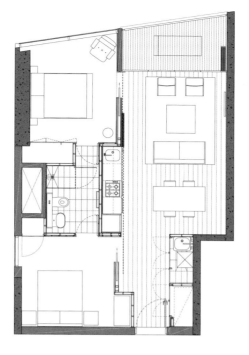

A spacious urban apartment with minimalist formal language, pleasant materials and a natural colour scheme.
One Central Park East, Sydney, Australia; Koichi Takada Architects

Wellness and design deluxe in this country hotel.
Lanserhof, Lans near Innsbruck, Austria; DRDI – reginadahmeningenhoven

MICRO-STRESS FACTORS IN HOTEL DESIGN: *DO IT SIMPLE DO IT STUPID*

In my mind's eye, I see a hotel advertisement: *Fantasy Hotels & Resorts are first class, full-service hotels that combine a stylish and contemporary approach to design with a culture of innovative thinking designed to meet the very specific needs of its guests.*

These innovations include its "Yes I Can!" spirit of hospitality, a great choice of concept rooms with Nespresso® coffee machines in Business Class, a 100% Guest Satisfaction Guarantee Programme, an Easy Connect approach to IT with free high-speed Internet access for all guests and meeting delegates, and a fantastic range of destination bars, restaurants, leisure facilities such as spa and wellness centres and meetings and event venues.[2]
– Daily newspaper
– Nespresso® machines with an assortment of coffees
– Free pay-TV movies
– Lifestyle magazines
– Fluffy bathrobe & slippers
– … and much more!

Most hotel chain advertising sounds something like this and features a long list of amenities and fancy-sounding services that are supposed to sound appealing, but in actual fact only add to the bewildering plethora of choices the customer faces. In the end, of course, it almost always boils down to the cost of a room for the night. After all, what the hotel guest really needs is just the basics: a place to stay for the night, a clean room, a good night's sleep and a hot shower.

But staying in a hotel is no longer as simple as that. The stress and confusion that hotel guests have to cope with begins the moment they are given the key. Nowadays, hotel room keys are not the sort that can be left at reception and picked up again later: today's hotel rooms are unlocked with a credit-card-sized "key". This is, of course, a size that is a little too easy to lose track of, causing frantic searching through pockets, wallets and handbags for the all-important piece of plastic on return to the room, hoping all the while that it has not become demagnetised while in contact with other cards or mobile phones. Sooner or later, guests find themselves having to return to the lobby at 2 a.m. to ask the night porter to fashion a new card.

Along with the card, the hotel guest receives an induction in the use of the practical guest entry system. The market economy has, of course, brought forth a variety of systems, so that hotel guests invariably have to deal with a new system for each hotel: insert the card in the slot from above, microchip facing downwards; slide the card sideways into the lock; pull the card through the slot in the lock (from top to bottom, of course); touch the card against the lock; swipe the card close to the door frame at the height of the handle, and so on. Once the hotel guest has passed this hurdle, the procedure continues with the "What do I do with the card once I'm in the room?" ceremony. But because hotel staff have learnt that guests are already overburdened with remembering the room number, where the lift is, where the breakfast room is, the price of breakfast, how to open the door and what to do with the card to activate the electricity, this last detail is often left unexplained. Guests are then left to find out what to do with the card, keeping one foot in the door to allow light into the room so that they can locate the cardholder of the guest entry system.

And here we encounter another old favourite of building technicians and hotel managers: the lighting system. Always on the lookout for new selling points, general managers are often keen on embracing new trends and technical advances. Ostensibly installed to reduce energy wastage and provide guests with added comfort, these complex lighting control systems provide a series of pre-programmed lighting scenarios controlled from a touch panel. The guests end up spending more time trying to work out how to actually switch off what they do not need than enjoying their stay. The list of pitfalls and surprises to be found in a hotel room is surprisingly long and the interior designer's battle to reduce these to a minimum is only sometimes successful.

Thankfully there are investors, hotel owners and managers who have understood that hotel guests do not really want to have to learn how to use their room, and that *Do it simple do it stupid* is often a better and more desirable approach to many of these issues. By way of example, the Hudson Hotel in New York has well-designed vending areas in the upper-storey corridors, the Soho Hotel in London has a self-service honesty bar in the lobby, replacing the need for a minibar in the room, and the Renaissance Hotel at London Heathrow has simply a fridge for guests to store the drinks bought from the kiosk in the hotel lobby. The same principle applies to cupboard storage – the less room one devotes to a cupboard that is rarely used anyway, the better. Some managers have realised that an open cupboard is just as useful for most guests and that what is really needed is a proper, stable luggage stand (Renaissance Hotel at London Heathrow).

Unfortunately, there are very few visionaries in the hotel business and only a small number have the courage to go new ways. One of the few pioneers in this oversaturated field is Ian Schrager. He has consistently pushed forward the boundaries and put new ideas into practice. The lobby of the Hudson Hotel in New York, for example, becomes a party cellar after 10 p.m. with music, drinks and everything else that belongs to a good night out. Philippe Starck's perfectly designed ambience turns a space that would otherwise be vacant – or being cleaned – at that time of day, into a good profit generator and at the same time into an in-location in New York. Ian Schrager has a talent for tapping into the zeitgeist and finding the right partners. Together with Andrée Putman, he created the Morgans Hotel in New York, the first boutique hotel of its kind, and with Philippe Starck he created the "design hotel" category. He also knows when it is time to move on, and was already working on new ventures as others were just beginning to experiment with design hotels. As other developers were eagerly launching the Hotel Puerta América in Madrid – a project more overcrowded than a techno-flyer – with much song and dance and designer name-dropping, despite the fact that the design hotel trend was waning, Ian Schrager was already working on 40 Bond Street in New York.

For some incomprehensible reason, most hotel rooms are planned around the TV and not, as one might expect, around the bed, which is after all the main reason for spending a night in a hotel. This seems all the more incomprehensible given the television companies' concerted efforts to provide the most mediocre television programmes possible. A digital television concept where films or programmes can be viewed on-demand and without advertising, much like a DVD, would be a much more relaxing alternative to television. Making this downloadable wirelessly to an iPad would make a perfect television evening. Accor together with Microsoft have developed the multimedia hotel room concept "Room 3120", which combines pay-TV and similar offerings with an in-room Wii area and computer games to provide a broad spectrum of entertainment options. Despite the degree of sensory overload in this project, it does at least represent an attempt to explore new directions.

All too often, the planning of hotels lacks plain old common sense. Instead, they are interpreted as profit generators, driven by the demands of banks, hotel chain standards and general managers. For example, the rooms of a luxury hotel in the Swiss Alps are air-conditioned, so that concerned visitors can be sure that the rooms will not be too warm, despite the fact that at 1600 m above sea level the temperature hardly ever exceeds 20°C. The same project contains a series of restaurants akin to a theme park with cuisine from their visitors' homelands so that, in accordance with the hotel's *100% Guest Satisfaction Guarantee Programme*, guests can partake of their favourite food in the respective ambience. The lobby opens onto the burger grill, the Swiss fondue cabin and the sushi restaurant, leaving the guests wondering which continent they are on. And, for the rare occasion when the hotel is fully booked, a multi-storey underground car park has been blasted out of the mountain to ensure that no one need venture out into the snow for an evening meal. Simple answers to simple questions and a greater focus on the essentials have become all too rare.

Surprisingly, the most innovative hospitality concepts are currently to be found in the budget and B&B sector and not in the luxury segment (for example in pentahotels and Meininger Hotels or in the Hoxton Hotel in London). By cutting back on the general excess so typical of the hotel industry, progressive hoteliers are demonstrating that they can offer guests what they need in a simpler form while still providing a sense of lifestyle. The guests are relieved of many of the micro-stress situations and can enjoy their stay without having to think about how things work. →136

Clean sheets. Just a simple, clean soft bed.
VIP WING, Munich Airport, Germany;
Tina Aßmann Innenarchitektur

The sweeping organic form of the concrete shell lends the unadorned restaurant a cave-like character.
Hoto Fudo Restaurant, Fujikawaguchiko, Japan; Takeshi Hosaka

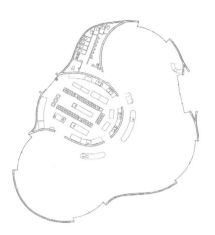

Clean, pure, organic – diffuse grey, clear lines, old farmhouse lamps, knitwear and candlelight – a good counterpoint to the stress of everyday life.
"Emotion" set design for canteens, Deutsche Steinzeug AG, Alfter-Witterschlick, Germany; tile design – Christiane von der Laake, set design – 100% interior Sylvia Leydecker

This restaurant exudes the refined elegance of a traditional hotel.
Garamond Restaurant, Berlin, Germany; Gisbert Pöppler

LIVING: FROM THE LIVING ROOM TO THE SKYSCRAPER AND BACK

"Living" – what does that mean exactly? The primeval cave was a place to seek shelter, warmth and to congregate. Since then, our forms of dwelling have developed over thousands of years, but our basic needs remain in principle unchanged. In old farmhouses, everything happened in one room: people ate, slept, cooked and spent time together in the same space, and when people bathed, that also took place in that room. In the houses of the bourgeois, in manor houses and castles, the different living functions were separated from one another. Each activity had its own room. Cooking was done in the kitchen, usually by a housewife or servants; sleeping took place in the bedroom, either alone or as a couple. In exceptional cases, there were more people, but then the room was for more than just sleeping; or it was the children's room. Work went on in the study and eating in the dining room – usually just the family, but sometimes also with friends, acquaintances, business partners, the vicar or other invited guests. People washed in the bathroom and lived in the living room. Very early on in the historical development of living, the way in which people lived and came together started to be separated into different facets, each with a distinct room of its own. In the houses of the nobility and in castles, there were appropriately prestigious formal reception rooms, which were only used for semi-public and social purposes, and separate private living quarters for being together. This illustrates how important social interaction with others was in everyday life. The layouts of the separate living rooms – private and formal – were completely different and they contained other items of furniture. In commoner's houses where it was not possible to separate the formal and private functions into different rooms, the furniture was re-arranged to suit the occasion.

The concept of spatially separated living functions remains the basic formula of living patterns today. Modern apartments and houses are still divided into separate living functions, and the purposes of the rooms are more or less the same as before. In more exotic constellations, such as lofts, one can even see the old pattern of living from the farmhouse: all functions are contained in one large space and with luck there is a fireplace to play the role of the hearth of yesteryear. Taken at face value, it would seem that in hundreds of years little has changed about the way we live. But there have been some radical changes. The basic needs are, of course, provided for in much the same way: we sleep, as before alone or as a couple…; we wash and go to the toilet (thankfully, much has improved here); we cook, eat, live and maintain social contacts with others. But it is this last area that has changed most.

In the past, everyone lived together, cooked together, ate together and talked, argued, played, enjoyed one another's company, or annoyed one another all together. People spent the day together conducting activities largely of a private nature. In the houses of the nobility and in castles, they played music together, wrote letters, passed the time of day with needlework or the like; even pursued hobbies. Guests were also received in these rooms, but they were no longer slept in. The activities were therefore not entirely private as before, but extended to encompass social interactions with others, i.e. functions of a more public nature.

The advent of modern technology has accelerated this tendency dramatically. The different forms of media started to play a role in how we live our lives: grandfather sat alone in the living room on Saturday afternoon to listen to the soccer on the radio; the family sat together to listen to a concert or the news. The advent of television changed not only our living activities but also the layout of the room: a comfortable couch now sits opposite the television and ever more living activities take place in front of the television. People now eat, peel vegetables, do their homework, sleep, pray and have sex in front of the TV. The furniture industry has responded accordingly with TV-oriented furniture: the sofa can be converted into a bed for watching TV while lying down (although no one seems to have developed a TV that automatically changes orientation when the viewer decides to lie on his or her side). Many of the activities that previously took place together now only appear to take place together as everyone is actually interacting with the TV. On the other hand, many people now come together to watch television: neighbours watch weekly detective series together, friends meet to watch cult music shows, in the 1980s there were "Dallas" and "Miami Vice" parties and, of course, mates meet up to watch soccer or other sports.

Alongside this development, social interactions have also acquired increasing importance. People now leave their houses to socialise. In cities, people have much more to do with each other than ever before: they go out to the pub, to a café or to a restaurant. In the past, eating out was reserved for special occasions, but as food concepts have become increasingly affordable, restaurants now cater for even the simplest of snacks. On Sunday afternoons, entire families visit McDonald's or Burger King. At the other end of the price range, posh restaurants and in-bars have become social arenas in which seeing and being seen is as important as the food itself. More and more living activities have shifted into the public realm, and ever new forms of going out are being born. In the 1960s there were tea dances where young people danced to rock 'n' roll and jazz music, in the 1980s nightclubbing was at its peak, and in the 1990s techno followed with mega events like the Love Parade and Mayday. Now that socialising takes place mostly outside one's own four walls, dwellings are getting smaller again. The number of single households is rising and landlords are gleefully renting out 15 m² shoeboxes for more money than they ever imagined. Cooking is done in the microwave, the shower replaces the bathtub, beds fold out of the wall and clothes are washed in the launderette. Skyscrapers are an extreme example of this tendency, in which a small city is squeezed into the vertical, the shops, offices, hotels, cinemas, restaurants and dwellings stacked like lots of small living rooms on top of one another. And there we can see the same principle once again: all functions united within a small space, except that now one spends much less time in one's own four walls.

People now often live their lives separated from their loved ones by large distances. As such, they need to re-create and re-organise their families. Social contacts are made in the sports club, or on the Internet and Facebook. Spaces for lounging are being created, along with WiFi areas for permanent connectivity. People go to Starbucks to chat on their laptops, grandparents sit in airports and skype with their grandchildren, and friends meet up in iPhone conference calls. More and more aspects of everyday life are taking place in the public realm.

WiFi areas and various well-meant approaches to lounging concepts are springing up everywhere, but very few have really got to grips with the issues at hand. Privacy, electrical sockets, theft protection (so that I can get a drink without having to pack up everything), table sizes and many other aspects are given too little attention. There is much that can still be done (and perhaps I would be better advised to keep quiet about it and get rich quick marketing my own solution). →142

**Voluminous and inconspicuous –
a lot of one's possessions can be made
to "disappear" into fitted cupboards.**
Loft apartment, Cologne, Germany; Birgit Hansen

This conversion is characterised by spacious and flowing open interiors with a strongly linear formal language.

Conversion of S House, Pegnitz, Germany;
Berschneider + Berschneider

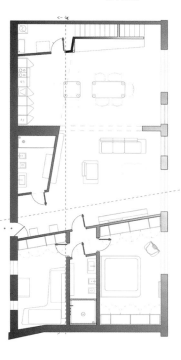

**"To each his own"
is the motto of this
private refuge.**
Casa Micheli, Florence, Italy;
Simone Micheli Architetto

**An underwater world with
reflective chrome-coated
and blue-illuminated
bubbles that reflect in the
water's surface, flanked by
cave-like wall structures.**
Atomic Spa Suisse, Milan, Italy;
Simone Micheli Architetto

Soft cushions: a comfortable corner sofa nestles naturally into the corner of the room.
Monterosa Department Store, Zurich, Switzerland; atelier zürich gmbh

Loft conversion with bathroom and open kitchen and living area – a typical example of an interior designer's staple work.
Private residence, Holzkirchen, Germany; Anne Batisweiler

The cultural awareness of children is stimulated from an early age in such interiors, here with ample storage space and light-coloured communal work surfaces.
"Kinderkunsthaus", Munich, Germany; ateliersv Innenarchitektur

A small, well-organised personal workspace and the corner of a living room – quality of life in everyday interiors instead of the lifestyle interiors of glossy magazines.
Private residence, Cologne, Germany; Innen-architektur. Daniela Haeck

THE QUALITY OF LIFE AND WORK: *THE GLORY OF BORE*

Today we spend as much time at our workplace as we do in bed. A plethora of studies, scientific investigations, norms and health and safety regulations exist covering every conceivable aspect of the design of workplaces. Many of these are without doubt valuable as a means of preventing basic mistakes, but so much has now been regulated these days that an entire industry sector produces only laminate-covered desks, monstrous seating machines and fluorescent lamps. Even carpeting may only have tiny dots or diamonds to avoid offending anyone's taste.

Paradoxically, when it comes to the design of our work environments, the best efforts of interior designers and architects are the first to fall victim to the red marker. As a consequence, our work environments end up as mediocre, risk-free spaces made using the cheapest possible products, justified by a need for cost-effectiveness and to adhere to regulations. People have forgotten that offices are one of the most important spaces in our lives. It seems that an entire army of office furniture manufacturers have agreed that it is cheaper and easier to create ugly office furnishings than it is to create beautiful furniture. One can, of course, use the same investment sum to create a nice working environment as opposed to an ugly one, or a good environment as opposed to a poor one. The difference lies in the choice of aims. The first question should establish what is really needed and what the main priorities are. For example, armrests are generally not necessary for executive chairs; in fact they can be obstructive, preventing the chair from turning while ruining the leading edge of the desk. The same applies to the many features touted for such chairs, such as syncro, body-balance-tec-joints, adjustable headrests, relax mechanisms or adjustable seat inclination. As most people generally do not know what setting is best for them, or even how to operate these features, the best approach is to adopt the method used when faced with long restaurant menus: order the familiar features and ignore the fancy extras. The focus should be on ordering a chair with the minimum necessary features, but one that looks good and is robust to use; after all, every additional feature is a possible source of defects.

The situation is very similar when it comes to lighting. To ensure that each workplace has sufficient lux levels to fulfil the norms, a large number of offices are unnecessarily bright. It is, of course, vital that the room has a sufficient degree of general illumination, but that does not mean that this has to apply for every square centimetre of the table, especially given the fact that 90 % of work takes place in front of a screen, which has its own particular requirements. In general, the aim should be to create an atmosphere similar to that of a pleasantly lit living room rather than one reminiscent of a football stadium. This cannot be achieved with an illuminated ceiling. 90 % of lighting situations can be resolved with individually controllable lighting and the remainder with indirect lighting.

The illuminated ceiling is a feature that arose with the development of open-plan offices, which today still remain the most popular type of office space. What continually motivates decision makers to choose this type of office layout is its apparent flexibility, but if one investigates whether this much-vaunted flexibility is actually exploited in practice, the sad reality is that this practically never happens. Nevertheless, offices continue to be arranged as expansive areas rather than as rooms. It is like working on a large platform with furniture on it. The window desks are therefore highly coveted, while the heads of department get an aquarium office of their own. Meetings are held in the middle, but this is also where the noise level is at its greatest. A change in thinking seems very difficult to bring about, as the problem lies with the decision makers at the top, who are not immediately affected.

This scenario stubbornly persists as the standard approach despite the many positive examples of alternative solutions that can be found. For example, offices in existing old buildings invariably make more user-friendly work environments, and firms with different company philosophies, such as Google or Grey, have demonstrated that it is possible, with a little creativity and courage, to create efficient and attractive work environments. Along with more pleasant lighting, the office furnishings have been designed to encourage staff to identify with their work environment and feel motivated. In the end, this is what it is all about: creating an atmosphere in which people can pursue their work with enthusiasm, where they are motivated and feel stimulated and where each and every person believes in what they are doing. That will not come about in a run-of-the-mill work interior.

All too often, product manufacturers and decision makers get waylaid in technical details and lose track of their vision. A visionary idea, the courage to do things differently and the discipline to question whether the prevailing option is always right should be a constant part of our work as designers. →150

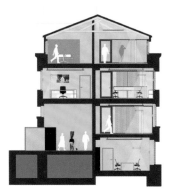

The interplay of spatial structure, patterns, colours and textures is inviting and recalls an over-sized doll's house – in the best possible sense.

Monterosa Department Store, Zurich, Switzerland; atelier zürich gmbh

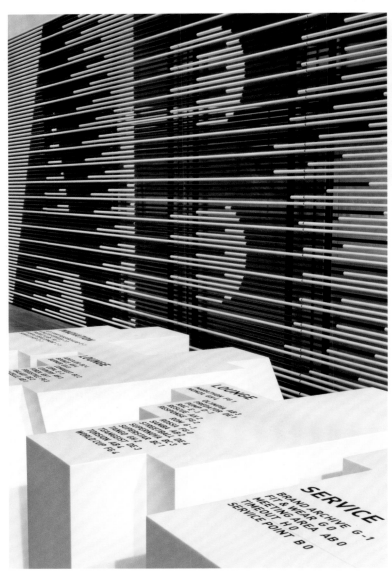

Signage as a decorative and dynamic element of space – from small detail to over-sized wall elements.
Adidas Laces, wayfinding system, Herzogenaurach, Germany; büro uebele visuelle kommunikation

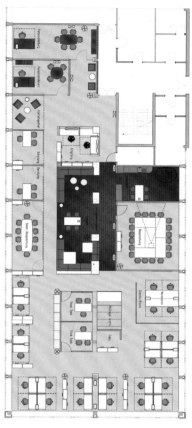

Good quality office design caters for the different working processes of large enterprises – providing open-plan areas, office groups to individual work cell offices.
Siemens HR Department, Karlsruhe, Germany; andernach und partner

Unconventional inspirational redesign with a fun factor and recycled furnishings.
Rebirth of Saatchi & Saatchi Thailand, Bangkok, Thailand; Supermachine Studio

Dining areas to spend time in – simple tables and benches for the staff of a huge IT company.
Google offices, Düsseldorf, Germany; Lepel & Lepel

Reduction – this globally operating agency presents a clear and dignified face to its clients.
Ideenbotschaft Grey G2 Group, Düsseldorf, Germany; two_Claudia de Bruyn, Cossmann_Jacobitz Architekten – Uta Cossmann
GREY Worldwide Advertising Agency, Hamburg, Germany; two_Claudia de Bruyn, Cossmann_Jacobitz Architekten – Uta Cossmann

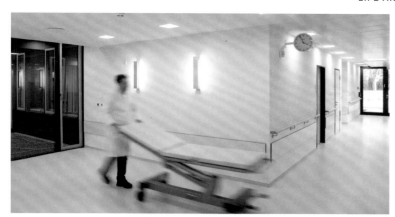

Corridors in clinics can often be rather cheerless – this interior attempts to enliven this oft-forgotten type of space.
Paracelsus Hospital, Osnabrück, Germany;
ruge + göllner raumconcept

Clear display cases and carefully designed consultation desks in an optician's store.
Multiópticas Omega Opticians, Murcia, Spain;
Moho Arquitectos

Quality of life in the workplace: spacious contemporary interiors with selected, stimulating, comfortable and timeless furnishings.
F&S Solar Concept, Euskirchen, Germany; 100% interior Sylvia Leydecker

EMOTIONALITY:
ANYTHING GOES, BUT...

From Chambord to Disneyworld and from Tadao Ando to Versace: the breadth of design approaches ranges from one extreme to the other. All kinds of different experiences are being created, and with them all manner of emotional responses (from enthusiasm to shock). Ever since industry and investment groups have discovered the value of designers, architects and interior designers as a tool for marketing, no stone has been left unturned. There are now motorbike helmets with rabbit's ears and sofas that look like variegated pebbles, skyscrapers are being erected on mountains, star designers paint their nails white and double as DJs, and bathroom taps come shaped like pink cow's teats.

Anything goes... and the merry-go-round of emotions spins onwards and ever faster. The highest building in the world reaches almost to the gates of heaven, entire groups of islands are being created, the first seven-star hotel is being built, not to mention the most expensive car. Good taste and far-sightedness rarely play a role. The competition departments of architecture offices are booming and property developers are busily creating new pipe dreams to sell. The Internet is awash with renderings and it is becoming increasingly difficult to tell what is real from what is just a house of cards.

The economic crisis sent shock waves through the entire system: bank credits, building projects, leasing contracts all came to a standstill. Or so it seemed: the marketing gurus have since recovered and are bombarding the ailing global markets with new empty slogans: sustainability, deceleration, go green... Armed with the argument of global warming, entire industrial sectors have managed to convincedpoliticians that light bulbs are the work of the devil and that in future huge piles of hazardous waste are a better alternative. Consumers have no choice in the matter, and so a few new horses are placed on the merry-go-round of emotions so that the journey may go on. But where is it heading? When such venerable institutions of craftsmanship as Rolex and Cartier in Geneva are no longer able to properly repair their own products, one begins to wonder. Quality no longer seems to interest anyone anymore.

Even architecture has descended into the bargain basement: the facades of houses are built out of strangely bent pieces of plastic, glued together with silicone; architectural models are produced a dozen at a time using stereolithography; the facade has become more important than a functioning building; and details are now downloaded from the Internet.

A few companies have, however, understood what true sustainability and satisfied consumers mean. Bags by Hermès or Louis Vuitton are still being repaired and looked after with the same care even after 20 years of use – they have not gone out of fashion and some are even worth more than before. Le Corbusier's LC2 armchair is still a bestseller 40 years on, historic buildings are now trendy (Hôtel Costes in Paris, for example) and fashionable restaurants are illuminated not by LEDs but by candlelight (Spice Market in New York, for example). In the ups and downs of the emotional merry-go-round, we are beginning to find our balance. Not without a sense of relief are we discovering that there are companies and designers who are able to unite creativity and responsibility under one roof.

1   Pierre-Alexis Dumas in the introduction to the 2010 Hermès Catalogue, http://www.paperblog.fr/3985389/la-maison-hermes-le-catalogue/.

2   Text collage based on excerpts from the websites of Radisson Blu Hotels & Resorts and the Rezidor Hotel Group.

Who wouldn't want to sit here and enjoy the time of day?
Monterosa Department Store,
Zurich, Switzerland; atelier zürich gmbh

The early bird... a contemporary interpretation of the old-fashioned rustic-style German bedroom.

Recycling – Artistic room concept for a hotel, Cologne, Germany; Raumkleid – Anke Preywisch, os2 designgroup – Oliver Schübbe

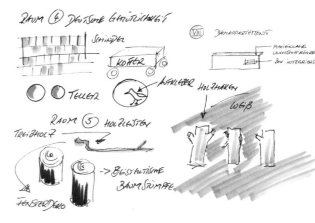

With just a hint of luxury and elegance, this Paris apartment employs a carefully chosen palette of materials, colours and surface qualities to create a comfortable living environment.

Apartment, Paris, France; Studio Catoir

Fine details in an exclusive hideaway residence that mixes historical reminiscences with a clear graphical formal language.
Apartment, Milan, Italy;
Studio Catoir

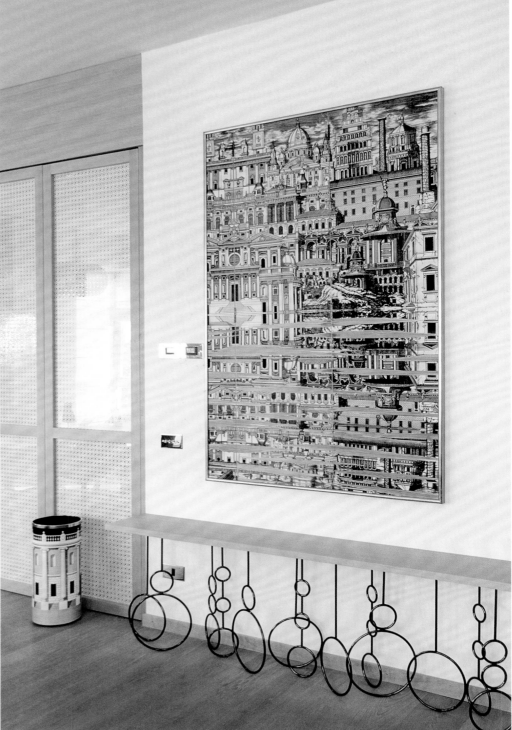

Light, mirrors and glass for a transparent and coherent interior.
Apartment, Milan, Italy;
Studio Catoir

Through the use of layering and folding behind glass, this "fossil site" provides a suitable backdrop for the fossils it displays.
"Zeit und Messel Welten" Exhibition in the Messel Pit Visitor Centre, Messel, Germany; Holzer Kobler Architekturen Zurich

TRADITIONAL MATERIALS

CHRIS LEFTERI

GLASS

Glass is the silent material. It performs its duty as the backbone of the modern age, silently and quietly in the background of many aspects of our daily routines. From the screens on our interactive, touch-sensitive phones and tablets to fibre-optic cables that carry the mass of digital information, through to more exposed products such as glass that is self-cleaning, glass is the base material onto which technology is driving ahead. All of these innovations go beyond the extensive use of glass in modern architecture.

Perhaps one of the reasons glass is used in such abundance is that society has reached a point where we can actually change the physical characteristics of the material altogether to make it more suitable or appropriate to our specific needs. By combining it with other materials such as plastics we can enhance its properties and mend some of its inherent flaws. Examples include glass that can block out UV-rays, glass that resists bullets and glass that will not shatter.

As an example in terms of interior design, shatterproofing provides reassurance by eliminating the risk of injury when broken. Safe from breakage, we can use shatterproof glass for large table tops, mirrors and door panels that come under heavy use or impact on a daily basis. Not only are new grades being developed but entirely new breeds of glass are being conceived. For example, the US company Corning are achieving some spectacular performances with Gorilla Glass: treated sheet glass that combines lightness in weight with exceptional flexural strength and toughness. This has given resurgence to this material born in antiquity and allows it to forge an alliance with new technologies. Predominantly used in consumer electronics, Gorilla Glass provides scratch-resistant screens for mobile phones, MP3 players and computers. In the future we will see this kind of lightweight and strong breed of glass being used for home appliances. The kitchen is filled with huge panels; on the front of the oven, the worktop, the microwave and the fridge. The point will come that through glass these surfaces will become interactive. Through glass and this interaction our kitchen will become smarter, linking the digital and the physical in new ways.

In addition, the craft production of glass situated at the opposite end of the scale is utilised for the visual and aesthetic qualities within decorative applications. Its fragility and brittleness could turn a piece into a thousand tiny fragments within a second, which helps glass to take on a unique persona vis-à-vis the material world. It has even been possible to capitalise on this inherent flaw by turning it into something of a value. Fragility makes it seem more precious and valuable, revered because it could so easily be destroyed. When hand-blown, this diverse essence of glass can be captured in that each piece is slightly different and unique, owing to the craftmen's incredible skill in achieving such beautiful shapes. But it also allows them to capture glass in its fluid form and manipulate it in ways that could not be achieved through mass production. It is the time, artistry and skill involved that turn handcrafted glass into objects of desire and admiration.

This dual personality is one of the unique characteristics of glass, whereby the mundane is transformed into the precious simply by the way that it is processed. You could even go as far to say that glass is really defined by its processing; blow it by hand and it becomes this beautiful, sculptural and almost magical form, yet at the same time when it is mass-produced it is almost invisibly functional.

Besides the pragmatic properties of glass such as transparency and strength, glass is also a deeply sensorial material with an ability to evoke powerful emotions through both its unique visual and tactile qualities. The capacity to interact with light can create visually stunning effects by altering the shape of glass, as witnessed in Japanese designer Tokujin Yoshioka's installation entitled *Spectrum*, an impressive facade that exploits the unpredictably beautiful phenomenon of refraction. 500 glass prisms stacked 9 m in height manipulate the outdoor light seeping in, and the natural light is transformed into a mesmerising display of rainbow colours scattered across the exhibition hall. This beautifully simple concept could be applied within commercial spaces as a separating wall to maximise natural light while providing a degree of privacy and space division.

Similar optical effects and interactive properties are explored in the shaping of glass tiles. For instance, convex-shaped square tiles add an element of depth and dimensional distortion, causing objects within view to attain a surreal and bulbous quality. This effect is not only useful for creating privacy; the novel optical effects of such tiles are playful and inviting. They could be used within both commercial and domestic environments to add a sense of depth and texture to a space while injecting an element of surprise.

However, interactivity need not be confined to the visual opportunities of glass surfaces. Touch and heat are exploited through the inclusion of thermochromatic pigments, for instance in sensitive tiles that change colour when heat is applied – even touching the surface of the glass with your hand will generate a dynamic coloured imprint. Although unabashedly novel, the idea of a shower tiled with this heat-sensitive glass is particularly alluring, changing colour as the hot water touches the surface.

The places from where glass is sourced are also changing in response to environmental concerns. Glass processing is incredibly energy-intensive due to the high temperatures required for forming. Manufacturers address the issue of sustainability through the re-use and recycling of post-consumer glass from the drinks industry in the production of new glass products. Identifying the opportunity to create decorative surfaces more responsibly and cost-effectively by exploiting the high reflectivity and fragility of glass, this post-consumer waste is crushed into small fragments, which are then mixed within a resin matrix to create a hard-wearing and decorative surface material. The recycled glass is sorted and divided by colour to allow for a plethora of colour opportunities to be facilitated, from subtle white hues for the minimalist interior to dynamic-coloured mosaics in bespoke designs. With a speckled shimmering aesthetic, this composite material is ideally suited for kitchen and bathroom surfaces, as it is incredibly versatile and capable of being formed into complex solid shapes including baths and sinks. It is also particularly suited to commercial environments such as offices or public spaces as table surfaces, seating or sculptures. Embedding a fascinating narrative within the formed object, the idea that "I used to be a Coca-Cola bottle" contextualises the material and object in a life-cycle to imbue a greater sense of value.
→161

Detail of a crystal chandelier.
Serviced apartments,
WAK Wohnen am Kurhaus,
Hennef, Germany; 100%
interior Sylvia Leydecker

Transparent: modern conference rooms are now often glazed.
Samas Office Furniture
Headquarters, Worms, Germany;
100% interior Sylvia Leydecker

Translucent: the interior of this law firm employs a reduced palette of diffuse glass and light.
Schlüter Graf & Partner, Dortmund, Germany; 100% interior Sylvia Leydecker

Feminine touch: roses behind glass in the marble wall.
Norton Rose, Frankfurt am Main, Germany; 100% interior Sylvia Leydecker

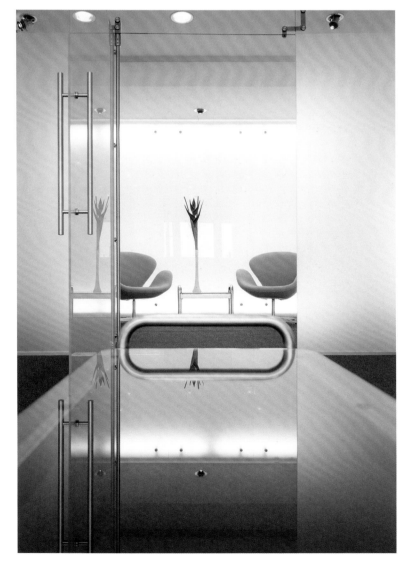

Crushed ice: a single facade panel made of glass ceramics was used for the design of the seamless back-lit reception desk.
Schlüter Graf & Partner, Dortmund, Germany; 100% interior Sylvia Leydecker

Silver green: painted glass, mirrored ceiling and a mosaic mirror in combination with an epoxy floor, grass panels and lino.
Practice for Paediatric Medicine and TCM, Drs. Schumann-Winckler-Schumann, Cologne, Germany; 100% interior Sylvia Leydecker

WOOD

Wood, along with ceramic, is one of the oldest materials used by man. As such, objects and elements made of wood have an innate perception of honourable reliability. We started using mud and turned that into clay, we then started chopping down trees and turned wood into timber. These two materials are perceived as some of the most reliable materials in the design palette, but are going through a huge transformation because they are fighting to keep up with materials like metals and plastics. The plight to remain in the running alongside these other established materials has prompted a complete modification and enhancement of wood's capabilities through extensive experimentation with material combinations in a Frankenstein-esque fashion to align wood for the mass-produced or technical markets.

Materials like Glulam, a structural timber composed from reconstituted pieces of wood glued together to form beams that exhibit much greater strength over long lengths than traditional timbers, are widely used wood composites. On a more advanced level there is injection-moulded wood, the child of the marriage between wood and plastic. This hybrid material consists of wood dust mixed with thermoplastics to create a material with the viscosity and mouldability of a plastic but the appearance and machinability of a wood product. These new advancements create new definitions of wood, imparting properties that you would normally attribute to plastics, such as being extrudable or injection-mouldable, and thus changing our entire perception of this essentially reliable, humane and hand-workable material.

Wood is also undervalued with regard to the sheer diversity of species available. We talk about types of plastics in a very specific sense, referring to grades, etc., but we usually talk about wood in a very general sense. Yet any number of different species of trees will give you a vast array of different properties – similar to the range of plastics. The properties of wood are also affected by how the trees are cut. Wood species all have very different personalities and consequently differ tremendously in the ways they can be utilised or how they grow. There is a beauty and wonder in understanding these properties and applying them in truly sensitive ways, as you would assign polystyrene for its impact-absorbing protective properties or polycarbonate for its durability and scratch resistance. Wood has this abundance of characteristics and uses, and only the best craftsmen who experiment with wood know how to tailor a tree into beautiful objects.

As a renewable resource, when responsibly managed, wood is accepted as an environmentally friendly material. Designers are beginning to fully explore the efficiency of all the elements, including waste, of this natural resource in order to eliminate waste through unconventional shaping and the use of diseased or damaged woods. The Bolefloor hardwood flooring panels, for example, embrace diversity and exude a surreal quality with their curved edges that snake seamlessly, unlike the traditionally straight-edged boards that we have become accustomed to. This unusual shape is not merely for aesthetic purposes, as it maximises the use of the timber by following the natural curvature of the tree growth. Whereas conventionally straight-edged flooring production cuts away a great deal of the timber to create a uniform size and shape, this innovation employs a scanning system that assesses algorithms to optimise the placement and cut of the lumber. Every piece cut is as unique as the tree it came from. This beautifully "imperfect" flooring solution is a conversation starter for all environments including residential, commercial and retail. It has an intimate and natural quality that prompts curiosity and questioning. These boards could equally be used for walls and ceilings.

In a similarly unorthodox approach to sustainability through an acceptance of "deformity" or flaws, manufacturers are gradually beginning to investigate the use of diseased woods. Contamination can often leave a distinctive marking that is considered unmarketable. More than often, an infestation will devastate entire forests and the wood is simply burned to allow new forests to grow, culminating in huge wastage. A collective of speciality millworks are beginning to emerge that deal exclusively with the salvage and processing of diseased and killed trees for the interior and architectural industries. Investing extra time and effort, this lumber can be brought up to scratch and often cut and laminated in such ways as to create an incredibly strong and robust alternative for structural elements in construction. With unique aesthetic qualities and markings, these timbers are ideal within the home either as veneers, flooring or furniture.

Another way of re-imagining the use of wood comes in the form of manufacture. When thinly sliced, wood takes on an entirely new genre of use and tactility. Flexible and lightweight, these paper-thin sheets are intended to cover surfaces and can even be applied as a wallpaper to add dimensionality and warmth with its natural grain effect. Moreover, the slicing of wood has led to the development of "transparent wood" that is used as a striking lighting feature, as the thinness allows light and shadow to become visible through the grain pattern. The resulting effect is a subdued lighting solution with a calming ambience that is visually unusual yet humble. Imagine using this veneer-like wood as a functional back-lit bed headboard, cabinet doors or even on a facade that is transformed from a traditional wood product into a compelling surface once the lights are turned on. →172

Private residence, Cologne, Germany;
Innen-architektur. Daniela Haeck

Long-time classics: stone, wood, glass and ceramics – materials that have not grown obsolete.

Sternen Grill & Belcafé in the Glatt
Shopping Centre, Zurich, Switzerland;
atelier zürich gmbh

Rounded Loft, Prague, Czech Republic;
A1Architects

Simply wood: timber planks on the walls of the corridor.
Matrix Technology AG Headquarters,
Munich, Germany; Plan2Plus

Wood everywhere: the entire room and furnishings formed out of exposed oriented strand board.
OSBox, Kortrijk, Belgium; 5AM

Wooden benches inserted into the exposed concrete stairs – a perfect and poetic symbiosis of wood, concrete and graphics.
School 03, Amsterdam, Holland;
i29 interior architects

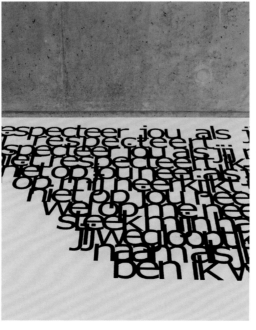

Traditional wood shingles decorate the rear wall of this lounge and make reference to the genius loci of the original context from which they derive.
VIP WING, Munich Airport, Germany; Tina Aßmann Innenarchitektur

Wooden planks used from top to bottom – uncompromisingly authentic.
House, Oostduinkerke, Koksijde, Belgium; SAQ Architects

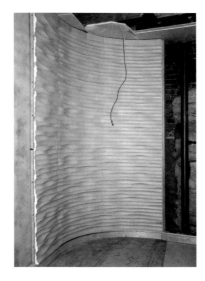

Pure white as a neutral background and impressive water-inspired scenery – a wave pattern, hand-cut in MDF, counteracts the supposed sterility of white.
OLIVOMARE Restaurant, London, England;
Architetto Pierluigi Piu

An attractive plywood veneer as flexible sandwich panels unites mass production with craftsmanship and engineering.
Flex, Sado, Japan; ply project – Kenichi Sato, material – Takizawa Veneer Co., manufacture – Takumi Kohgei Co.

The organic lines produce a naturalistic formal language.
Wilkinson Residence, Portland, Oregon, USA; Robert Harvey Oshatz

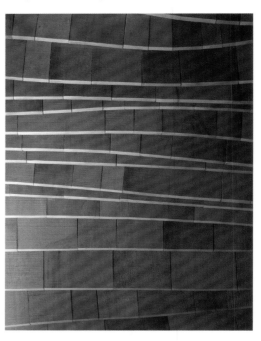

On the move: wood used as a cladding material for "train compartments" of a restaurant and as a rustic-industrial framework for the wall in the background.
Fabbrica Bergen Restaurant, Holland; Tjep.

Voluminous and curvaceous, these elegant and sculptural wooden elements bathe in the light-flooded interior of this high-end showroom in the former swimming pool of the Lutétia Hotel.

Hermès Rive Gauche, Paris, France; RDAI

Layered: cut split firewood forms a natural backdrop in this spa.

Ostseeblick Beach Hotel, Meerness-Spa, Seebad Heringsdorf, Germany; Susanne Kaiser

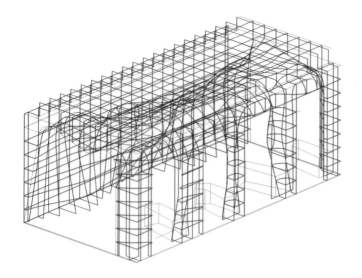

An attractive play of light and shadow on the wall produced by light, wood and grasses.
Hilton "Edge" Restaurant, Pattaya, Thailand; Department of ARCHITECTURE Co. Ltd.

The surfaces of this room are clad entirely with plywood.
Carlos Ortega House, Mexico City, Mexico; ROW Studio

Curvy: computerised design methods and CNC milling were used to create this room-filling shelving.
Estación Glocal Design, Mexico City, Mexico; ROW Studio

 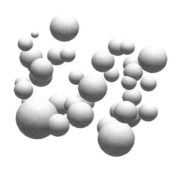 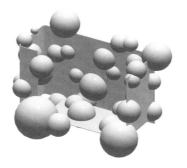 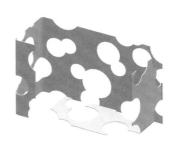

Say "cheese": the views in and out of these negative bubbles cut out of plywood remind one of a gigantic piece of Swiss cheese.
BOOLEAN – Tokyo University Tetsumon Café, Tokyo, Japan; Torafu Architects

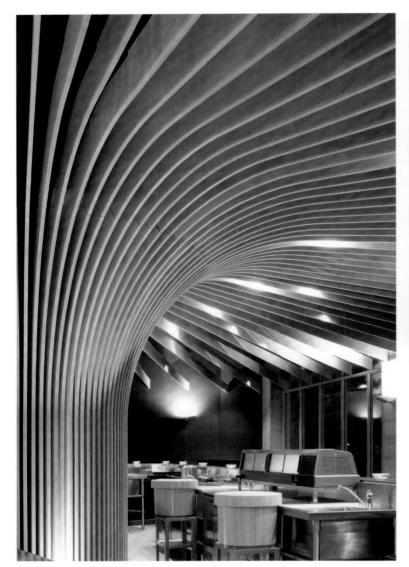

Under a tree: an abstract tree made of wood dominates the restaurant and creates a poetic, protective atmosphere.

Tree Restaurant, Sydney, Australia; Koichi Takada Architects

Comfortable minimalism: strong, graphically clear forms, light and shadow, all made with one material – wood.

Niseko Village Look-out Café, Hokkaido, Japan; design spirits co., ltd. – Yuhkichi Kawai

The warm atmosphere of this restaurant in a shopping centre is a product of the material "wood" with elegant curves, translucent structures and a pleasant haptic and acoustic quality.
Nautilus Project, Singapore; design spirits co., ltd. – Yuhkichi Kawai

METALS

Metals are valued and can be aspirational, but at the same time they are invisible in a certain sense, due to their abundance. It is also possibly the only material group in this book that is a natural requirement in our bodies. In the future metals will be defined more by the way they can be processed than by the introduction of new types. This is highlighted by the many new forms generated by metal being used in new ways, like for instance the wealth of metal fibers that are woven into new textiles for interior design and structural applications. Another example are injection moulding metals that borrow from plastic processing techniques to create new shapes from high-temperature metals like stainless steel. Not to mention aluminium foams, an evocative, visually striking family of metals that are waiting to be used in mainstream consumer applications.

However, there are also innovations in metals that are being driven by designers (rather than engineers) who manufacture with innovative processing and forming techniques. For instance, the designer Oscar Zeita introduced the concept of inflated steel, a technology that works much in the same way as inflating a plastic – imagine blowing up a pair of armbands. This whimsical form of manufacture came in answer to the question of how to turn a simple steel sheet into something strong and dimensionally stable. With a great love for and knowledge of metals, combined with tireless experimentation, Zeita's process was born and refined. In a first stage, two sheets are laser-cut into two identical shapes and welded along the edges. Air is then pumped in at great pressure, causing the sheets to deform and inflate into a hollow three-dimensional shape that is actually very strong and sturdy in its structure. Using this fast, easy and precise process, Zeita has produced a range of characterful pieces of furniture including stools, chairs, tables and lamps. With a cartoon-like appearance that reflects their unique form of manufacture, these products use very little material as a result of their hollow structure and benefit from containing solely steel so that they can also be easily recycled. Similarly, the process of hydroforming is based on the same principle but in place of air uses water to activate the intended deformation. New machinery and new ways of converting a flat sheet into a three-dimensional form are the driving forces behind innovation within the realm of metals use. This aspect of a designer working with metals is something that is common with many practitioners as highlighted by Tom Dixon and Ron Arad, two designers who started their careers through a hands-on approach to designing by using metal as the medium for their experimentation.

New processing techniques are also being accompanied by innovations in new forms of materials. One of the most interesting deals with smart metals made of nickel and titanium that retain a memory and change shape when heated. These are materials that emerged from the medical industry and are manufactured in specific shapes. Their shape can be distorted and by the action of heat will automatically revert back to the original shape, a process that can be repeated many times. Imagine for example a straight piece of wire, which is coiled into a spiral and then, by applying heat, will instantly revert to being straight.

Another area that metals appear to be having a big impact on are magnets, in particular innovations in liquid magnets and ferro fluids and also increasingly powerful neodymium magnets. These magnets are so strong that disks with a diameter of 45 mm can carry a weight of 64 kg. Once the cost lowers this will provide a new way to potentially assemble and disassemble furniture.

Elaborating and exploring further the user-related aspects, a recent study has revealed the anti-microbial properties of copper, forcing us to think about this ancient material in new ways. These antibacterial properties have been implemented and exploited to the full extent within Chile, whose main export is copper. Besides the patent of copper combs that are claimed to combat hair loss and grease, this lustrous pink metal has been used to coat surfaces within hospitals including bed rails, trays, buttons, table surfaces and poles to prevent the spread of germs and bacteria with outstanding success. These findings have opened the door to a broader range of applications throughout public spaces, where germs culminate and can be easily spread, including restaurants, transportation and bathrooms. This fascinating application explores the full potential of materials within the realm of well-being and healthcare.

Alternative perspectives also emerge from an eco stance, where technology becomes the focus of material breeding. Proposing an ingenious new use for discarded electronic devices, an innovative sparkling surface material exploits the reflectivity of metal components, including silicon chips, by blending these waste parts with a natural quartz in a selection of colours. The resulting composite surface is durable and hard but at the same time decorative and desirable, so it can be used throughout the home for kitchen countertops and bathroom units. Capturing and manipulating light on the surface, this material affords a unique and engaging story through re-appropriation of materials for a second life.

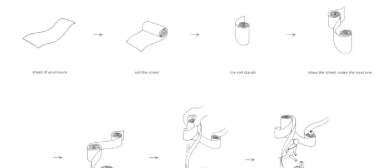

sheet of aluminium   roll the sheet   the roll stands   draw the sheet, make the next one

repeat again   hung up one of them   filled with continuous aluminium roll

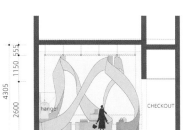

Flexible rolls of aluminium – hard and bendy at the same time – are the dominant elements of this room installation.

Rolls, Tokyo, Japan; sinato – Chikara Ohno

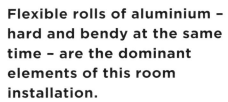

The gentle curves of the ceiling made of plasterboard panelling redefine the boundaries of the space and create a sense of intimacy and height at the same time.
M Coffee, Tehran, Iran; Hooba Design

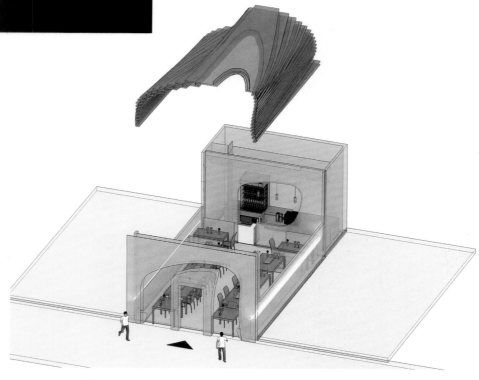

The exposed concrete of the ceiling contrasts with the interior, lending it structure and a refreshing degree of tension.
HOEY Loft, Herent, Henkel site, Belgium; Archiblau & Partners

Unadorned concrete blocks, placed and illuminated to dramatic effect.
Viet Hoa Mess Restaurant, London, England; Vonsung

"You are mine": the edge of this baptismal font made of white cast concrete has this phrase engraved in its edge by computer.
Altar in the Lutherkirche, Düsseldorf, Germany; Lepel & Lepel

ROADS OF MATERIAL INNOVATION

CHRIS LEFTERI

MOOD

The history of interior design, until very recently, was focused around decoration and simple functionality. The concept of mood and how materials could affect the way a user feels within a space is a relatively new phenomenon. One of the biggest influencers on mood is light.

Light is not just an entity, it can be used as a tangible material to enhance our sensory perception and enrich our immediate environment. Seen as a material, light distinguishes itself through the ease with which it can be explored through simple experimentation.

Bright and direct lighting can be very harsh and may negatively impact a space by making it feel cold or unwelcoming. A simple remedy can be found in the form of intelligent diffusing films that provide a dampening effect on light, creating a softened ambience. With numerous grades in various percentages of light transmission at a designer's disposal, one can create a wide variety of lighting effects for either single- or double-sided coatings. The films with a lower percentage of light transmission create a dim glow, whereas those with a higher percentage will give a bright light with a slight glow. Traditionally designed and used for backlighting applications within the electronics industry for mobile phones and LCD screens, these films could be turned into decorative diffusers or applied to glass to transform the lighting conditions within a given space. There are all kinds of thicknesses available, ranging from thin and flexible films to hard and rigid sheets.

With similar mood-enhancing qualities, coloured spectrum films that are traditionally used within the movie industry can transform a normal lighting element into the glow of an early morning sunrise or even crisp bright moonlight. They create colour by subtracting certain wavelengths in light to allow only specific colours to pass through, resulting in hundreds of colour options, each evoking a unique personality and character. Not only enhancing the appearance of a space, these films can alter the entire atmosphere simply through intelligent colour selection, for instance providing a flattering warming of skin tones through the use of rosy pink tints or a calming aura through the use of subtle amber and yellow hues. With just a simple thin film, dramatic scenarios and ambience can be attained, not only enriching the space and objects within it but also the mood of any person who enters, to provide more than just an atmosphere but an experience. →180

Lift me up: a banal lift lobby transformed into a dramatic experience that is guaranteed to "wow" its visitors.

W Hotel, London, England; Concrete Architectural Associates

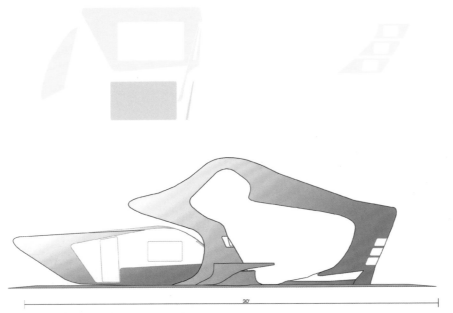

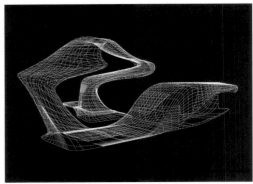

Spacey forms for that science-fiction feeling.
Sci-fi trade fair stand, Cornicon, San Diego, USA; Graft

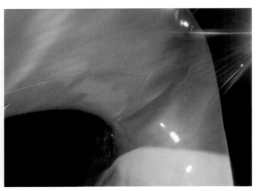

Hygienic and decorative:
a hospital corridor with applied graphics made of adhesive but removable translucent foil that allows one to see through but also creates a sense of privacy.
Gynaecological practice, Maria-Hilf Hospital, Brilon, Germany; 100% interior Sylvia Leydecker

Visionary: this concept bathroom "for Albert Einstein" uses just two materials, reflective dichroic foil and mirrors, to blur space and time.
Kaldewei "Pioneers", A Bathtub for Albert Einstein, Cologne, Germany; Kaldewei and DDC, 100% interior Sylvia Leydecker

PROTECTION

The 1950s witnessed a massive cultural shift in all forms of design, facilitated by the inventions of new materials, largely plastics. These new plastics created a bright, optimistic-looking world. However, the future of materials is going to be increasingly filled with a more invisible functionality. We will not see a huge change in the way interiors look due to new materials, like we did in the 1950s, but instead we will be surrounded by materials that we cannot necessarily see but that will certainly instead change the way we feel.

One example is that of smart films that can also provide protection within the home against external elements. The fading of interior paint, carpets, textiles, wood or really any coloured object is often the direct result of sun damage. When applied to the inside of the windows, these films reduce the amount of infrared radiation and UV rays that penetrate the glass to prevent furnishings and decoration from colour loss and alteration, thereby greatly extending the lifespan of the interior contents. They have typically been implemented within galleries and exhibition spaces to protect paintings, photographs and other artworks from colour alteration. In addition to sun protection, these films can reduce the amount of heat transferred to the room from the sun by up to 55 %, a capacity that can significantly lower the amount of energy required to cool the home in the warm summer months. In the winter, the same film can also keep the heat in, reducing the amount of energy and therefore cost of heating.

The film does not only have aesthetic protection value but also safety benefits. With their crystal-clear clarity, window films are virtually invisible, yet they provide a cost-effective form of security along with helping to reduce injury. Constructed from several layers of polycarbonate, there are a variety of grades and levels of protection available for specific areas of application. For office buildings or large public spaces such as train stations, where there is often a great amount of glass, the risk of injury from broken glass is great. A heavy-duty variety of protective films would be implemented as a safety precaution against the danger of flying glass in the unlikely event of a bomb blast or earthquake. If the pane of glass were to break, the broken shards will remain stuck to the film in one piece rather than dispersing in tiny splinters. Not only does this provide protection from injury, but it also makes it far more difficult for a potential intruder to break in and enter. Windows are the quickest and easiest way of gaining illegal access to a home or building, but when the glass does not shatter, the intruder will have to make their way through the plastic films, which will make entering far more difficult and time-consuming. Special tinted coloured films also provide privacy in addition to security, for instance

An arabesque pattern cut into sheet metal adorns all the surfaces of the room; to the eye it appears like a delicate white, shiny foil.
Beijing Noodle No.9, Las Vegas, Nevada, USA; design spirits co., ltd. – Yuhkichi Kawai (this page and opposite page, top)

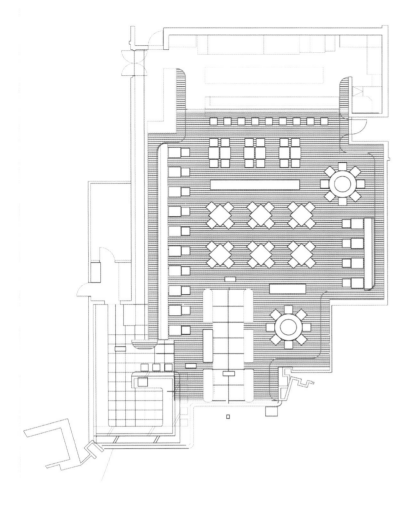

reflective films can prevent those outside from peering in whilst allowing those inside to see out and let natural light in. They have excellent scratch resistance and do not easily suffer damage during installation or cleaning. These films can be used in other areas of the home besides exterior windows; for example they could also be applied to coat mirrors or tabletops in the event of breakage, which is often a big issue when there are small children around. When broken, the pane can simply be removed in one piece and disposed of easily without the need to rigorously search for any tiny splinters stuck in the carpet. Beauty, safety and protection, it is amazing what a thin plastic film can do.

WELL-BEING

The concept of well-being is relatively new. Until recently hygiene, noise pollution or enhancing safety where non-existent topics in any discussion on interior design. Instead, over the last 50 years our increasingly urbanised lives have put a new set of requirements on the agenda that materials are helping to facilitate. This emerging trend directly impacts interior design as it corresponds with the merging of living spaces, as for example the kitchen is increasingly taking on the role of other living spaces within the home. It can be difficult to envision a simple fusion of the living room, traditionally associated with soft furnishings and carpets, with the kitchen surfaces typically made with hardened, solid and inert materials. The materials world approaches these issues with the help of advanced nanotechnology in order to develop coatings that include active ingredients capable of improving air quality, preventing the spread of bacteria or even self-cleaning. Besides this influx of active ingredients, researchers are also unveiling the hidden power of patterns and structures inspired by nature as a driving force in the development of innovative new materials for healthier and safer living. The groundbreaking technology of Sharklet™, developed by Sharklet™ Technologies Inc., is capable of inhibiting bacterial growth by using a surface constructed from millions of microscopic diamonds. These are arranged in a distinct pattern that mimics the microbe-resistant properties of shark skin – hence its name. This pattern disrupts the ability for bacteria to colonise and develop into biofilms, making for a simple, cost-effective means of controlling bacteria. At present this remarkable surface structure is being used in high-touch, germ-prone areas including bathroom doors, push doors in food service areas, hygienic receptacles, hospital bedrails, bedside control panels, nursing call buttons and tray tables. Although particularly beneficial within the healthcare industry, the discreet nature and aesthetic of this marvelous material could lend it to a wider spectrum of applications throughout public spaces or even areas of the home.

The thermochromic surfaces of this chair react to body heat and leave traces of past visitors.

Yala Sofa; Elliat Rich

ACOUSTICS

Invisible functionality is a consistent occurrence across the spectrum of future materials around the theme of well-being. Although inconspicuous to the eye and often disguised as ordinary materials, their effect can dramatically affect our senses. This is particularly accurate in respect of sound. Large open spaces often have poor sound quality, as noises tend to resonate and echo within the area, making it feel uninviting, stark and cold. Good acoustics can imbue an essence of peace, tranquility and warmth. In particular, office spaces are prone to noise pollution that can affect performance, concentration and thus efficiency. There are a number of materials including Sonoperf® that can insulate acoustic noise by diffusing sound waves thanks to tiny perforations made into a sheet metal that is backed with layers of wool and fleece. These sheets are extremely thin and can be used throughout commercial and residential environments for ceilings, canopies, screens and furniture fronts to reduce the reflection and scattering of sound.

Sheet panels are just one solution, as innovative coatings have also proven to dampen noise and vibration while being easy and inexpensive to apply. QuietCoat, for example, developed by US manufacturer QuietRock, is a sprayable polymer coating that can be applied to almost any surface including metal and plastics to reduce noise and vibration; in addition it lends anti-rust and anti-mould properties.

PERFORMANCE

Besides an increased awareness towards well-being, another growth area in performance materials for interiors is in "family-proofing". Multifunctional living spaces have focused the spotlight on the development of new surface materials to enhance product safety, durability and maintenance, with areas such as scratch resistance, easy cleaning, acoustics.

Flooring manufacturers in particular have devised extensive measures that include water-, scratch- and impact resistance in response to this growing set of needs. In the laminates area, Belgian flooring supplier Uniclic have developed Aqua-Step®, a product that is completely impermeable to water, tested to the point where it can be fully submerged without damage. Designed for use in virtually any environment including gyms, restaurants and shops, this impressive flooring does not swell like traditional laminates and comes in an array of wood grain and stone patterns, colours and finishes. The flooring industry has pushed the boundaries and capabilities of surfaces, a trend that has given rise to an elitist breed of specialised dynamic laminates that are prepared for any eventuality. These new surfaces exhibit extensive properties such as fire resistance, anti-static, scratch protection and sound absorption to cater for even the toughest of environments.

DYNAMIC DECORATIVE SURFACES

There are also those materials that are concerned with the purely visual. No longer confined to such prosaic concerns as colour and texture alone, emerging aesthetics explore new fields of depth through three-dimensional surfaces, layering and personalisation.

The appearance of surface depth presents designers with many possibilities. Variation and irregularity in otherwise flat surfaces evoke a sense of movement through reflections and shadows, as well as providing a tactile dimension. One example is Muraspec 3D wall panels that apply the multi-axial CNC cutting technique to plastic or wood to transform typically flat walls into a dynamic display of sculptural shapes with extreme texture to resemble works of art rather than wall coverings. These panels are available in a huge variety of patterns, from more linear and repetitive constructions to an off-beat selection of asymmetric and experimental shapes. These finishes are comparable with the hand-sewn textile creations of Anne Kyyrö Quinn that craft bold-coloured felts into geometric three-dimensional forms. Inspired by nature, these structures are applied to all kinds of interior furnishings and decoration including cushions, throws, table runners, wall panels and blinds.

A subtle oriental aesthetic has been created using overlaid layers of laser-cut material – including sandstone, light-coloured wood and high-tech foil.
Shang Xia, Shanghai, China; Kengo Kuma & Associates

This art shop has been "pimped" using adhesive foil – a low-cost and effective solution.
Artshop 09, Basel, Switzerland; ZMIK

Sophisticated digital cutting technology has been used here to perforate an otherwise smooth mineral composite material, creating an ultra-modern spatial continuum.

Open Lounge Raiffeisenbank, Zurich, Switzerland;
NAU Architecture, Drexler Guinand Jauslin Architekten

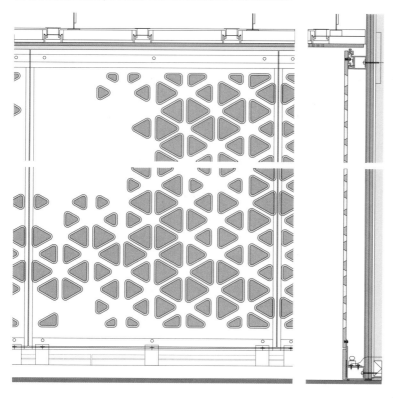

PERSONALISATION

The experimental approach to surface design is being taken to new extremes with the introduction of digital print technology that facilitates the personalisation of interior surfaces. Industrial-scale digital printers are able to produce very short runs of custom sheet materials at a reasonably low price to allow anyone to add their own images, logos or graphics to any surface. Italian supplier Gruppo Frati have released NEXT Floor, which is printed directly onto high-density fibre board, while FN Digiprint in Germany supply custom printing for three-dimensional parts including skirtings, laminate floorings and shelving panels. Even the acrylic material Corian® can be printed, as demonstrated in a showroom kitchen designed by Arik Levy. This process means that one-off surfaces can be created for all kinds of jobs, like small independent shops or children's bedrooms, to add a personalised touch. Other emerging alternatives to traditional laminates include a process developed by German flooring supplier Egger. The company can print patterns, colours and images directly onto MDF and sheet materials that can then be coated with multiple layers of clear varnish for protection. IKEA's Billy bookcase is a well-known application for the process. For solid colours, two-part polyurethane paints are also emerging as an alternative to laminates. Although laminates are still superior in terms of durability and overall toughness, these two processes are expected to improve to comparable levels as they evolve over the coming years.

RESPONSIBLE

High-quality materials, surfaces and tools are no longer not just supposed to perform well during their useful life, but are also to be disposable in a responsible way. Flooring supplier Forbo, perceived as one of the leaders in the field of "eco", produces a durable and hard-wearing Marmoleum® exclusively using natural raw materials such as timber resin, plant inks and jute textiles. Recycled raw materials are also becoming more widespread, as recyclers are able to offer high-quality and often less expensive alternatives to virgin resources. Laminate manufacturer Omnova have released their EFX Eco-Friendly 3D Laminates that contain no PVC, plasticisers, phthalates or lead. Besides flooring and laminate products, the textiles industry has long embraced the use of natural or recycled fibres in both fashion and upholstery. With the Precious Waste project, Dutch designer Michelle Baggerman proves that innovation within the development of responsible materials can also stem from the production process and a re-use of materials, as demonstrated in a process invented for spinning notoriously prolific plastic bags into strands that can be woven into beautiful textiles. With their exceptional durability, strength and beauty these textiles are ideal for use throughout the home for all manner of interior furnishings from curtains to upholstery.

Woven carbon textiles can have quite different structures – here it is used to imitate parquet, which can be used, for example, for making furniture.

Carbon parquet flooring, Aachen, Germany; Institut für Textiltechnik (ITA) of RWTH Aachen University

SPACE-DEFINING SURFACES: FLOORS, WALLS, CEILINGS

CHRIS LEFTERI

Materials define spaces in so many ways, not only in the more obvious form of channeling light or allowing designers to create intricate geometries. They define our environments also through association and through the stories they embody and communicate to a user. In an age where we are increasingly dependent on, and needy of, the knowledge about the provenance of the ingredients of our material world, the stories that these materials embody become more important. For instance, if designers specify materials that are in some way energy-efficient in their production, this will be communicated to the users and will become part of the personality that will define the building or space. On many levels our environments are becoming more defined by the personalities who shape them, for example, those of the architect, the owner or a company brand, each of which tells a different and personal story. We are also becoming more and more reliant on experiences that new materials are bringing to interiors. No longer just passively using a space, surfaces are beginning to give feedback. Reflections and refractions create spaces that 20 years ago would have needed very smart and advanced electronic devices to make them work.

MATERIAL LIGHT

For a surface that cries out for attention to generate a "wow" factor there are some wonderful new material combinations that capture light and channel it out in unexpected ways. As you walk across certain types of tiles you will be captivated by a dynamic spectrum of tiny shimmering lights flickering below. It may sound as if some pretty advanced technology is involved, but this surface simply relies upon the use of fibre optics embedded within a resin or concrete block. The fibre optics pick up changes in light and disperse them onto the surface, where they magically shift and move in a rippling effect. The colour and movement created all depends upon the intensity of light, whether it be natural or artificial, with more dramatic contrasts being produced when light is directed onto the surface. For instance, as you pass over the tiles, your shadow will block the incoming light, making the surrounding areas appear to light up. As the tiles contain no electrical components, they can even be used within areas exposed to moisture such as kitchens, bathrooms and even outdoors. This material should not be limited purely to flooring applications: its intriguing behaviour can enhance countertops or wall panels, as the blocks are available in custom sizes and shapes to suit the desired use.

It is important to consider not only the additional or decorative surfaces that we can incorporate into an interior space but to get right down to the fundamental elements. Even something as mundane as wall plaster can have a huge impact on a space. There is a chameleon-type technology that has been incorporated into a variety of substrate materials that are classified as phase change materials (PCMs). These materials previously congregated within the industrial sector for packaging and storage applications, but they have branched out and their technology can now be found within the building industry to create a variety of very smart materials that actually moderate the temperature of a room. The novel appeal of these materials is that to some extent they actually work like a heater and air-conditioning unit combined by both storing and emitting heat when needed.

Phase change materials exist in a constant state of flux, adapting themselves to the environment. Made up of several layers, these materials contain microscopic beads that change state – like water does when it changes to ice – depending on the temperature. When they change from one state to another they are continually storing and emitting heat. For instance, when applied to a wall plaster, as the room begins to heat up on a hot day, the beads will start to melt and as they do they begin absorbing some of the inside heat to cool the room down. By contrast, when the room begins to cool down, the beads will begin to solidify and release the stored heat to raise the temperature back to the desired level. Using this plaster helps to keep a room at a constant temperature. The beads can be programmed to activate at specific temperatures so that the liquefying and solidifying is controlled depending on the climate. Not only do these materials enhance comfort, but they also provide significant energy and cost savings in heating and air-conditioning systems.

Along a similar theme of incorporating energy systems within a material surface, lighting is currently going through incredible advancements that are rapidly redefining the way light is applied in our environments. The traditional concept of light being contained in a glass bulb will become redundant. Instead, light will soon be available as a liquid.

This can already be seen in lighting no longer needing be restricted to fixtures or fittings, as developments in organic LEDs (OLEDs) and chemical alternatives are dematerialising our traditional perception of light and affording the opportunity to integrate it seamlessly into the surrounding surfaces. Flooring, walls, tabletops can all become light-emitting surfaces, opening up an abundance of creative opportunities in the development of ambient environments.

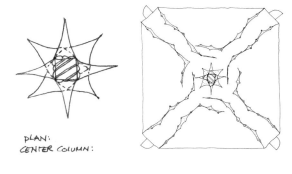

PLAN:
CENTER COLUMN:

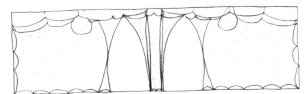

Flexible textile room sculptures, white, transparent and back-lit, create a bright atmosphere in the windowless showroom.
Elie Tahari Fashion Showroom, New York City, New York, USA; Gisela Stromeyer Design (top and opposite page)

Organic LEDs have dramatically transformed the lighting industry with their flat electroluminescence that is incredibly energy-efficient. A technology that has typically been used within electronic devices, its benefits are now being recognised further afield beyond the limits of the screen. We are seeing the opportunity to integrate this flat film into flat surfaces such as wallpapers, to produce shapes or patterns of light any way you wish. Accenting elements, creating focal points or simply making a bold statement, these dimmable and switch-operated films are indistinguishable from traditional wall coverings when in the off position. Switch it on and the embedded OLED coating will glow softly to add an atmospheric element to both commercial or domestic environments. When combined with motion sensors, there is even the opportunity to mediate user-interaction where a person passing causes the light to animate.

Aside from decorative and stylistic possibilities, other chemical coating technologies are being developed that imitate natural light in low-lit or windowless environments. The product acts like painted light and when applied all over the walls, a very slight glow can be generated throughout to mimic sunlight. Such possibilities go beyond decoration and can actually help to enhance your mood and energy. This lighting solution changes light as we know it while consuming very little power and being fairly low in cost. →193

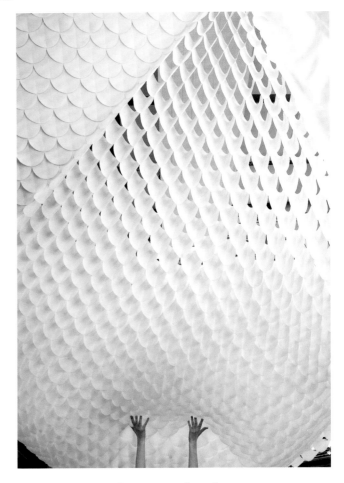

The ceiling of a room is often neglected – this laser-cut structure made of a textile or a foil creates a distinct atmosphere and conceals unsightly equipment.
The Ceiling, Hägersten, Sweden;
Boel Andersson

Bus stop: the wall installation made of laser-cut three-dimensional MDF lettering acts as an eye-catching display showing the stops connected by the public transport network.
KWS Kraftverkehr Wupper-Sieg Customer Centre, Leverkusen, Germany;
100% interior Sylvia Leydecker

Triangular: the space is defined by the strong geometric graphical pattern of triangles.
Arthouse Café, Hangzhou, China;
Joey Ho Design Ltd.

Rippling waves: the textile ceiling design of this hotel lobby echoes the view of the sea. Gentle waves, moved by the wind, are a never-ending poetic means of transposing the movement of nature to the interior.
Hilton lobby, Pattaya, Thailand;
Department of ARCHITECTURE Co. Ltd.

Hanging undulating ceiling elements made of LEDs and metal wire are digitally controlled and unite light and sound in a unique way.
Aura Light and Sound Suites – Nightclub, New York City, New York, USA; bluarch

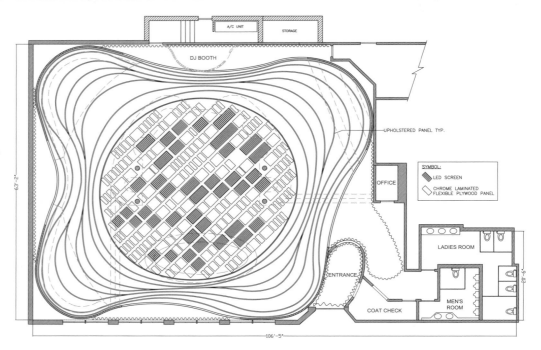

Light instead of lighting: the futuristic appearance of this hotel room is reinforced by the illumination that is integrated into the shape of the room.
Future Hotel Showcase, Duisburg, Germany; LAVA – Laboratory for Visionary Architecture

Moiré – interactive light forms graphical wavy structures.

OLED installation by Philips Lighting,
Langenthal, Switzerland

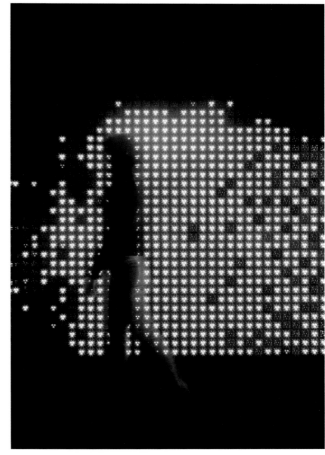

OLEDs will in future be an indispensable light source and will soon replace the use of LEDs – as interactive and normal light sources.

Post Digital Philips Lighting, Milan, Italy;
Studio Fabio Novembre

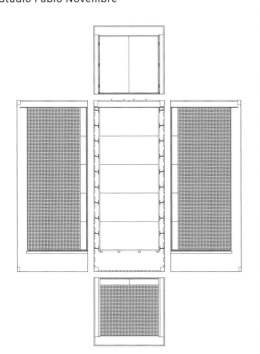

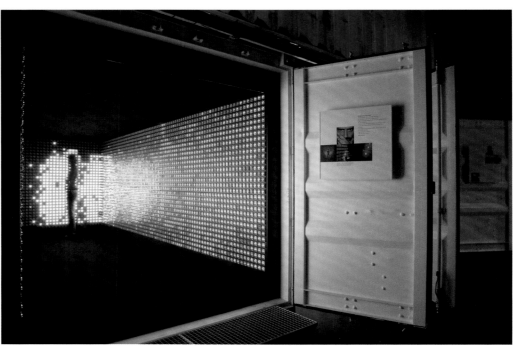

"Zahnarium" Drs. Stammen &
Partner children's dentist, Greven-
broich, Germany; 100% interior
Sylvia Leydecker

Translucent back-lit concrete – achieved using light-conducting fibres – is particularly fascinating for the small patients attending this dentist's practice.

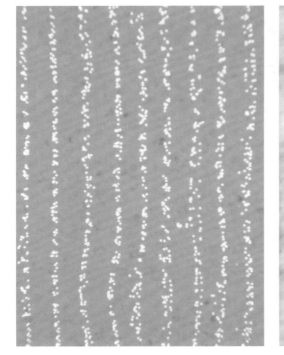  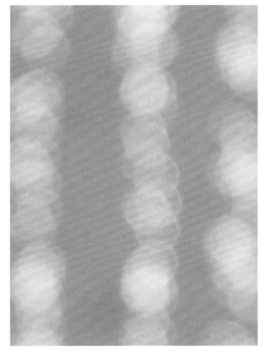

LIGHT CONCRETE

Experimental approaches to material development have also led to some other unusual and surprising concepts, none more so than translucent concrete. With the strength and appearance of traditional concrete at first sight, this material is indistinguishable until placed next to a light source where suddenly shapes appear through from the other side as shadows, almost like on a sheet of fabric. This mystical effect is not as high-tech as it first appears and is actually the result of a combination of just two materials from very diverse beginnings and backgrounds. Very tiny optical fibres are placed in a regular pattern throughout a very fine concrete matrix. Quite simply the fibre optics allow light to pass through from both sides and so give the appearance of translucency.

With the ability to induce an almost child-like wonder, the material invites you to interact with it and contemplate its illusive nature. By fusing a material so mundane and ubiquitous as concrete with something as high-tech as fibre optics, each material has been given a new lease of life as a new material altogether. The juxtaposition of strength and lightness, the mundane and magical, industrial and chic is poetry in physical form. Channeling urban industrial features with something so delicate and whimsical, the two personas compliment one another beautifully to create what you might classify as "ethereal industrial".

This extraordinary material would particularly lend itself to a partition wall between an outside space and the indoors. It would also be particularly effective in commercial environments from shopping malls to nightclubs where there is a great deal of movement and opportunity for interaction. It creates an enchanting environment that is both ethereal and tough.

Renewable resources: a plentiful supply of coconut fibres.
Seychelles

SPINNING A YARN

While materials can be revived and transformed by combining them with a modern technology, they can be given a new lease of life simply through introducing new manufacturing and production methods. For instance, a very conventional and traditional material like ceramic can be rejuvenated through experimentation in form.

As one of man's oldest materials, ceramics have over recent years gone through an expansion and modernisation phase. For instance, ceramic fabrics contradict any perception that we have of this brittle and hard material. They are made by spinning very thin strands of ceramic into a yarn and weaving them together to create a fabric that is surprisingly strong and has an incredible resistance to heat. This innovation has been put to use in some of the most demanding and challenging applications, from deflecting heat from jet engines, to military armour where other materials were unable to cope. These new applications have inspired other, more subtle and humble developments in the modernisation of ceramics for use within the home and interiors.

In the same way that ceramic can be given a new lease of life through experimentation in production methods or form, so can processing methods be redefined when used in conjunction with experimental materials.

RECLAMATION

Taking an economical approach to material selection and forming it using a traditional processing technique, we can transform the way we perceive waste or recycled materials. The idea of using plants to produce materials is nothing new, but taking seemingly useless elements of these plants, for instance coconut shells from the food industry, and combining them with the weaving technique is recontextualising the material and turning it into a functional and decorative surface. Panels and tiles can be woven from these reclaimed coconut shells that are left over once their edible content is removed and then combined with other natural resins and backings. They can be woven into various structures and patterns and dyed in a range of natural tones to add an exotic and rustic touch to any ceiling surface. The ensuing unique tactile and textured surface would compliment and contrast with the smooth finish of the walls to help bring a little of the natural outdoors in.

**Perforated semi-transparent surfaces
create interesting views while drawing
attention to the surface in-between.**
Home 07, Amsterdam, Holland; i29 interior architects

This futuristic capsule made of plastic, its vibrant colour and modern shape create an exciting frisson with the surroundings.
nhow Berlin Hotel, Berlin, Germany; Karim Rashid

Japanese cloud formations made of 2500 individual wooden rods. The carefully chosen spacing and lengths of the rods create a stereoscopic effect.
Tsujita LA, Los Angeles, California, USA; SWeeT co.,ltd.

As if in the process of growing, the graphical blocks on the ceiling also contain the lighting elements.
Rebirth of Saatchi & Saatchi Thailand, Bangkok, Thailand; Supermachine Studio

A reception desk in the shape of an "X" reflects the name of the company and is mirrored by a complementary element on the ceiling with integral lighting strips that respond to the changing natural light in the room.
Xella International GmbH, Duisburg, Germany; two_Claudia de Bruyn

The ceiling of this bakery starts with a chocolate-brown mosaic at its base, covered with cedar wood tubes and light bubbles.
Omonia Bakery, New York City, New York, USA; bluarch

WOVEN MATERIALS: FROM WOOL FELT TO SMART TEXTILES

CHRIS LEFTERI

Renaissance: the conversion of this loft looks at first sight like a historical painting but on closer examination one sees it has a modern twist.
Amsterdam loft, Amsterdam, Holland; UXUS

WOOL

With production at over 1 million tons per year, wool is one of the most prolific materials used today and its manufacture has been a prominent industry for over 5,000 years. Both a natural and traditional material, sheep's wool is one of the world's most sustainable and renewable materials that causes no harm to the animals that provide it. Every summer, a freshly shaven sheep will cool down after its winter coat has been shed before it grows back again the following winter. Besides being extremely durable, wool is completely compostable and will decompose in soil while providing nutrients to the earth. It can also be recycled, by being cut or torn apart and the fibres re-spun to form new products. With a crimped and elastic texture, it has a bulk particularly effective at retaining heat that makes it so comfortable as clothing, bedding or upholstery. One of the most versatile fabrics available, it can be found in all kinds of applications, often combined with synthetics but also some other more experimental substrates.

Although associated with wool felt or felting, felt can be made from a number of different fibres. With its brightly coloured fuzzy texture, felt is instantly distinguishable from any other fabric. It has a unique character and tactility that give it a sense of playfulness and fun. In recent years we have seen a felt revival where combinations of bold colouring and matte surface have been used to liven up and redefine upholsteries for sofas, cushions and even storage units. The "dressing up" of furniture units has a whimsical and animated effect that makes them appear cartoonish or exaggerated in scale. It is even possible to create felt from recycled plastics, allowing it to be pressed into sturdy and rigid structures such as seating. As a low-cost and low-grade fabric, felt can be enhanced through sensitive collaboration with high-end materials and textures and simplistic forms. Its appeal goes beyond its characterful appearance, as felt is actually durable to an extreme and can endure heavy use over prolonged periods of time.

Innovations in textiles is one of the leading areas of new materials, with new types of textiles being produced from sources as diverse as nettles and paper. Woven paper, which has been made famous by Lloyd Loom furniture, can be tightly twisted into a thread that is then combined with other textiles such as linen to create a rustic woven fabric that is flexible and durable. These fabrics can be dyed with natural dyes to suit the existing colour scheme. The texture is not restricted to one particular structure as different weave patterns can be created to suit the application desired, such as a strong and stiff, an open or closed pattern. This fabric makes a rustic alternative to cotton or wool and can be used for carpeting and upholstery. It can be woven together with linen, resulting in a flexible, durable textile. There are also a variety of weaves available to suit different end needs. Loomtex, for example, is typically used as carpeting, rugs, chair upholstery, storage units, tables or laundry baskets; it has a natural and rustic texture that is particularly suited to conservatories. These fabrics are an interesting combination of a low-cost and disposed-of material that is given a new lease of life when combined with a very different material to create end products that are rich in texture and story.

The fact that the curtains are just a little too long adds a sense of sumptuousness to this European house.
Single family house, Turgi, Switzerland;
Sabine Hartl Architektur + Raumdesign

Wool: the decorative woollen bubbles on the wall look like giant moss growth and also serve an acoustic function.
Högskolan i Halmstad, Kårhuset, Halmstad, Sweden; Wobedo Design & Lars Nordin

Felt: the acoustics in large open-plan offices is a constant problem – these striking partitions clad in grey felt counteract this problem and are also eye-catching.
Office 04, Amsterdam, Holland; i29 interior architects

THREE-DIMENSIONAL TEXTILES

Inspired by architectural design, three-dimensional textiles have an almost surreal appearance with their undulating surface. Available in various patterns from blocks to spheres, they not only have a unique appearance, but their tactile quality provides an intriguing, responsive interface to touch. With their structured texture and surfaces ranging from matte to gloss, they manipulate light in fascinating ways and invite touch, making them ideal for all kinds of interior uses including carpets and curtains. Metallic fabrics can be used to further enhance the changes in surface, while soft wools can create cushion covers and rugs; paper threads lend themselves to wall coverings; or even a combination of different materials can produce something unique. The structure also provides a sound-absorbing quality that could make for an innovative wall covering. These fabrics have been used within auditoriums as a sound buffer, but their tactile surfaces suggest uses around the home for cushioning or upholstery.

LASER-CUT TEXTILES

While the use of lasers for cutting materials has found its calling in the machining of plastics, many are unaware that this technique can also be applied to the cutting of fabrics. Experimental textures can be produced using the ability to cut detailed and complex shapes. Decorative screens that use light to highlight the cut-out areas are one such use. Inventive structural fabrics consisting of several layers and cuttings allow the user to alter and play with the patterns by hand, producing a craft-style effect.

WOODEN TEXTILES AND TEXTILE WOOD

Many innovations in materials are redefining our perception of wood as a rigid and flat material. When laser-cut wooden triangles are backed on to a soft textile material a new flexible and structural textile is created: the cutting pattern of the wood defines the behaviour of the fabric, causing it to fold and move in different directions. It is both hard and soft. There are various potential interior applications for floorings, curtains, drapes, plaids, upholstery or parts of furniture, of this attention-grabbing fabric that invites the user to play and experiment with its unusual tactility and structural form.

Textile wood by Finnish inventor Tero Pelto-Uotila is a coarse, dense and hairy texture made from the surface of Aspen timber. It gives the impression of a matted wool surface instead of the usual flat grain we associate with timber. Apart from being a completely new surface effect in timber, its main practical application is in sound dampening. Tero suggest applications such as wall cladding and space dividers, to create what could be seen as rugs for walls.

Folding surfaces: 2D printing is responsible for the 3D folding of this light and elastic textile – inspired by geometrical patterns found in nature.
Folding A-part, Israel; Mika Barr

Textiles to sit on and pull along: typically used for upholstery and curtains, textiles are used here as a room divider and seating sculpture.
Brownless Biomedical Library, Melbourne, Australia; McBride Charles Ryan Architecture & Interior Design

The laser-cut pattern of this suspended ceiling also has its origins in textiles.
Spaghetti Tales Restaurant, Hong Kong, China; Joey Ho Design Ltd.

Wondrous being – a translucent, glowing and delicate use of textiles.
OLIVOMARE Restaurant, London, England; Architetto Pierluigi Piu

METALLIC FABRICS

To most people the idea of a metallic fabric suggests cold, rigid sheet using interlocking metal wires as in architectural cladding. However, there are many fabrics that use metal fibres and combine them with soft fibres such as cotton or polyester, woven together to create a hybrid textile. The metallic often only makes up a very small percentage of the overall thread count, but the performance opportunities they provide are immense.

A steel and cotton fabric that provides protection against electrical charge and shields against static energy can be used for upholstery. Surprisingly, these fabrics act like conventional textiles in that they can be washed, cut and sewn. Contrastingly, metallic fabrics also provide conductivity to allow electricity to pass through them. One particular product is conductive Lycra, a fabric that combines the stretch of Lycra, a material well-known for its use in swimming suits, with electrical conductivity. Another example provides a resistive touchpad that consists of five layers of fabric, with the outer two being conductive to form an electrical circuit when pressed together. This opens up opportunities for electronics within interiors and furniture where rigid circuit boards could not compete.

On an aesthetic level, woven metal fabrics can also be used as a flexible ceiling cover delicately draped to create or enhance sculptural elements or as a lighting shade that uses its reflective qualities to manipulate and play with lighting elements. Combining metallics within textiles provides a variety of different effects besides the attractive shiny aesthetic.

SMART HYBRID TEXTILES

There is a breed of textiles that exhibit a chameleon-type behaviour by adapting themselves to both hot or cold in order to moderate the temperatures. These fabrics have a water-repellant exterior, while the other side is highly absorbent and breathable to allow humidity to pass quickly from the inside to the outer surface. You might expect such high-tech properties to translate into the feel and texture of the fabric but they are surprisingly stretchy and soft. While they are currently used for apparel, particularly sportswear as they absorb perspiration, these textiles could serve particularly well for bedding, cushions or upholstery as they can be produced in every colour imaginable and are washable – without any effect to the performance. For instance as bedding, this fabric's breathability could provide a light and airy sheet during summer that absorbs perspiration to keep the user cool, while its durable exterior could keep out the cold in the winter months. Imagine also a use for seat upholstery, where the fabric's water resistance could prevent against staining from everyday spills and marks. With an incredibly durable exterior that is resistant to abrasion and wear, these fabrics can withstand daily use and are ensured to last the lifetime of the product.

Floor coverings can serve multiple functions and be smart and intelligent. This project provides a glimpse of the floor of tomorrow…
"The future at your feet" project, Ulm, Germany; Uzin Utz AG

NANOTECHNOLOGY IN INTERIOR DESIGN

SYLVIA LEYDECKER

**Buckyball: while no nanotechnology was used
for this sculpture, it shows how beautiful
Buckyballs can be.**
Bang, Milan, Italy; Studio Fabio Novembre

Nanotechnology is a quiet revolution. Regarded as one of the key technologies of the 21st century, nanotechnology plays a role not only in construction but also in fields ranging from aerospace to medicine and automotive engineering to architecture and interior design. In the design of interiors, however, its potential has yet to be fully exploited. Interior designers are in the special position of being able to contribute inspiration as well as develop initial ideas for new product developments in this field due to their ability to connect product development with specific usage requirements.

But why "nano" anyway? Nanotechnology as an innovation is neither an aim in itself nor a flagship topic for political backing; it offers a variety of concrete and practical uses. Whether optimisations or entirely new creations, nanoproducts and nanomaterials consume fewer resources, have a smaller CO_2 footprint and make things more comfortable to use. In both the field of new construction as well as the renovation and modernisation of existing buildings, a traditional domain of interior design, the days in which investment costs were the sole concern are behind us. Today, the life-cycle costs (LCC) are gaining greater focus. So why is the pace of development of nanomaterials and nanoproducts from the laboratory to the market so difficult and slow? Aside from the cost, a primary reason would seem to be the lack of communication between the realms of science, industry, design and architecture. For this reason, this chapter takes a look at what nanotechnology is all about.

WHAT IS NANOTECHNOLOGY?

The word "nano" derives from the Greek word nanos (νάνος) meaning "dwarf". A nanometre (nm) is a millionth of a millimetre: 1,000,000 nm are 1 mm and 1 metre is a billion nanometres (1,000,000,000 nm). While an international categorical definition of what constitutes the nanoscale is lacking, different nations or regions, such as the USA or the EU, have their own definitions. Generally speaking, nanotechnology describes the analysis and manipulation of materials with particles where at least one dimension is smaller than 100 nm. This threshold reflects the fact that at this point there is a "kink in nature" where the properties of materials begin to change, for example their colour or conductivity. Compared to their volume, nanoparticles have a very large surface area, which makes them potentially highly reactive.

The specific exploitation of these properties began long before these phenomena were explained by nanotechnology: nanoparticles are responsible, for example, for the ruby-red colouring of stained glass in historical church windows and for the extreme hardness of Damascene blades. Nanotechnology applies to all manner of materials. The term does not refer to a specific material but to the size of its particles and the properties they have at this scale as well as how these can be used.

A view of a typical laboratory – here for the development of nanocoatings.
Laboratory, anonymous

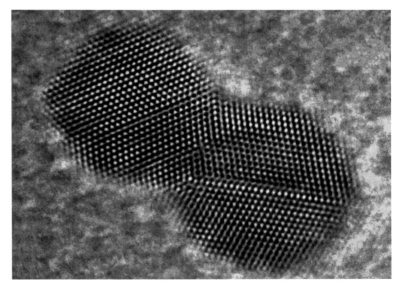

Microscopic photo of a gold nanoparticle showing the atomic structure.
INM Leibniz Institute for New Materials, Saarbrücken, Germany

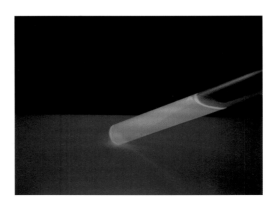

The fluorescent effect of a nanosolution.
Test tube with nanosolution; INM Leibniz Institute for New Materials, Saarbrücken, Germany

Nanoparticles are invisible to the human eye because they are smaller than the wavelength of visible light. A good example of how the dimensions of particles affect visibility can be seen by looking at two solutions each with a 50 % proportion of suspended solids. When the particle size measures just a few nanometres, the solution looks transparent despite containing the same percentage of solids.[1]

The ability to impart specific functional qualities to surfaces with the help of nanotechnology can make materials exhibit properties that are quite different to their own. Surfaces can also be given multifunctional properties. In general, however, interior designers will employ commercially available products or materials. Instead of choosing a standard catalogue material, they employ materials that have already been optimised using nanotechnology, for example with surface coatings, to offer particular properties or functions for specific uses.

So, what is available on the market? The majority of the many currently available applications are surface coatings that make surfaces easy to clean or reduce soiling. Other functional coatings used to optimise materials include scratch-resistant coatings, thermochromic surfaces, tribological coatings for reducing friction, or antibacterial coatings. Insulation materials are a further interesting area of application with much potential in the context of green building. Similarly, nanotechnologically optimised concrete has the potential to become the lightweight building material of the future. Because the value chain in the construction industry is long, it can take a correspondingly long time for the finished product to reach the market, and eventually the consumer or client. Many applications, such as fire-retardant hemp-straw insulation boards, are already possible but not yet in production. Some materials and products that are already available do not achieve market penetration due to a lack of appropriate marketing and market visibility. When marketing strategies switch back and forth between "nano" and "no nano", as is the case with some producers, consumers are understandably confused. While the hype surrounding nanoproducts has receded somewhat, and the field of bionics now stands in the marketing limelight, properties such as the oft-cited Lotus Effect® are used interchangeably to describe both fields.

Some products are not yet viable for the mass market due to their high cost compared with conventional solutions. Other materials, products and applications are simply ahead of their time and will require staying power and the necessary financial backing before they become more widely adopted. Innovation is generally regarded as desirable, but few are prepared to bear the risks involved, especially in hard times. Cultural approaches to taking risks and embracing innovation also vary.

Dimensions: in relative size, a football is to the earth as a fullerene is to a football.
Buckyball; graphic by 100% interior Sylvia Leydecker

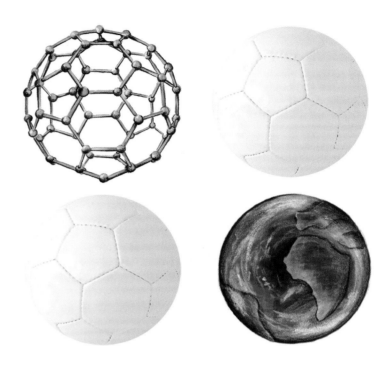

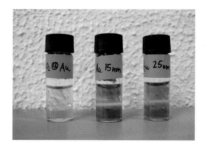

Dimensions: a solution with the same proportion of solids becomes transparent when the particle size of the solids approaches the invisible nanoscale region.
INM Leibniz Institute for New Materials, Saarbrücken, Germany (left); University of Kassel, Germany; Dr. Dietmar Stephan (bottom)

Carbon nanotubes are lightweight and strong, hence of great interest for developing powerful and ultra-light materials.

Nanotube, graphic by 100% interior Sylvia Leydecker

Graphene layers are the next promising candidate for pioneering research after Buckyballs and nanotubes.

Graphene layer, graphic by 100% interior Sylvia Leydecker

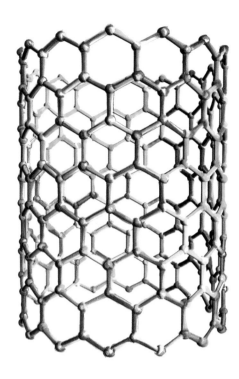

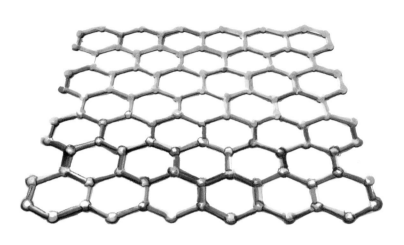

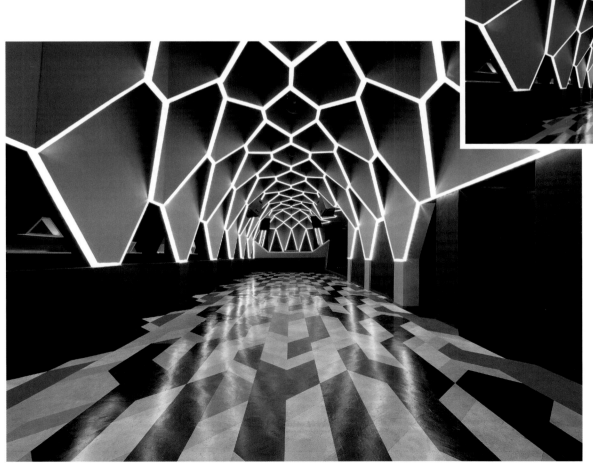

Nanotube: this futuristic entrance recalls the structure of a carbon nanotube.

Roxy/Josefine – Pista Principal, Belo Horizonte, Brazil; Fred Mafra Architect

207

Scratch-resistant coatings on various three-dimensional materials.
Cologne University, Germany, Institute for Inorganic Chemistry, Prof. Dr. Sanjay Mathur; Nurgül Tosun

Hydrophobic and vapour-permeable anti-graffiti coatings protect surfaces against undesirable graffiti spray.
East End, London, England

Hydrophobic and self-cleaning surfaces emulate the principle of the lotus flower – bionics and nanotechnology go hand in hand.

(ALMOST) SELF-CLEANING

Three functional enhancements that have become more widely established around the world relate to cleaning. Nanomaterials can be used to make materials easy to clean and reduce the frequency of cleaning. This in turn lowers maintenance costs, minimises the use of environmentally harmful cleaning agents, which conserves resources and reduces staffing costs and material wear and tear.

Of these three, the most popular is the Lotus Effect®, a term often used synonymously to mean "nanotechnology" although it is actually only licensed for a select group of applications on the market. This effect is used on surfaces, such as the painted facades of buildings, so that rainwater simply runs off the surface due to the hydrophobic (water-repellant) properties of the coating, taking any dirt deposits with it. At a microscopic scale, the surface is not smooth but rough and covered with tiny protuberances so that there is little contact surface for droplets of water to settle on. Artificial lotus surfaces do not have the self-healing properties of a natural lotus flower if the surface structure is damaged and are not resistant to mechanical abrasion. As a result they are not suitable for many uses and are rarely used in interiors.

Water-repellant surfaces are also often used for sanitary facilities such as shower screens, toilets, washbasins or similar, although these are called Easy-to-Clean (ETC) surfaces. These have a diminished surface attraction and exhibit both hydrophobic (water-repellant) as well as oleophobic (oil-repellant) properties. They are more resilient than artificial lotus surfaces, but only to a limited degree and can be damaged by abrasive cleaning agents. Easy-to-Clean surfaces are relatively widespread, easy to maintain and help to ensure general cleanliness.

Photocatalytic self-cleaning is a third variant already in use around the world, and especially in Japan. Water falling on one of these surfaces spreads to form a film of water that washes off loose dirt deposits, cleaning the surface in the process. While this does not replace the need for cleaning, it reduces the cleaning intervals significantly. This variant is most commonly used for smooth surfaces such as membranes, glass and ceramics in outdoor areas. Self-cleaning tiles are, however, also used in interiors, for example for bathrooms or operating theatres. In contrast to hydrophobic surfaces, photocatalytic surfaces have hydrophilic (water-attracting) properties: rather than running off, water falling on such surfaces spreads out in a thin film. In combination with UV light, a catalyst is activated that decomposes organic dirt on the surface, allowing it be washed off by the film of water. In most cases the active compound is titanium dioxide (TiO_2).

Tiles with photocatalytic properties are also available in combination with additional antibacterial properties that are particularly effective at improving hygiene. Silver has historically been prized for its antibacterial properties, and nanoscale silver particles are that much more effective in preventing bacteria biofilms due to their large surface area. Silver ions have a triple effect, destabilising the bacteria's cell walls, inhibiting their reproduction and halting their metabolism. This antibacterial function is also available on its own and can be used for surfaces and textiles – curtains, upholstery, work surfaces, light switches and door handles – in kitchens or in healthcare environments, such as hospitals and care homes, where hygiene is especially important. To prevent the build-up of resistance, antibacterial silver nano-applications should not be used for end consumers but rather only in healthcare environments. Their usefulness should ideally be tested on a case-by-case basis because the industry testing standards do not correspond to real-world requirements in practice.

Fingerprints are generally regarded as unsightly. With the help of nanotechnology, their visibility can now be inhibited using surfaces with anti-fingerprint coatings that alter the refraction of light, rendering them invisible to the eye. As such, building material concepts using glass and steel can also be employed in the interior of buildings without fear of aesthetic or functional impairments. In the same way, anti-fingerprint coatings can be applied to especially smudge-prone materials in interiors, such as stainless steel and frosted or coloured glass, to achieve a consistently lasting appearance and also to integrate these materials in a holistic interior design concept.

Inspired by bionics: from a tree branch to an ultra-lightweight, strong, three-dimensional woven carbon element.
ITV Denkendorf, Germany

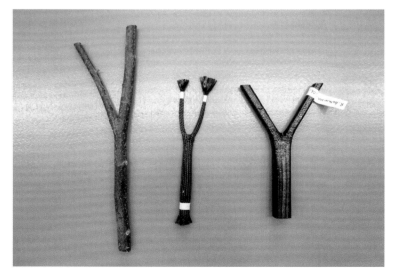

A roll of ceramics: ccflex "Stardust" wall covering – hydrophobic, vapour-permeable, non-combustible and impact-resistant thanks to nanotechnology – is a product designed in the context of interior design.

100% interior conference room, Cologne, Germany;
100% interior Sylvia Leydecker

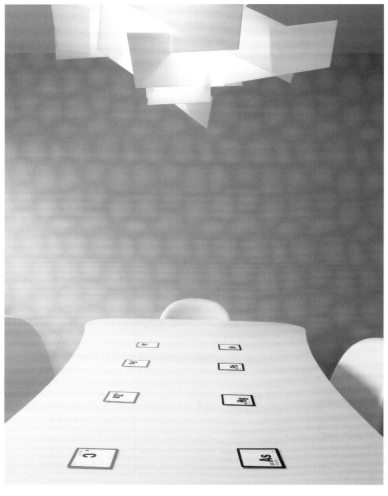

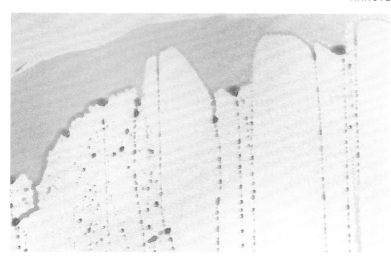

Its hydrophobic properties can even withstand green syrup, as our own tests show.
100% interior conference room, Cologne, Germany; 100% interior
Sylvia Leydecker

IMPROVED INDOOR AIR QUALITY

How comfortable we feel in an interior also depends on the quality of the indoor air, both in terms of smell as well as freedom from pollutants. The quality of indoor air can be improved by using air-purifying materials, which can range from plasters and building boards to textiles such as curtains and carpets. To be effective, there must be sufficient unobstructed material surface for the volume of air in the room. In a catalytic process, unpleasant odours as well as pollutants in the air such as formaldehyde or nicotine are broken down into their constituent parts and destroyed. This represents an especially interesting option for tackling the widespread sick building syndrome (SBS), although it only combats the resulting conditions and not the root causes. This method does not obviate the need for adequate ventilation with fresh air and cannot remedy high levels of relative humidity and related problems such as mould formation. The products of the catalysis, such as carbon dioxide (CO_2), also need to be extracted from the interior.

Air quality has long been the focus of environmental protection initiatives. More recently various pilot projects have examined the use of nanotechnologically enhanced road surfaces and facade paints in inner-city areas subject to heavy traffic, as the process of catalysis is reportedly even more effective outdoors.

HIGH-PERFORMANCE LOW-THICKNESS THERMAL INSULATION

In the context of energy conservation initiatives and building certification by organisations such as the DGNB, LEED or BREEAM, the use of nanotechnologically optimised thermal insulation materials offers very promising results. These include vacuum insulation panels (VIPs), renders or plasterboard panels with integrated latent heat accumulators or phase change materials (PCMs) as well as insulation panels and glazing filled with aerogels.

Vacuum insulation panels exhibit extremely efficient thermal insulation properties and are very thin, making it possible to build very compact constructions. VIPs achieve the same insulation effect as normal insulation materials at a tenth of the material thickness. Put another way: the effect of VIPs is ten times greater than traditional insulation materials. For new construction, VIPs are especially attractive as they maximise the amount of lettable space. In the renovation of existing buildings they enable the insertion of narrow constructions that would not be possible in the available space when using conventional materials. The planning and installation of the panels are, however, more complex. The layout of the panels needs to be precisely planned as the panels cannot be cut to size for this would puncture the vacuum. For the same reason, they may not be drilled, screwed or perforated in any other way. VIPs are comparatively susceptible to damage and are available integrated into sandwich panels of different shapes and sizes and surface qualities. The benefits must outweigh the disadvantages and the effort required when using them. As such, this variant is not a standard means of insulation.

THERMAL NANOMATERIALS FOR REDUCING HEATING AND COOLING REQUIREMENTS

The indoor room temperature can be maintained at a comfortable level with the help of phase change materials as a means of latent heat storage. Using PCMs, a room stays cool or warm for longer without the need for additional energy input in the form of heating or cooling – offering a further means of saving energy. The PCM consists of minute paraffin-filled globules, each encapsulated in a sealed plastic sheathing, that change their state from solid to liquid or from liquid to solid at a predefined switching temperature, for example 24°C. During this phase change period, warmth is given off or absorbed and the wax stores this "latent heat" until the material changes its state again. The paraffin PCM therefore acts as a temperature buffer. PCMs are available as additives for plasterboard panels or plasters to even out temperature fluctuations. The material is easy to work and can be sawn and drilled without damaging it.

Aerogel is another thermal material that is as visually fascinating as it is functionally impressive. It consists of 99 % of air, is ultra-lightweight, appears to float with a cloud-like quality and has a translucence to it that seems out of this world. This association is not as far-flung as it might sound, as aerogel was originally developed by NASA to protect people and equipment from the extreme temperatures of outer space. The pores are so small that molecules are unable to pass between them and therefore to conduct or give off heat. The excellent insulation properties of aerogel are not limited to heat: it is an equally effective acoustic insulator and can be used for noise insulation. Aerogel-based products include glass panels with aerogel filling or innovative insulation panels, both of which have mass market potential.

ELEGANT AND VISIONARY ARCHITECTURAL FORMS USING UHPC

New architectural forms for spatial enclosures are now possible using especially lightweight and slender concrete constructions made of ultra-high performance concrete (UHPC). This nanotechnologically optimised high-density concrete also offers other means of construction. It can be glued, which makes it much easier to handle. UHPC concrete makes it possible to realise complex 3D geometries, including decorative perforations, and has the potential to change both the aesthetics and construction systems of buildings.

In this context, UHPC represents a perfect material for parametric design. Nevertheless, the market will probably be dominated by prefabricated modular elements. In the realm of interiors, UHPC is used for flooring, wall panelling or other fittings or furnishings such as tables or planting containers. Compared with conventional concrete, UHPC is more environmentally friendly as it reduces the quantity of material needed and therefore the CO_2 footprint of its production, as well as the life-cycle costs due to reduced need for maintenance and repair.

OTHER APPLICATIONS

Nanotechnology contributes to many other areas, for example when used to make ultra-thin fire-resistant fill material for fire safety glass, or glass-like coatings using silicon dioxide (SiO_2). In construction, the bonding of components can be enhanced with nanotechnology to provide increased adhesion using contact adhesion principles similar to those used by geckos.

For a long time Buckyballs (C60-fullerenes), then a newly discovered carbon allotrope, were the rising stars of nanotechnology, but today carbon nanotubes (CNTs) have taken over this role. They are now produced at an industrial scale, and the strong and lightweight materials made possible by CNTs offer great potential for the future of product design. Products originally developed for space technology have now found their way into automobile mass production. The materials of the future may be two-dimensional crystalline graphene layers, which are at least as promising as their predecessors: conductive, lightweight, mechanically stable, transparent and ultra-flexible.

ENERGY-EFFICIENT LIGHT: SUPER-FLAT AND FLEXIBLE

Light-emitting diodes (LEDs) are today a widely used modern source of artificial light and are extremely energy-efficient. The next generation – organic light-emitting diodes (OLED) – is, however, already in sight and has the potential to give rise to completely new products. Using OLEDs, light can acquire another dimension: lighting will not come from a single tangible light source but from large surfaces made of lightweight, flexible illuminated foils. Paper-thin, super-flat, large-format OLED foils can, for example, function as screens in conference rooms. While this vision is still a little way off, it is no longer science fiction: OLED displays are within reach.

These thin foils give off a warm light strong enough to illuminate a room. The materialisation of light in the form of surface leads to the dissolution of the boundaries of spaces. Light is fused with the boundaries of spaces, lending light architecture a new quality. In future, light may also be used in three dimensions: three-dimensional OLEDs have already been created in laboratories. Currently the available formats are still very small – more suitable for a mobile phone than an entire wall. Different lighting manufacturers are currently experimenting with OLEDs for relatively traditional uses such as desk, floor or ceiling lamps.

Daylight is a fundamental aspect of interiors. Hand in hand with this is the need to darken a space, usually using an additive measure such as a blind or similar. Nanotechnology offers another, elegant and minimalist variant: thermochromic glass that darkens automatically or switchable electrochromic glass that can be used to change the atmosphere of a space but does not require a constant electrical current.

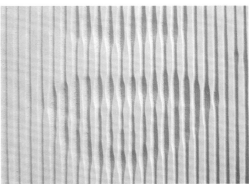

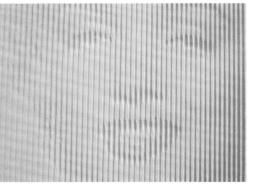

Ultra-high performance concrete (UHPC) makes it possible to construct slender constructions with interesting forms – here in the likeness of Marilyn Monroe.
Surface pattern

PAINTS AND LIGHT

Without light there is no colour. Light is essential for us to perceive colour but it can also have a detrimental effect: UV light can accelerate degrading, which is why many wood surfaces, for example, are coated with a transparent UV protection varnish. Conventional varnishes consist of organic particles that sooner or later degrade of their own accord. With the help of nanotechnology, transparent varnishes can be made of inorganic particles that do not degrade and provide lasting protection.

Paints can be given new qualities using effect pigments. So-called flip-flop effect paints employ special effect pigments to create new variants of painted surfaces. The colour changes with the angle of view, shifting from pink to green and blue. Thermochromic paints, on the other hand, respond to changes in temperature and were originally developed for military purposes – in the realm of interiors there are as yet no specific areas of application.

Thermochromic paint reacts to an increase in temperature, produced for example by body heat.
Linger a Little Longer Table; Jay Watson design

INFORMATION TECHNOLOGY

Information technology (IT), Ambient Assisted Living (AAL) and interior design are becoming increasingly intertwined. IT systems and AAL components are increasingly miniaturised, which would not be possible without nanotechnology. Their sensors are being integrated into textiles, RFID (Radio Frequency Identification) systems are used to allow access to particular rooms and track operating processes, computers make it possible for the user to control energy consumption and IT is increasingly being used to communicate with the building as well as with the outside world. IT is changing the design of interiors, whether they are in office workspaces, restaurants and hotels or private houses. Many processes are changing and with them the requirements that rooms need to fulfil.

True progress consists of useful innovations that improve on what we already have. Today and in the future we will need to carefully weigh up the benefits and risks of such progress. Interdisciplinary teams of scientists, industry, architecture and interior design are called upon to push forward the development of energy-efficient buildings, and politicians need to create the necessary conditions to make this possible. Good interior design should likewise address the challenges facing society and help to conceive new solutions for the future.

1 Leydecker, Sylvia, *Nanomaterials in Architecture, Interior Architecture and Design* (Basel, Boston, Berlin: Birkhäuser, 2008).

Organic: this light consists of individual OLEDs and showcases new lighting technology.
OLED Lighting; Philips

**Thermochromic coating
on the seating surface and
rear wall of a bench.**
Thermo.Bench, Berlin, Germany;
J. Mayer H. Architects

**Low-energy production: the
use of nanotechnology means
that the moulding process
can be conducted at a lower
temperature, saving energy.**
Myto Chair for Plank in collaboration with BASF;
Konstantin Grcic

**Space illumination:
this installation unites
a projection, graphics,
light and sound to an
aesthetic whole.**
BBASS installation, Ghent, Belgium;
SAQ Architects

THE AESTHETIC QUALITIES OF LIGHT, AIR AND ACOUSTICS

PETER IPPOLITO

Light, air and acoustics – are these design elements? Although often perceived merely as a functional necessity, the integration of technical installations, the aesthetic potential of which is not immediately apparent, offers fascinating design possibilities. The design of light, air and acoustics can help shape the direction, zoning and layering of a space, and can significantly influence its atmosphere and impression.

The breadth of design possibilities offered by these three "building materials" is diverse. In this respect, it is important to utilise the design potential of all elements that enclose and define space, whether furniture, walls, floor or ceiling. The ceiling in particular is a surface whose design potential is often overlooked. Typically serving just a functional purpose, the design of the ceiling should be seen as an opportunity to shape the identity of a space. Very often it is the only surface that cannot be concealed and as such has the potential to significantly influence the aesthetic impact of a space. An innovatively designed ceiling can tell stories, awaken desires, dreams and longing or alternatively be calming. It activates cultural or personal memories and consequently plays a key role in helping people identify with a space.

LIGHT – A SENSUAL BUILDING MATERIAL

Over and above its functional purpose, light is one of the most sensual design elements in the palette of technical installations. In all its dimensions, it is not only an aesthetic but also a dynamic building material, capable of lending spaces structure, shape and identity – as well as a distinctive atmosphere.

The visual appearance, experience and form of spaces can be influenced through the use of artificial and natural light. A good lighting design concept is a product of an intensive study of the spatial context. It creates backgrounds, defines visual axes, establishes relationships, highlights elements and helps direct how we perceive the hierarchy of a space. Light is essential to our perception of space. To fully exploit the great potential of light, it is important to understand the effects of the different qualities of light. → 220

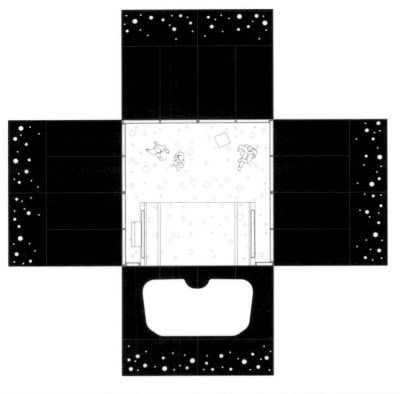

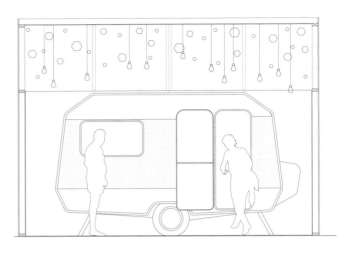

**Into the dark: as part
of the Trailerpark
Festival, the night was
illuminated with an
interactive starry sky
of light and sound.**
Black Box Revelation, Copenhagen,
Denmark; Re-Make/Re-Model
Architecture

**Meow: lighting scheme
for an out-of-the-ordinary
veterinary surgeon's
practice.**
Veterinary Clinic for Small Animals,
Lübeck, Germany; Monz + Monz |
Innenarchitektur und Design

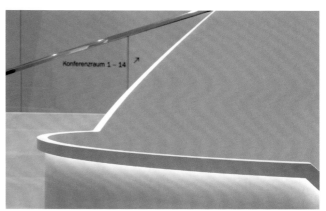

**Lines: strips of concealed lighting
subtly demarcate the contours
of the space.**
Office interior for the ICADE Premier Haus,
Munich, Germany; landau + kindelbacher

QUALITIES OF LIGHT: FROM RICHARD KELLY TO THE PRESENT DAY

Richard Kelly, one of the pioneers of modern lighting design and architectural illumination, who worked with Louis Kahn on the Kimbell Art Museum and with Ludwig Mies van der Rohe on the Seagram Building, used different qualities of lighting to give elements in space a particular meaning. His pioneering light compositions influenced several generations of lighting designers and architects and his elaborations on architectural illumination, although now half a century old, remain as valid as ever. His lighting concepts visualise emotions, but relate these emotions to a particular function. As a consequence, light does more than just create a comfortable environment; it also provides orientation. For his lighting concepts, Kelly always started from the viewpoint of the user. He united psychological findings with his experience of stage lighting. The theatrical style of his lighting concepts results in spaces that are not only aesthetic but also have depth and meaning.

Richard Kelly grouped light into three basic types: *"ambient luminescence"*, *"focal glow"* and *"play of brilliants"*. The use of these three basic types defines the character of a space and creates spatial complexity. Targeted lighting is used to accentuate the specific characteristic of a space and creates and communicates information about the space and its structure.

"Ambient luminescence" forms the basis of the lighting concept. Here diffuse light is used to assist orientation by uniformly and evenly illuminating the room, including all its elements and objects, without throwing shadows. The meanings, relative sizes and forms are not important. Instead the light focuses on the room itself and its geometric dimensions. It creates a spatial sense of security.

In the next step, *"focal glow"* is used to create a second level of thematic accents in the space, providing the viewer with a more directed sense of orientation by separating the important from the unimportant. This glow lends conceptually relevant elements in the space importance by giving them different levels of brightness, directing the viewer's attention and creating focal points. Like a theatre spotlight, it orders and accentuates our perception of space. A chain of meaning can be created through the use of several instances of *"focal glow"* within one space. The *"focal glow"* helps us perceive a space.

The *"play of brilliants"* places emotionally inspiring accents on particular details of the space. The magical light captures the viewer's perception and creates brilliant highlights that help in experiencing the special quality of the space. These visual highlights deliver moments of vitality and an ambience with a clear thematic structure that is visually attractive, informative and interesting, as well as functionally logical in its structure. It is the dazzle that lights up our eyes by appealing to our senses.

These three functions of light can be combined individually with one another to create unique lighting concepts and spatial impressions. Using this palette of possibilities, the lighting designer can underline a particular facet of a space, or create a particular spatial experience, visually enhancing the overall impression of the interior's architecture.

Today the use of light-emitting diodes (LEDs) has extended the breadth of design possibilities considerably by exploiting their key characteristics: cost-effectiveness and minimal requirements in terms of technical installations.

The reservations voiced in the early days of LED technology at the beginning of the 1990s have long been overcome. Initially only employed for very specific uses, LEDs are now used in almost all areas of architectural lighting and for artistic installations and more recently have become available on the mass market. The key benefits of LEDs are their long life and efficient energy requirements. Due to their extremely small size, they can be used in all manner of situations and, unlike other light sources, LEDs do not produce UV or IR light. Consequently light-emitting diodes will not cause works of art or goods in stores to fade or discolour. LEDs are energy-efficient and can produce a remarkably bright light with low energy loss and little heat.

In architectural lighting compositions, LEDs offer design advantages unachievable with other light sources. Light-emitting diodes can be used to create interesting visual effects over large surfaces, bringing them to life. They require very little space, allowing them to be used on almost all kinds of surfaces, substrates and geometric forms, which gives architects unprecedented freedom in designing architectural lighting concepts.

Using LEDs, video installations or screens can be used not just to illuminate spaces or produce lighting effects, but also to create complex three-dimensional spatial theatre. LEDs make it possible to create pulsating, dynamic spatial constellations that play with the colour and intensity of light. By equipping them with sensors, they can be used to dramatic effect to visualise the movement of people passing by, creating a direct interaction between people and space. Surfaces can be made to come alive, to respond dynamically and to communicate content in three dimensions. The use of LED technology therefore opens up new interesting possibilities for perceiving and portraying space.

Intelligent systems are able to control individual LEDs to modulate the desired atmosphere, colour or warmth of a space dynamically. Any conceivable content, any kind of abstract graphic information can be presented visually. LEDs that present graphic information, or alternatively video content and films, serve equally to help shape the space, to communicate content and to provide orientation.

→ 226

Drama: the focused use of light creates an appropriate atmosphere for a theatrical experience – in this case a restaurant interior.
Viet Hoa Mess Restaurant, London, England; Vonsung

Dreamland: a skilfully illuminated bedroom creates a luxurious atmosphere.
Numptia Super Yacht; Achille Salvagni Architetti

Time tunnel: the changing colour of the light makes the interior feel like a space capsule.
SHOEBALOO Shoe Shop, Amsterdam, Holland; Meyer en Van Schooten Architecten (MVSA)

Weightless: the pure white interior is steeped in rose-coloured light to create a sense of relaxed weightlessness.
CocoonClub Silk, Frankfurt am Main, Germany; 3deluxe

Supper Club: dining in a relaxed fashion and appropriately illuminated – a restaurant model that has caught on around the world.
Supper Club, Singapore;
Concrete Architectural Associates

Coloured light effects in combination with a strong graphic pattern used to dramatic effect in this interior.
Cienna Restaurant, New York City, New York, USA; bluarch

Light and acoustics are united in this specially made ceiling construction.
"DER SPIEGEL" canteen, Hamburg, Germany; Ippolito Fleitz Group

Swarm: the light installation made of illuminated glass tubes appears to fly – controlled by sensors the tubes respond interactively creating ever-new patterns.
Flylight, Moscow, Russia;
Studio DRIFT, Philosophy of Design
(left and bottom left)

The project in the studio.
Flylight; Studio DRIFT (bottom right)

LIGHT IS EMOTION

An important element of architectural illumination is the emphasis light places on the intended effect of the interior design, thus making that effect more apparent to the viewer. Because, by employing combinations of the various qualities mentioned above, the medium of light has the power to influence emotions in different ways, it is important to understand the requirements of the space: should the space be stimulating or exciting, inspiring or relaxing, creative or calming, should it facilitate communication or contemplation? When the illumination of a space supports the needs and desired effect of a space, it provides a platform for communication and interaction for its users.

If, by contrast, the intention of the space and its illumination are not concordant, the viewer will be disconcerted by the discrepancy between the subjective perception and the spatial impression of the space. A space intended for communication but swathed in a cold light conveys conflicting messages that users find subconsciously unsettling, and they are therefore most likely to feel uncomfortable in the space.

It is, of course, possible for the lighting planner and the interior designer to use lighting concepts in a manipulative way to elicit a particular emotional response from the user, to give the space a particular function or to create a moment of surprise. The design should, however, always take into account the fact that if lighting situations are not immediately understood they may not always be perceived as elements of surprise or entertaining provocations but could be annoying and generate a negative response.

If lighting is to support how we see and perceive our environment, it must satisfy our need for functional and sensory coherence. Lighting concepts as well as the spaces themselves should support human needs and not be used solely for design effect.

Good lighting concepts give attention to how we perceive spaces and which elements of a space the viewer should take note of. Materials and details can be emphasised and dramatised through lighting concepts. Light can be used to draw attention to particular motifs in the interior design that may otherwise go unnoticed and therefore not communicate their meaning.

Lighting design makes it possible to draw attention to the special communicative possibilities of a space, its aesthetics, formal design and functional meaning. Light can be used as a means of metaphorically interpreting a space, not just in a level-headed intellectual manner but as something experienced with the senses. It can underline the poetry of a space, or reveal it in the first place. The sym-biotic relationship between light and interior design is fundamental to how we experience spaces. As such, an integral approach to designing architecture and light is of central importance and enriches the qualities of both.

The interior designer and lighting designer need to work in close cooperation to develop a lighting composition that creates specific visual highlights with a view to communicating an artistic and functional interpretation of the space. It is important that both designers align their concepts during the early phases of the design process. An early dialogue between the two designers ensures that building measures and the choice of materials support the architectural design as well as the lighting concept of the space. Because the lighting designer has precise knowledge of the behaviour of light and knows how best to achieve the intended effects and suggestions, this dialogue needs to take place at an early stage so that the interior design and lighting act together to form a *Gesamtkunstwerk*. What spatial and visual aspects need to be accentuated in the space? What different uses does the space need to fulfil and how should these be communicated through the architectural design and lighting of the space? What atmosphere and mood should greet people as they enter the space? These and other questions need to be explored and clarified in a joint constructive working process.

The motto "a good light is one that cannot be seen" illustrates the principle that a successful lighting concept achieves its effect through indirect visual perception. Successful lighting schemes conceal the light source in such a way that they are integrated into the interior design so that the light appears to be intrinsic to the architecture. An alternative approach highlights the light source itself, which through its shape and positioning in space creates the desired atmosphere and reinforces the intention of the interior design concept. →230

Highlight: pools of light used to accentuate specific areas such as the bar or a table.

Chan pan-Asian Restaurant and Bar in The Met Hotel, Thessaloniki, Greece; Andy Martin Architects

This space uses light and shadow to accentuate the arrangement of surfaces in the space and its volume.
Lighting laboratory, Rüdesheim/Nahe, Germany; planungsbüro i21

The deliberate exclusion of colour and use of light is an effective means of increasing dramatic effect.
Viet Hoa Mess Restaurant, London, England; Vonsung

The exhibits take centre stage in this illuminated exhibition – the route through the museum combines light and typography, maybe in a nod to Jenny Holzer's installation at the Guggenheim Museum in 1989.

BMW Museum, Munich, Germany; Atelier Brückner GmbH

LIGHT SCENERIES

Given that interior design and lighting enter into an inspirational symbiosis, to be mutually supportive the spatial concept needs to be reflected in the lighting composition and the lighting composition needs to fit into the spatial context. Accordingly the composition of the architectural lighting concept can be used to create a sense of tension.

Lighting can order a space, creating zones or layers by precisely defining points of rest and points of activity marked by differing degrees of illumination. When the character and atmosphere of a space is clearly and implicitly understood at an emotional level through the senses, it gives people a sense of security and location in their spatial and social context.

For example, the changing structure of work patterns has given rise to new requirements in the lighting of office spaces. To respond to these changing demands, the lighting of office workspaces needs to create different zones for different tasks. The creativity and productivity of staff can be improved through lighting by ensuring that light sources are as flicker-free as possible to prevent fatigue. The brightness of the light and the degree of daylight also play an important role. The colour of the light needs to be pleasant, and reflections and glare must be kept to a minimum. The intensity of illumination should reflect the demands of the task at hand, the focus of the work as well as the space itself. Finally, the work environment should be evenly illuminated.

In the same way that spaces should respond to the changing zeitgeist and pace of work by being variable, the lighting concept needs to exhibit a high degree of flexibility. Similarly, a space can also contain areas for relaxation and areas for activity that can be described with the help of light. Relaxation zones should be places for contemplation that can improve the productivity of staff, and visual focus on interesting architectural details can stimulate the imagination, provide inspiration and a generally pleasant working environment. One-dimensional, flat lighting scenarios are no longer appropriate; targeted accentuation and dynamic, variable lighting concepts are more suitable for supporting the changing functions of spaces.

Dynamic lighting scenarios likewise need to respond to the changing time of day by emulating the gradual changing colour of light over the course of the day. The illumination of a space responds to the individual needs and requirements of a predefined rhythm of the day and of how we live. The dynamic response of such lighting systems needs to be gradual and continual so that the users do not notice the changing lighting conditions, i.e. in the same way as daylight changes throughout the day. Users should experience the changing lighting conditions subconsciously.

A dynamic lighting composition also influences the patterns of movement and the time spent in a room. In office spaces, for example, it is generally pleasant when the connection with the world outside is not lost but the illumination inside is nevertheless continuous to help staff concentrate and feel comfortable. Light can also shape the experience of visiting a restaurant. How long should a diner spend in a restaurant? Should the quality of light be cool or make them feel comfortable? Should the lighting separate the diner from the world outside or create an explicit connection with the surroundings? The lighting of a hotel lobby can invite people to enter the lobby as well as to sit down and spend time there. Today, static, monotonous lighting setups have been replaced by dynamic compositions that create spaces with narrative structures and meaning.   →234

Striplight: back-lit illuminated walls and spotlights dramatically transform this corridor.
Matrix Technology AG Headquarters, Munich, Germany; Plan2Plus

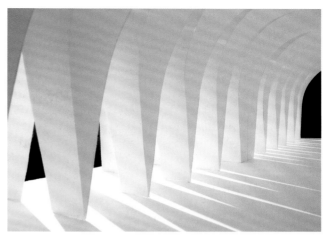

Heavenly: the arches in this hairdressing salon are highlighted by indirect lighting that gently illuminates each seat.
mizu Hair Salon, Boston, Massachusetts, USA; Níall McLaughlin Architects

Atmospheric lighting in a modern inner-city apartment.
Penthouse B27, Frankfurt am Main, Germany; Hollin + Radoske

Light wave. A lobby and staircase transformed by a lighting installation to create a sensuous atmosphere.
Hilton lobby, Pattaya, Thailand;
Department of
ARCHITECTURE Co. Ltd.

Accentuated light lends the space a different and stimulating atmosphere that is particularly apparent in the more enclosed rooms and at night.
Penthouse B27, Frankfurt am Main, Germany;
Hollin + Radoske

Translucence, texture and structure are heightened to dramatic effect through the careful use of light and shadow.
Hilton "Edge" Restaurant, Pattaya, Thailand; Department of ARCHITECTURE Co. Ltd.

CULTURAL ASPECTS OF LIGHT

When different interpretations of the meaning of light are considered, some interesting aspects arise that, when used for architectural lighting, can illustrate different cultural responses to light. Today, light also functions as a medium, communicating messages and metaphors that originally arose in a religious context before later becoming mainstream, and now still retain some of their connotations in our secularised world – for example with regard to light and shadow. In architectural lighting, intelligent lighting schemes sometimes exploit certain religious connotations of light and shadow, luminance and darkness, and good and evil. A lighting scheme inspired by religious associations can lend an elegant boutique a sense of drama and significance. Such approaches create narrative nuances and meanings that establish a cultural connection to our collective memory or to our personal lives.

The use of light in a cultural and political context reveals further interesting aspects that once again underline the essential importance and effect light has for us as human beings. Understatement and representation play a major role in the development of a lighting concept. The respective weight these are given reflects an image of society and reveals a politico-cultural intention. Depending on the cultural background and the desire for representation, buildings and spaces may be illuminated at nighttime to a greater or lesser degree: to create a certain external impression and communicate this outwardly; to demarcate the nighttime surroundings visually using light; or to leave the building's appearance to the shadows of the night.

Light is therefore a design element that can also evoke culturally specific responses. In addition light has always determined and influenced the biological rhythm of all living beings. Because most people nowadays spend a large part of the day indoors, this plays an important role and must be taken into account in the design of architectural lighting. The state of people's health can be positively influenced through the considered use of lighting. To feel comfortable in spaces, as well as to be able to concentrate, people generally require much more light than they need to simply see or to take in information.

This aspect is of crucial importance in the northern countries of the northern hemisphere. Here, as a result of their geographical location, daylight hours are shorter in winter, which can lead to depression. The architecture must respond to this by providing spaces with sufficient natural and artificial illumination. Lighting designers and interior architects must accordingly develop lighting compositions that create the desired and necessary contrast to the darkness prevailing outdoors and lend the living environment a sense of vitality.

Special light boxes and daylight lamps with different and varying light colour temperatures are used not just in the northernmost latitudes to compensate for a lack of available daylight. These lamps, which emulate the changing quality of light over the course of the day, support the human biological rhythm.

The light of more southerly countries, which is characterised by a pleasant, warm atmospheric colour, is often emulated in the design of architectural lighting in northern countries when the intention is to improve the well-being of people in indoor areas. There are, however, significant differences in lighting design in northern and southern countries. In northern countries, warm light and large windows are installed to compensate for the lack of daylight while in southern countries, small windows are used to restrict the amount of direct sunlight and illumination to protect against the heat. In Greece and Turkey, for example, fluorescent lighting is often used because the diffuse, cold and neutral light emitted by fluorescent lamps creates a sense of coolness that contrasts pleasantly with the blinding light of the sun.

Sun deflectors equipped with sensors and slatted blinds are increasingly being used to deflect daylight into rooms. It is important when using such systems to ensure that they do not produce glare. In addition to the emotional and biological sense of well-being that daylight creates, these systems also offer a spatial and temporal connection to the outside world. Because the colour of daylight changes dynamically over the course of the day, this can be emulated with artificial lighting that imperceptibly changes its colour temperature over time. A combination of warm and cool light colours lends a lighting scheme a sense of organic depth that most people find pleasant and natural.

In addition to all of the above, trends, fashions, the zeitgeist, local conditions, contemporary tastes, the prevailing light culture as well as artistic and other cultural movements and manifestations also play an important role in shaping the concept of a lighting composition. And even when cultural preferences concerning light and lighting undoubtedly play a role, spaces used privately should ultimately take into account the personal needs of their users.

Let there be light: the combination of pleasant lighting and light-coloured wood creates a contemplative atmosphere – a metaphor for purity of faith.
The Cathedral of Christ the Light, Oakland, California, USA; SOM

Daylight filtered by translucent curtains in combination with back-lit foil displays and a gentle colour scheme create a calm atmosphere for an infusion therapy room in a doctor's practice.
Private Practice for Naturopathy, Dr. Radecki, Cologne, Germany; 100% interior Sylvia Leydecker

Bright sunlight baffled by panels serves as a backdrop for a pompous chandelier suspended from the high ceiling.
Villa Chnanir, Lebanon; Bachir Nader – Interior Architect

Shop illumination with bright lighting to show off the products in the best possible light. Individual spotlights in an otherwise comparatively dark space illuminate the products as if they were precious wares.
Shiseido the Ginza, Tokyo, Japan;
Klein Dytham architecture

LIGHT FOR SENIOR LIVING

A further aspect for consideration when developing lighting concepts is the demographic shift in society. In many countries, and in the Western nations in particular, the population is growing ever older. A good lighting concept will therefore need to increasingly take into account the worsening vision of older people. Spaces used by older people in particular, such as hospitals and housing and care homes for the elderly, need special lighting to alleviate the risks arising from their users' gradually failing eyesight and to help them perceive visual information more easily. In addition to the atmospheric and design aspects of light, it is very important that older people can find their way around their spatial surroundings. Such spaces should be evenly illuminated to reduce the risk of accidental falls and eliminate disconcerting visual effects. Reflections, strong shadows and bright surfaces should be minimised as they can be misinterpreted as obstructions or a threat. Older members of society often require light that is two to four times brighter, and their sensitivity to glare also increases with age. The brightness and colour temperature must also be chosen to lend a space sufficient depth so that people with impaired vision have sufficient contrast to discern the three-dimensional size of the entire space.

To provide optimal orientation cues for older people, spaces should be given a defined arrangement with different zones marked, for example, using different characteristic kinds of lighting. The function that a space and its zones provide should be visible from the way they are illuminated. An especially important aspect of orientation for older people is their day-to-day life, which follows a pattern anchored in time and place and is therefore determined by the rhythm of the day. Here too lighting can be used to recreate the natural progression of light and its atmosphere during the day to support the biorhythm of the body.

Adequate lighting conditions and well-designed lighting compositions are important not only for older people but also for children and young adults. Their sense of well-being, ability to learn, even their health and biological growth can be positively influenced with light – the needs of body, spirit and soul can be brought into harmony with the right kind of light.

Healthy light: daylight is not only good for one's general well-being but also supports one's natural biorhythm and structures the day.
Hospice, Stiftung Marienhospital, Euskirchen, Germany; 100% interior Sylvia Leydecker

Carefully orchestrated lighting is used here to highlight the shopping experience – the reflections and curves of the room help create a dynamic and stimulating space.
SHOEBALOO Shoe Shop, Maastricht, Holland; Meyer en Van Schooten Architecten (MVSA)

Light for reading: this library would not be half as impressive without the appropriate lighting.
City Library on the Mailänder Platz, Stuttgart, Germany; Yi Architects

LIGHTING DESIGN AND A SENSE OF IDENTITY

Lighting compositions can create spaces with an individual character that is distinctive and memorable. The expressive dimension of light can be used to create unique identities. *Corporate lighting* is used to create personalised spaces that offer space for interpretation, imagination and desires without neglecting the functional requirements. The specific memorable character of a space creates a sense of identity that people recognise. *Corporate lighting* can be used to visually emphasise the familiar and trusted character of a logo or company and to reinforce how it is perceived.

Through its identity-strengthening character, light can serve as an information medium, creating and highlighting messages and communicating these to the viewer. The ability of light to impart information is what made it a communication medium able to keep pace with changing society over the centuries. Light can actively influence the cultural spirit of an era. It is not a passive design element but an active, dynamic element that helps shape information, aesthetics, order, structure, well-being, functionality and opportunities for identification and communicates this visually to society at large. The interplay of contemporary impulses and lighting innovations that respond to them results in lighting compositions that are a reflection of human life and interactions: a manifestation of the current spirit of the time that shapes how we identify with the here and now.

Light for added safety: the illuminated stairs not only underline the poetry of the arcing staircase but also help one to safely register each step.
Clayton Utz Head Office, Sydney, Australia; Bates Smart Architects

The use of moss as an ornamental "climbing plant" in this interior brings nature into the house and improves the indoor air quality.
Private residence ("Moss House"), Tokyo, Japan; Nendo

INDOOR AIR – AN INVISIBLE DESIGN ELEMENT

The air in a room is an invisible design element with the potential to influence people in significant ways. We live in an age dominated by technology in which natural aspects are slowly but surely being displaced. However, technical innovations lead to technical dependencies that in turn awaken a desire for greater naturalness. Interestingly, what most people appear to long for is often just an image of naturalness. But even then, we can still observe an increasing tendency to incorporate natural and sustainable materials in technical solutions.

Natural indoor air concepts that function without technical assistance or concepts that employ ecologically friendly technologies can consequently be interpreted as a response to the current situation. The cultural, moral and social transformations in society have caused many people to take a closer, more honest look at environmental issues that goes beyond politically-correct statements of belief and in turn have led to a greater focus on sustainable materials.

A pleasant indoor air climate has a positive effect on spaces and the people who use them. It facilitates and inspires communications and interactions between people. In spaces for private use, it heightens the sense of comfort and sensuality; in workspaces good air conditions improve concentration and productivity. The aim of a pleasant indoor air climate is to achieve a symbiosis of aesthetics, function, natural feel and sustainability. If this can be achieved, it is possible to reduce the energy consumption of a space considerably. In response to the environmental problems of our time, environmentally friendly solutions are being devised that reduce the degree of technical equipment required to a minimum, resulting in a pleasant, natural and healthy atmosphere.

COMPONENTS OF INDOOR AIR CONCEPTS

The most important component of an indoor air concept is the elimination of harmful or toxic substances. For this it is necessary to examine the proposed materials and ensure they do not pollute the indoor air with unpleasant or toxic smells or emissions. In addition to analysing the materials, numerous other factors and processes must be considered that can also lead to pollution of the air with harmful or undesirable substances, for example CO_2, which may arise as a product of human metabolism, germs, mould, gases, dust, plant pollen, steam, solvents, chemical substances and more. Numerous sources of hazardous substances can be found in the ground, in construction materials or are introduced during the construction process. In addi-

tion, the user may inadvertently cause pollution through incorrect use. For example, insufficient ventilation may result in the formation of mould, which can be a health hazard. In such cases, air-conditioning systems can be useful as they regulate the air exchange and can be optimally adapted to the conditions in each room. Biological, physical and chemical pollutants can affect humans and the environment. Only a precise analysis of the levels of emissions to be expected from the materials to be used and of all other possible sources of contaminants, as well as of the function of the spaces and the activities that go on within them, can avoid or reduce the possibility of health risks.

Good indoor air quality appropriate to both the function and aesthetics of a room can lend it a tangible sense of dynamism. This spatial dynamism can exert a real pull, drawing people into the space, inviting them to linger and making their stay comfortable. When, for example, the quality of air in an entrance area is similar to that of fresh air, people bring the outdoors with them as they enter the building. Well-planned indoor air concepts consider each room with an individual concept that corresponds to the specific requirements of that space.

Every user perceives the air and the scent it transports very subjectively and what one person finds pleasant is unpalatable to another. This means that the air in a room is a transparent "building material" to be handled with a sensitive awareness of its aesthetics. Artificial fragrances should not be added to the air as this can trigger allergies, transport harmful substances into the room or simply be the cause of general indisposition. Everyone can recall visiting a perfume department of a large store where the many competing fragrances cause shoppers to catch their breath.

Indoor air climatology is the study of the biological, material and construction-related aspects that influence the air climate in an interior. It involves the analysis of physical parameters such as air humidity, air temperature and ionising radiation. These various analyses make it possible to develop a concept for an indoor air climate that can create healthy work, living and recreation environments. When the climatic parameters of air velocity, air humidity and air temperature are evenly balanced, the resulting indoor air climate is beneficial to the human organism.

INDOOR AIR AND SUSTAINABILITY

The development of sustainable and natural indoor air concepts shows just how much nature and culture influence and depend on one another. The qualities of indoor air as a building material and creative design element prove themselves in their ability to respond directly to changing external environmental factors and changing cultural policy. The causal but also creative relationship between environmental climate and room climate illustrates how both systems react to external factors and how both must be protected as they have a great effect on human activity and well-being.

Because energy conservation measures have led to buildings and rooms being better insulated than ever, it is important that intelligent indoor air concepts ensure rooms are supplied with sufficient fresh air. Draughts and significant temperature variations in the fresh air should be avoided. As many people dislike air-conditioning systems, it is desirable to achieve a comfortable indoor air climate either using natural ventilation systems or by developing indoor air climate concepts that skilfully combine modern technology with traditional, environmentally conscious knowledge gained and proven over hundreds of years.

Key aspects in the supply of fresh air include the prevention of audible noise and the occurrence of draughts, the provision of sufficient air humidity, a pleasant temperature and air pressure and a high level of energy efficiency. The air-conditioning systems of old often resulted in room climates with insufficient levels of high-quality fresh air, causing a condition known as sick building syndrome (SBS), which manifests itself as headaches, tiredness and an inability to concentrate. A causal relationship cannot be established here because many air-conditioning plants produce air of better quality than that of the air outdoors. Nevertheless, if the decision is made to employ mechanical ventilation systems, these systems, however complex, should still allow the user to control the system individually so that it can be adapted to the user's personal preferences. It should be possible to open windows manually in private rooms and offices so that the user can actively influence the indoor air climate.

Natural ventilation systems attempt to eliminate health risks by minimising the use of technical equipment and maximising the atmospheric well-being of the users. Such indoor air concepts may also employ plants, using them as natural "air-conditioning units". The biochemical processes in plants cleanse the room air and provide a level of humidity. Plants also reduce emissions, absorb audible noise and have a general calming effect on many people. The combination of functional and health-promoting properties with their well-known aesthetic qualities means that plants are a valuable part of a sustainable ventilation concept.

Present-day energy-saving measures include extracting any remaining energy from exhaust air before it is released into the environment. Sustainable materials reduce health risks and do not pollute the environment. An ethical aesthetic concept involves the use of recyclable and regionally sourced materials wherever possible. To improve the indoor air climate, materials are used that in addition to their aesthetic function also offer further properties that help improve the quality of the air in a room. Biochemical processes can absorb pollutants in the air and neutralise them.

In ethical aesthetic concepts, the temporal dimension of the use of such materials also plays a major role. Many people find that natural materials and indoor air concepts have an invigorating and revitalising effect in which energy is set free; humans can feel part of the biological life-cycle themselves.

INDOOR AIR AND INTERIOR DESIGN

Although we cannot see indoor air, its consideration in the design of spaces offers numerous design possibilities that are not solely related to the olfactory system but have a positive effect on our aesthetic sensation. Both the visible and the invisible integration of air vents in the design of a space present a challenge for architects and interior designers. The visible parts of the ventilation system can be used as a design element to support movement through a space and enhance the spatial concept of the room, its aesthetic design as well as its zoning.

The indoor air supports the functional and thematic impression of a space in a manner that is felt but not seen. The indoor air climate can structure a space by creating areas of different temperature, air flow, humidity and quality that in turn create zones with different degrees of comfort, concentration, work, privacy or contemplation. Each zone is supplied with the kind of air required for its function.

The development of natural indoor air concepts requires interdisciplinary cooperation to bring together the technical, physical, cultural, social, meteorological, chemical, biological and economic aspects. For example, the flow of air can be pushed into buildings or spaces and then sucked out again to ensure sufficient mixing of the air. Such concepts make use of the laws of physics to draw air into a room and to circulate it with as little technical assistance as possible. Similarly the power of the sun can be used to produce air circulation. Such systems employ the natural advantages of the elements sun, air, wind and water to generate their own independent eco-systems.

The mixing of different styles, different knowledge and cultural influences enriches the aesthetic integration of air in space. Art installations, for example, can help promote the aesthetic design of the indoor air and extend the possibilities of integrating and designing with this element. Air membranes, for example, can be arranged in the form of an ornament and parts of the indoor air can be given a visual structure with the help of light. Multi-dimensional spaces result through the combination of art and functionality, offering users a pleasant indoor air climate coupled with visual enjoyment.

Living walls: vegetation-covered green walls are popular as vertical gardens in buildings.
Home 06, Amsterdam, Holland; i29 interior architects

Country air: this landscape in the interior of a marketing agency communicates at least a comforting sense of good air.
TBWA / Hakuhodo, Tokyo, Japan; Klein Dytham architecture

ACOUSTICS – AN AESTHETIC DESIGN ELEMENT

The acoustics of a space is an auditory design element controlled by technical installations whose aesthetic qualities are not immediately apparent. The seemingly paradoxical assertion that the acoustics appeal not just to the auditory but also the visual senses has been deconstructed in the contemporary design of spaces. The design of the sound of a space can be adapted to the requirements of the architectural space and can strengthen the functional and thematic purpose of the space as well its form.

Acoustics is an interdisciplinary field that unites physical and psychological principles with experience from the field of materials science. The elements of acoustics important to interior design include how the sound arises and how it spreads, the correlation between architectonic materials and sound and the effect of sound on the space and people.

Sound produced by the oscillation of air molecules and perceivable by people is known as airborne sound. People, machines and technical installations create sound waves, which spread as airborne sound through the air. In this context, sound is considered as either signal or noise: the signal can be the sound of a conversation or the melody of music, while noise covers intrusive sounds such as traffic noise or the noise of machinery. Architectural and acoustic concepts attempt to minimise the noise to support the desired signal so that this sound can be heard optimally.

Vibrations caused by the physical movement of materials, bodies and building elements are known as solid-borne or structure-borne sound. Sounds of this kind can only be felt by people to a limited degree. Usually people are only able to physically sense low-frequency vibrations caused, for example, by a passing train. What we hear is the airborne sound caused by the object. Solid-borne sound caused by impacts, such as walking across a floor surface that is not decoupled from the structure, can however cause materials to vibrate. If these materials have a sufficiently large surface area, the solid-borne sound impulses can also cause the air to vibrate. These vibrations we then hear with our ears. For example, this is how we hear the footsteps of someone crossing the room above us. For the architect and interior designer, it is important to know that both the excitation of a building element with a sound event as well the transmission of the sound can be influenced positively and negatively through the design of the building. Depending on the desired effect, sound events can be supported, minimised or even largely eliminated through the acoustic and architectural concept.

Acoustics have a poetic aspect that every person feels and experiences intuitively. All the surfaces of a space reflect, absorb or scatter sound. As a result, every room has an individual tonal quality that triggers a subjective response in the listener. It is interesting to see how the unusual sound of a space makes people more conscious of their hearing. Sight-impaired people are particularly sensitive to the sound of a space and need to establish a realistic relationship between their auditory impression of a space and their knowledge of its function. When developing an acoustic concept, the designer must take into account that the acoustic impression of a space is a product of the subjective perception of each individual.

Technical developments present a variety of possibilities, through the use of acoustic floors, ceilings and wall elements, to improve the acoustics of a space and with it to enrich the visual quality of a space. The combination of the design elements light, air and acoustics can lend a space an unmistakable and unique atmosphere. The spatial functionality of a space is always reflected in its aesthetic concept. Interior designs create atmospheres whose expressive power lives from the balance between form and function, restfulness and energy and dynamism and aura.

FACETS OF ACOUSTICS

The sound of music and the spoken word has motivated people since ancient times to examine acoustics with a view to improving the sound quality of special spaces. As far back as the 3rd century BC, the first tonal systems in music were established in China, which is now widely regarded as the first treatment of acoustics. In antiquity the Roman architect Vitruvius examined how sound spreads in amphitheatres. He had clay vessels placed beneath each seat to absorb the low-frequency sounds, improving the clarity of the spoken voices. In the Renaissance the effects of spaces and their requirements were examined in detail to improve the musical sound in each room. Finally, the manifold investigations into acoustics in the 20th century have increasingly been applied to improve the acoustics of spaces and to provide a more pleasant listening experience.

Music in the air – the perfect acoustics ensure a pleasurable concert while the dynamic arcing structure appears as if manifested melody.

J.S. Bach Music Hall, Manchester, England; Zaha Hadid Architects

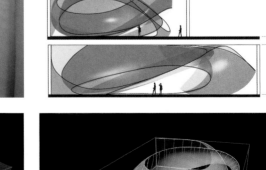

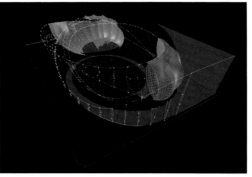

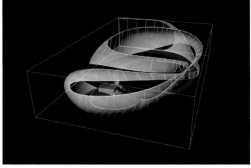

The degree of reverberation and the reverberation time are the most important acoustic qualities of a space. The time a sound takes to fade away is termed the reverberation time or decay. This physical unit affects the sound of a room and its quality. The reverberation time is influenced by the volume of the space and the degree of absorption of the surfaces of the space. To achieve a pleasant-sounding acoustic concept, the reverberation time needs to be adjusted to the space, its size, geometric form and intended function. If the reverberation time is too long for the spoken word, some syllables fade too slowly and overlap one another. The clarity worsens and the listener has to make an effort to follow what is being said. For music, a long reverberation time causes the individual sounds to blend into one another and the music loses its brilliance. If the reverberation time is too short, the sound does not carry across the room. This can be a problem in large spaces where the volume sinks so low that one cannot hear at the back of the room.

The reverberation describes the acoustics of a space. It is influenced by the reflective and absorptive properties of the bounding surfaces and elements in the room and is characterised by the duration of the reverberation time. The time it takes for an acoustic signal to fade determines the subjective acoustic impression a listener has of a space and its spatial, temporal and acoustic extension.

ACOUSTICS AND WELL-BEING

Good acoustics create spaces that are pleasant to be in, providing people in these spaces with a sense of orientation and enabling them to focus on what is essential.

The fact that the acoustic design of a space is not achieved solely by invisible means, but also employs aesthetic and haptic materials and elements, shows how much creative potential there is in this design element. What is fascinating about this technical building material, which is subject to the laws of physics, is that it has a sensory component. When people enter a room, they perceive it with all their senses. If the acoustic impression is different to the functional and spatial impression of the space, this is unsettling. A private room whose acoustics do not permit an intimate conversation is not felt to be comfortable.

The acoustics of office buildings are an issue not only in the workplace but also in conference rooms and reception areas.
Office interior for the ICADE Premier Haus, Munich, Germany; landau + kindelbacher

The acoustic sound and its design underscore the identity of a space through auditory and visual means. This potential to strengthen identity can be employed in all kinds of spaces.

A well-designed acoustic space "embraces" the people in it and pleases the senses. The acoustics set in motion mental, psychological and emotional sensations and processes and enable, create and structure the way we perceive a space, both in terms of how we take in information intellectually as well as the emotional impression we have.

The sense of enclosure in this cave-like interior is heightened by the folded and perforated acoustically-active surfaces.

Wellington Airport International Passenger Terminal ("The Rock"), Wellington, New Zealand; Studio Pacific Architecture in association with Warren and Mahoney

ACOUSTICS IS COMMUNICATION

The acoustics serve as a medium of communication. This aspect of acoustics can be seen in its ability to act as a communication channel, to communicate information and to produce information itself. As such it has the potential to respond to contemporary influences and needs. When the acoustic design supports the function of a space, it facilitates interaction and communication between people as well as between a person and the space. Good acoustics support the intellectual communication of information. When the listener can take in auditory information clearly without having to strain to distinguish it from distracting noise, the acoustics corresponds well to the function of the room.

Flexible acoustic concepts make it possible to accommodate varying individual uses with different acoustic requirements in one room. Through acoustic structuring, several individual qualities of sound can be accommodated in a single space. Acoustic zones can be defined according to different purposes and functions and adapted to different functional requirements. An auditory room atmosphere that provides a sense of general emotional well-being but also facilitates intellectual communication, creative work and peaceful contemplation is enriching because it provides visual, haptic and auditory inspiration and endowes the room with an emotional breadth and depth.

Acoustic concepts must respond to the different needs of people. When, for example, quiet, introverted people need to work with and communicate with loud, extroverted people, both groups need to feel comfortable in the space. The acoustics designer must create acoustic zones within the space so that individuals can feel comfortable and interact according to their respective personality.

When acoustics are considered in terms of culturally inspired aspects, an awareness of different acoustic preferences and patterns emerges, which in turn demonstrates the sensibility required when developing acoustic concepts and how important the spatial, cultural, social, political and societal context is for acoustic design.

An analysis of different cultures and nations shows that, without wishing to fall back on generalised clichés, temperaments differ strongly from country to country and sensitivity to loudness in the spatial environment varies accordingly. In many parts of the world, loud activity is regarded as normal, as a sign of *joie de vivre* and vitality, while in other regions it is regarded as intrusive and annoying. In southern countries of the northern hemisphere,

for example, loud and vibrant atmospheres are a place-making, characteristic aspect of a space, and the acoustic design must take this into account, for example by simply omitting noise-dampening measures. In northern countries, by contrast, great emphasis is placed on acoustics tailored to the function of a space and on the creation of a quieter listening atmosphere with as little intrusive background noise as possible.

The different preferences of people in rural and urban areas should also be taken into consideration when planning good acoustic concepts. The acoustics of spaces in the loud environments of large cities have to be handled differently to rooms in quieter rural areas. Should spaces in urban environments pick up the driving pace and rhythm of the city or provide islands of tranquillity and contemplation? Do rooms in rural regions need to offer a dramatic contrast to the quiet countryside, or is it precisely this quality that should be reflected in rooms? To answer these questions, it is crucial to analyse the target groups precisely, and to determine the functional purpose of the spaces. In addition to individual needs, regional and cultural particularities also play a major role.

Acoustics as a building material forms spaces and makes it possible, through auditory zones, to orientate better in space. Open-plan workplaces in particular require solutions to ensure that the different areas have the appropriate acoustic characteristics for promoting better concentration and quality of work. The design of furniture to meet acoustic needs is likewise important: by using sound-absorbing materials, for example, calm zones can be created for areas of greater privacy and contemplation in the midst of a large communicative space. The acoustic quality can therefore be used to define different functional areas.

The open-plan structures of modern workspaces require suitably flexible and adaptable acoustic concepts. Sound-insulated booths, acoustically separate telephoning areas and special furniture offer areas for different uses. Open-plan workspaces where people and teams work close by one another can result in a level of background noise not necessarily conducive to other work processes. Using individual elements inserted into the space with an appropriate visual and haptic design, flexible acoustic spaces can be created within the workspace to promote concentration, communication, relaxation, high-quality work and creativity. In such spaces the reverberation time should be kept short and sound-reflecting elements should be clad with sound-absorbing materials.

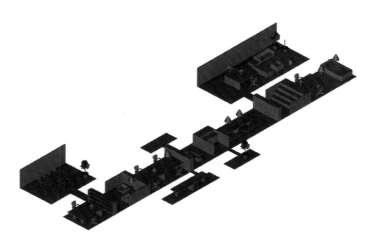

Spray job: a standard acoustic ceiling grid and stock office furniture transformed into a dramatic office interior by spraying the floor and furniture grey.
Office 03, Amsterdam, Holland; i29 interior architects

The conference room has the right acoustics.
Norton Rose, Frankfurt am Main, Germany;
100% interior Sylvia Leydecker

Headphones or baffle ceiling – both help one to hear what one wants to hear.
Google Engineering Headquarters, London, England; Penson

ACOUSTIC DESIGN AND INTERIOR ARCHITECTURE

Every spatial function requires a special acoustic concept. Is the spoken word more important, or music? Should the room be calming? Should it be a creative working environment or a quiet area for concentrated work? Is the space publicly accessible or privately used? Does it serve just one function or does it have to be multi functional? These are some of the questions that need to be considered when developing a spatial and acoustic concept.

A well-designed acoustic concept can employ a wide variety of design possibilities. Depending on the treatment and use of acoustic materials and room elements, the effect they have on a space may be perceived only subliminally or quite consciously. Materials that influence the acoustics often offer great aesthetic potential, as they are not typically restricted by the demands of mass production. The most important acoustic tool, which offers a wide variety of design possibilities, is the use of perforated surfaces with a sound-absorbing surface arranged behind it. The design possibilities of perforated surfaces are vast. A plain plasterboard ceiling, for example, can be transformed with very little effort into an individual design feature. Patterns created by perforations, for example, can contribute significantly to the identity of a space.

The forms of individual elements can also play a significant role in determining the acoustic quality of a room. Flat surfaces, for example, scatter sound differently to undulating or corrugated surfaces. Hard surfaces reflect sound while soft surfaces absorb sound. What makes the acoustic design of a room interesting is the interplay of different textures and the different sound qualities they produce. The contrasts between different haptic materials offers numerous possibilities for designing surfaces. Different textures and textural qualities – soft and hard, loud and soft, coarse and fine, textiles, leather, carpets, marble, wood, metal – can be included in all manner of combinations to influence the sound of a space and its aesthetic articulation.

The development of an appropriate acoustic concept requires interdisciplinary collaboration in the planning process: architects, acoustics designers, electrical engineers, interior designers, media planners and operations planners should bring their various competences to the table at an early stage in the design process. The interdisciplinary planning process illustrates how complex acoustics is as a building material: there are many different possibilities and many different requirements. Perforated surfaces, textile coverings, curtains, surface maximisation, acoustic plaster, coffered ceilings, ceiling-mounted sails and baffles are just some of the many possibilities for designing and influencing the acoustics of a space.

A further aesthetic aspect in the development of acoustic concepts is the question of whether sound-affecting elements should be visible or invisible in the room's design. The shape of a wall, the floor and ceiling can have a decisive, or a barely perceptible, effect on the acoustics of a space. Acoustic surfaces in the furnishing of a space can alternatively be used to create focus in a space. The same applies for sound-absorbing, sound-insulating or sound-dissipating materials: when invisibly embedded in the design, their effect can be subtly incorporated into the overall design and function of the space; when made visible, they can help define its visual character. The acoustic design then determines the form and style of the space.

The acoustic design of the floor, for example, plays a key role in defining how comfortable the atmosphere of a space is. Unlike the ceiling, the floor can be experienced haptically by people in the room. As people walk across a hard floor, they produce sounds that influence the acoustics of the space. To eliminate these, floors are fitted with absorbent materials, which dampen the sound. Soft carpets can absorb sound, are nice to look at and communicate a haptic sense of cosiness. People crossing such a room do not inadvertently attract attention to themselves because the sound of their footfalls is almost entirely absorbed. The opposite effect can, of course, be achieved using a hard floor surface, focusing attention on the floor and the people crossing it.

Acoustics as a design element can foster identity by creating an auditory symbol for the aesthetic and functional meaning of a space. Using aural and aesthetic means, the acoustics of a space can underscore the special quality of that space.

Acoustic screens in a restaurant interior.
Flex, Sado, Japan; ply project – Kenichi Sato, material – Takizawa Veneer Co., manufacture – Takumi Kohgei Co.

Acoustic panelling in an events room needs to be able to cope with different kinds of events.
Hilton Frankfurt Airport Hotel, Frankfurt am Main, Germany; JOI-Design

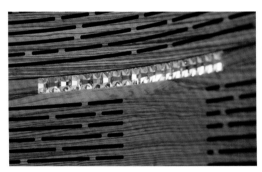

Bubbles: a sprinkle of holes in the acoustic ceiling of this waiting room is incorporated into the design of this "underwater world"-themed interior.
"Zahnarium" Drs. Stammen & Partner children's dentist, Grevenbroich, Germany; 100% interior Sylvia Leydecker

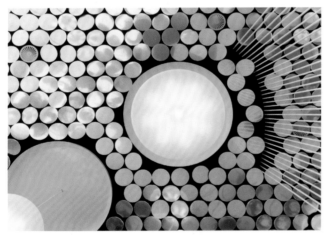

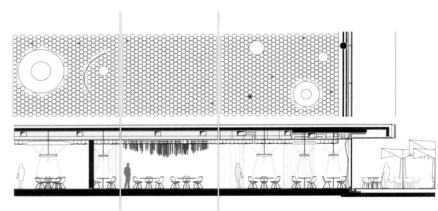

Talking point: the publisher's canteen has an acoustic ceiling consisting of micro-perforated aluminium mirrors applied to a sound-absorbent backing material.

"DER SPIEGEL" canteen, Hamburg, Germany; Ippolito Fleitz Group

EXAMPLES OF THE USE OF TECHNICAL INSTALLATIONS AS DESIGN ELEMENTS

An integrated approach to designing the elements of spaces and the skilful use of light, air and aesthetics offer new perspectives in which space creates an endless number of possible viewpoints beyond its limits. As described here, the use of the technical design elements light, indoor air and acoustics can strengthen the impression of spaces and through orientation, layering and zoning make its character perceptible. Furthermore, these building materials have the potential to contribute elements to a space that lend it a sense of identity. The two case studies described here illustrate the application of these three building materials and the technical installations behind them.

"SPIEGEL" GROUP CANTEEN IN HAMBURG, GERMANY

The building materials light, indoor air and acoustics contribute to the special character of the staff canteen at the headquarters of the SPIEGEL Group publishing house in Hamburg's HafenCity. The design of the ceiling unites functional requirements with aesthetics. The functional components of the ceiling conceal the entire technical apparatus, sprinkler systems, media systems, light, air ventilation and acoustics. The aesthetic component contributes to the identity of the space and creates a connection with the world outside.

The new staff canteen, like its predecessor, acts an advertisement for the SPIEGEL Group – not least due to its prominent position in the building and strong visibility from outside – and reflects its journalistic philosophy as much as its culture of dialogue. The floor plan of the canteen encompasses a large polygonal space whose horizontality is underlined by a band of windows along two of its sides. Given the dimensions of the space, the design needed to avoid creating the impression of monotonous, serially repeating elements and arbitrariness. Instead, the design aims to reproduce the culture of informal dialogue when eating that has developed over decades at the SPIEGEL. The staff canteen is a place to meet, a place of cultural activity and for informal exchanges of opinion. At the same time, all the usual functional aspects such as easy access and general clarity had to be fulfilled.

Because the room has to be able to respond to changing uses, the design focuses on the ceiling as the identity-giving element of the space. Accordingly a matt reflective ceiling was developed that draws its inspiration from the position of the building in the harbour, and reflects the light in a manner similar to light glistening on water. The ceiling consists of 4203 micro-perforated, matt-finish aluminium discs suspended at slight angles to one another. The individual discs are mounted on a sound-absorbing backing material. The natural atmosphere of the light therefore responds to the light in the surroundings. Using the ceiling has further functional advantages: the entire space above the suspended discs, including the technical installations, is painted black and is therefore not visible. Ceiling diffusers and sprinklers disappear in the ceiling. The top surface of the ceiling is sound-absorbing to supplement the acoustic effect of the micro-perforated discs. The ceiling design therefore unites aesthetic and functional aspects. It creates identity-giving elements, picks up the spatial context of the surroundings, improves the acoustics through the use of sound-absorbing materials and surfaces and creates a distinctive space that entertains the eye with warm light reflections.

Large circular ceiling elements create zones in the space through their strong colour. The colours create a positive atmosphere in the space, even on grey days. Dimmable pendant luminaires are located directly above the tables and the degree of illumination can be regulated in fine steps. In the evenings, the circular ceiling elements transform into indirectly illuminated light reflectors. The warm-white "ambient light" of the pendant luminaires defines the basic mood of the canteen. Indirect light in some of the pendant luminaires gently illuminates the coloured discs on the ceiling. Focused downlights placed at strategic locations hidden in the ceiling add accentuated light to the general high-quality atmosphere. Wallwashers integrated into the pattern of the ceiling illuminate the wall surfaces evenly. They ensure there is a balanced relationship between horizontal and vertical illumination and balance the feeling of the room in the evening – also by reflecting in the glass surfaces.

The communicative round tables rest on black, powder-coated steel bases that appear to grow directly out of the floor in a soft movement. The tabletops are made of granite with a laser-engraved screen pattern on its surface, which permits the ceiling lights to be bright without causing glare.

The tables are freely placed in the space in three main groups and provide an organic counterpoint to the polygonal floor plan. The circulation zones are clearly visible. Three lines are inserted into the otherwise seamless white terrazzo floor screed: these lend spatial definition to the tables along the main circulation areas and give visual structure to the space.

Arranged along four sections of these lines, lightweight, removable partitions made of vertical white rods are suspended from the ceiling, dividing off separate zones with an elegant semi-transparent screen.

The core of the building is given extra depth through the use of wood panelling. The whitened and oiled panels have a vertical wavy surface, similar in look to hanging textiles, which scatters sound in the room in all directions to produce a more pleasant acoustic quality.

A zigzag arrangement of glass partitions can be used to close off an area for separate events. A swarm of illuminated acrylic glass rods hang from the ceiling and provide glare-free illumination while making the space more intimate.

Using the three design elements light, indoor air and acoustics, the design supports the functions of the canteen as well as the identity and conversational culture of the publisher. The staff canteen is designed as a communicative meeting area, a place of cultural and political exchange.

INTERVAL FOYER OF THE PALACE OF INTERNATIONAL FORUMS IN TASHKENT, UZBEKISTAN

The interval foyer in the lower ground floor of the Palace of International Forums in Uzbekistan is an example of the interplay of the three building materials, which are used visibly as well as invisibly to give the room a functional and aesthetic structure. Numerous columns and a relatively low ceiling that slopes away to the back required a solution that could lend the space a sense of lightness and elegance.

The bright columns connecting the floor organically with the ceiling appear dematerialised through their illumination. Indirect light illuminates the flanks of the columns, shrouding their surfaces in light and lending the room an impression of expansiveness and structure. The materiality of the columns is given additional depth through the use of a shimmering mother-of-pearl effect produced by Venetian plaster, a smooth, polished white-coloured plaster with a marble dust additive. A slot of light in the ceiling around the top of the columns makes the columns look as if they disappear into the ceiling and illuminates the columns so that they appear to shine from within. All the visitor sees is the light of the sensual object, not its source. The light is reflected by the polished white marble floor and brings it to life. Through the elegant use of light and dynamic design of the ceiling, the room is given an expansive sense of depth and a festive atmosphere.

The arcing black channels in the ceiling add dynamism to the plan of the room and create a stimulating contrast to the floor, walls and columns. These channels contain all the technical elements: the air vents, lighting and safety fittings. The functionality of the acoustic ceiling has a minimal design but a great aesthetic impact. The coarse plaster of the ceiling contrasts with the smooth materials of the columns and the floor. The arcing channels draw the visitors dynamically into the depth of the room, inviting them to move around.

The visual patterning on the floor made of straight, narrow lines of grey marble inlay creates large, star-shaped ornaments, a characteristic motif in the national culture, and provides a sense of orientation in the space. The satin sheen of the floor and the light reflections contrast pleasingly with its hard materiality. As people cross the marble floor, their footfalls echo into the room. These sounds emphasise that the room is a place to mingle, a place to see and be seen.

The wavy glass facade of the restaurant adds additional dynamism to the room and simultaneously scatters the sound diffusely across it, contributing to the good acoustics of the space.

Light, air and acoustics are used here to support the architectural concept of a place of communication. The active treatment of the ceiling and the floor strengthen the character of the space while simultaneously lending it structure. The open and generous design of the room along with the ornamentation sends a signal of openness within the building. As a result the interiors unite a sense of grandeur and openness, which the visitors take with them into the outside world.

Hypostyle hall: a dynamic space full of columns is given a simple acoustic ceiling of coarse plaster.
Palace of International Forums, lobby,
Tashkent, Uzbekistan; Ippolito Fleitz Group

MEDIA

MARK BLASCHITZ

Ring-ring: not all that long ago, this was emblematic of modern communication.

Medium, the singular of media, derives from the Latin word for "middle". This original meaning is still used today, for example in the *Small*, *Medium* and *Large* labels of clothes sizes; but the word "medium", and especially its plural "media", is now used in many other ways, which can be broadly categorised into two meanings: to denote a bearing material or to denote a medium for conveying information. This differentiation is, however, provisional pending a categorical classification of technical media terminology according to a sensible and consistent definition of the term medium, or media.

At present there is no generally applicable media theory able to encompass the different understandings and interests of the fields of humanities, technology and art. There is an urgent need for greater clarification in the confused language and definitions used in association with the term media – which is an issue for the field of cultural studies – but this goes beyond the scope and subject of this short chapter. Nevertheless, I would like to briefly give a phenomenological overview of the broad and often contradictory use of the term. The intention is not to undertake a methodological, academic examination but rather to offer the reader a better understanding of the term.

The term medium is commonly used to denote materials that have a bearing or transporting function. In the field of physics, a medium can transmit all manner of waves, in chemistry a medium is a substance that can hold or absorb other substances, and in biology the term media is used to denote a nutrient solution for organisms. In the field of technical engineering, the term media is used as a collective term for liquid, gaseous or finely dissipated solid substances. In architectural practice, media commonly refers to the routing of infrastructure for utilities such as gas, water and sewage as well as cabling for electricity, telephone, TV and Internet.

In the field of media science, we differentiate between old media – which includes print media, gramophone records, audio and videotapes as well as radio and television – and new media such as CD, DVD and Blu-ray as well as Internet and e-mail. Here a further means of differentiation becomes apparent: between a storage medium and a transmission medium. Strictly speaking, however, we need to start by differentiating between the terms mediation, medium and means, and as a consequence between the producer and recipient, the sender and receiver, as well as between media that are monologic, dialogic, polylogic or interactive in the way they operate.

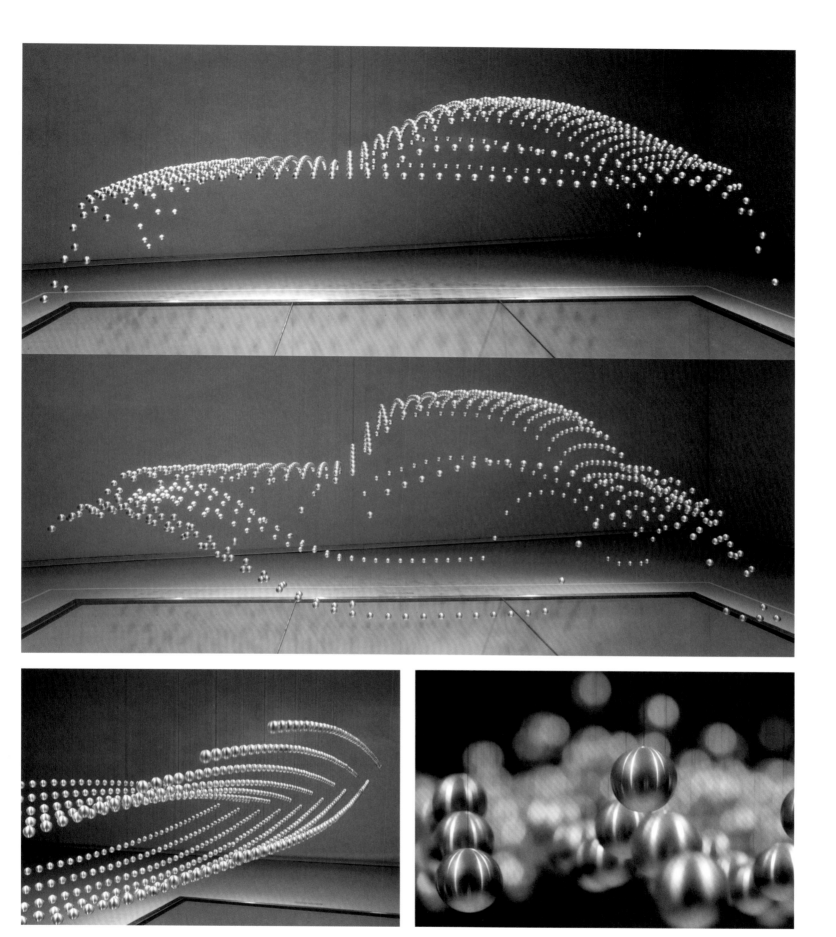

This kinetic sculpture translates the process of form-finding in art and design metaphorically in space. A chaotic jumble of 700 metal spheres forms itself with the help of a concealed mechanism, electronics and the final code into the contours of a BMW.

Kinetic sculpture for BMW Museum, Munich, Germany; ART+COM AG

MEDIA AND THE FINE ARTS

The fine arts have traditionally categorised media differently: painting, graphics and sculpture are termed old media and photography, film and video are new media. Architecture and its related fields are accorded a special role in this context as they have strived since antiquity to unite the different forms of art. As such, architecture not only integrates different art forms – both in the fine arts and applied arts – but also new and old media.

For quite some time, the fine arts have adopted an alternative means of differentiation between analogue media and digital media: in addition to the traditional carrier media, i.e. different pigments and thinners, or different kinds of tools, one can now add digital, electronically controlled hardware and software.

Currently inter-media or trans-media artistic production in both the so-called old and new media is being subsumed under the term multimedia as a new artistic genre. In this context it is important to note that in the history of art, the advent of a new medium has never actually fully displaced or replaced an existing, older medium – and this will not be the case either with the emergence of digital media in the 20th century. Analogue pictures will continue to produced using traditional media. Graphics will still created on different kinds of paper murals and frescoes will be continue to adorn the walls of architecture; tableaus will be applied to wood, metal sheeting, composite materials and plastics; oil paintings will be applied to canvas frames; and this will continue to happen manually, semi-automatically as well industrially in the form of drawings or paintings, silk screen prints or offset printing.

It is not hard to see that there are no limits to the variety of media and their inter-media or trans-media production in all forms of fine art. The fundamental role light plays in how the human brain perceives objects will ensure the continuing variety and vitality of traditional media. The appearance of surfaces is a product of how they absorb and reflect light, which is in turn influenced by the pigment and texture of the surface as well as the spectrum of light shining on it. The appearance is therefore dependent on the one hand on the colour, or colour temperature, of the light that illuminates it, and on the other on the qualities of the surface, and therefore how that spectrum of light reflects from the surface. The possibilities range from transparent and translucent materials to rough, opaque or shiny surfaces in all colours of the spectrum, to mirrored surfaces that reflect the entire spectrum of incident light.

The variety, simultaneous presence and sheer endless possible combinations of traditional media have had a strong and positive impact on the production of fine art that transcends the boundaries between disciplines. The now widespread existence of old and new media serves only to further accelerate this development. With the help of technical equipment such as projectors and screens, coloured light can be created, controlled and made visible using a wide range of analogue and digital optical techniques. More than ever before, graphics and painting are no longer confined to marking – or visually obscuring – the boundaries of space but now have the capacity to connect the pictorial and the physical realms in a dialogic and dynamic way. For architecture and interior design, this represents a major extension of the interface between the user and technically generated images and of the interface between these images and space.

What would happen if we were to relate the history of architecture in terms of the history of media? In a lecture entitled "The Crisis of Linearity" held in Bern in 1988, Vilém Flusser structured his text in eight chapters, in which he elaborates eight steps from the image to writing and beyond.[1] From Frank Lloyd Wright's open-plan houses from the turn of the last century, we have developed contemporary switchable floor plans. From Adolf Loos' flowing spaces of the modernism of the 1920s followed the informed space of our media society, and from Ludwig Mies van der Rohe's functional-modern boxes and Le Corbusier's cubistic spaces, we have the contemporary hyperspheres in which living, working and recreation take place simultaneously like the multitasking processor of a computer workstation.

The doors of cyberspace are open and it is rapidly being populated from all corners. What has been state of the art for more than a decade in finance, medicine and fine art – media-networked, decentrally organised spatial situations that are strongly shaped by the interaction between real material space and virtual action space – is only rarely to be found in the realm of architecture. If architecture is not to lose its value as an expression and reflection of society, this whole aspect is an area that will become increasingly important to address.

Vilém Flusser will almost certainly be proved right with his call for a new type of architecture and a new design for the house: "Home-as-one's-castle with its roof, walls, windows and doors now only exists in fairy tales. Material and immaterial cables have knocked as many holes in it as in a Swiss cheese: on the roof there is the aerial, telephone wire comes through the wall, the television takes the place of the window, and the door is replaced by the garage with the car. Home-as-one's-castle has become a ruin with the wind of communication blowing through the cracks in the walls."[2]

→262

The dynamic sensor-controlled mesh of LEDs generates an impressive life performance.

Dynamic Performance of Nature, Salt Lake City, Utah, USA; E/B Office

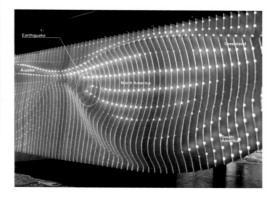

Nearly 100 hand-folded emergency foil blankets equipped with LEDs and connected to movement sensors sparkle in this interactive art installation.

BOTOXUTOPIA, Milan, Italy; The Principals – Drew Seskunas

Anamorphosis: this principle has been used to transform the logo of a bank into an abstract three-dimensional structure which one only perceives as a logo from a specific viewpoint.

The BrandSpace – anamorphic logo for Deutsche Bank Headquarters, Frankfurt am Main, Germany; ART+COM AG

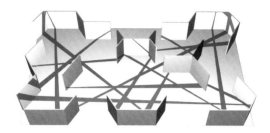

Visualisation of telemedicine and its application using a series of different stations such as at home, at the pharmacy, an emergency, the doctor's surgery, etc. The rays crisscrossing the trade fair stand represent the flow of data.
FutureCare at CeBit, Bitkom with Deutsche Messe Hannover 2010, Germany; 100% interior
Sylvia Leydecker

AT HOME IN CYBERSPACE

In future the implications of telematic communications will determine the concepts of new architecture. Frequency and density of information will become the new important design parameters. In the process, the look and rhythm of the facade will be of secondary importance. Digitally informed, switchable walls will serve simultaneously as the boundary of a room and as a connector (replacing wall and door), creating natural or artificial illumination (replacing the window and light) and forming the outer surface of individual buildings or entire sites. They may be transparent, translucent or mirrored, convey information through projections, screens or LEDs, be multi-coloured or of a single colour, and be mono-, bi- or multi-directional. "More is different," as Kevin Kelly[3] would say.

Fundamental changes are underway during an age in which the increasing media connectivity of households will have inevitable and lasting consequences for individuals as well as their living environment. On the one hand, individuals risk involuntary isolation – in the Western world, singles already account for half of all households – and on the other the public realm is making increasing inroads into private space through the vehicle of new media – we sit in front of screens, wear headphones over our ears, and we have swapped the comparative distance of books and magazines for the immediacy of laptop and mobile phone. As we become increasingly isolated from our immediate environment while simultaneously in direct contact with the far and wide, the question is how we should lead our lives in virtual space, i.e. in cyberspace, as well as how we should live and build communally in the telepolis, as Florian Rötzer[4] has called it. It seems apparent that space is undergoing a transformation, a transformation that borders on placelessness – although this placelessness has its roots and its correspondences both in the virtual as well as material worlds.

The question as to where home is in the midst of an increasingly decentralised media society is also a question about placelessness itself. In order to consider the issue of placelessness in the context of society, and therefore also of architecture, it is useful to research the principle of what place is. One possible approach to this is the creation of places – of artificial places. This way of place-making begins to form a topography as networks start to form, and it is through this artificial landscape that we can then derive an idea of what place is in its full complexity. So, the first step towards researching the phenomenon of placelessness is to examine a virtual landscape made up of places, people, things, terms, verbs, numbers and symbols. Virtual regions form as networks of connections between individual landscapes and through views – or links – to other places in the Internet, as well as through the form of their surfaces. It makes no difference whether we are talking about a real landscape or the creation of virtual topographies: the structure and poetry of real landscapes consists of materiality and distances perceived using all our senses, while virtual landscapes consist of pixels on a screen and time itself, perceived as colours, contrasts and design. The peak of a mountain in the real world corresponds to the depth of a link in the virtual world, the pattern of land parcels to the document and data structure, the rhythmic repetition of elements in the landscape to the colour and rhythm of words on screen, and the speed of travel in a real landscape to the load times and refresh rates when surfing the Internet.

The issue of placelessness and the accompanying question of how we find a home in the midst of this homeless architecture will in future lead to the development and design of new living environments and communal spaces. The task of the planner in the 21st century will be to design a binary world – a worldwide, electronically conveyed environment with omnipresent networks in which most of the artefacts (in all sizes from the nano-dimension to the global dimension) will have some form of intelligence and telecommunication capabilities. This hyperworld – according to William J. Mitchell – will superimpose itself over the agricultural and industrial landscape that people have lived in for so long, eventually succeeding it completely.

Today, the instruments of synchronology already exist with which all spaces can be present at once – spaces that according to Kant have a transcendental identity, i.e. that no longer exist once we remove the conditions that make it possible to experience them – spaces that are a purely predefined manifestation of our external senses. All designers and planners will have to work within the conditions described: conditions that will not only require changes to spaces themselves but also changes to the availability of spaces. The transition from dealing with spaces to controlling the availability of spaces means that our direct relationship to things will change. If we assume that space as a real entity will be a limited resource, that the post-industrial process of mobilisation has already exceeded its limits, and that people's desire for mobility – which includes their desire for imagined variety and curiosity – is likely to increase rather than decrease, we will need to develop new ways of experiencing our living environment. These are already on the brink of being realised in the new digital world, where technological possibilities are beginning to appear ever more real. The screen is starting to replace not only the window but also the traditional doorway. Reality will be replaced by observability.

Fire and heat: this showroom uses film and images that are projected onto a foil that encloses the interior of the room.

Jaga Experience Lab, Diepenbeek, Belgium;
SAQ Architects

TOPOLOGICAL TRANSFORMATIONS AND INTERSPACES

The emerging information society is meanwhile bringing forth image collators and data informants. The active communication of information (in Latin *informare* means to shape) involves the polydirectional generation of data. Only when the meaning of contributing own data is perceived as a socio-cultural opportunity and starts to become normal practice will it become more likely that the way in which we interact with media spaces will change more fundamentally. Of particular interest in this regard is person-generated content that is transported by the media machinery and the potential this has to influence the importance of the "interspace", which is discussed in more detail below.

The provision of spaces could be effected through their transformation into media-based fields of existence, which would make an evolutionary consideration of the phenomenology of space possible. With the help of digital information technology, it is possible to generate "common spaces", to make them interactive, to offer them access to isolated spaces of imagination and to experience how new levels of activity can be provided that can be individually changed and collectively experienced. The field of activity of an individual is transformed into levels that, through input and attention from others, may be transformed into common spaces, which may be developed and cultivated, and perhaps shaken up through intervening processes to form new constellations and systems of order making it in turn into a telematic place.

In response to these places, a new material and architectural reality is gradually stirring in the real, physical world: one that has conflicting functions. Hybrid action and living spaces are waiting to be designed that, reflecting the mobile society and its patterns of thought production and reflection, will take the form of network plans. The reciprocal influence of the design of digital networks and actual, material space in combination with emerging design parameters such as realtime, speed and scenarios, will bring forth new architectural living environments and action spaces.

The interspace denotes the immediate spatial transition zone and is the setting for this new interactive spectacle. It defines a new sphere of reality. Functions that society has kept separate, such as living, manufacturing, research and administration, services, offices, consumption, publicity, culture, etc., can once again interlock to form transformational constellations of greater complexity. By the same means, functions that were until now dependent on one another can be increasingly decentralised.

Parallel to the already available interfaces between the digital and analogue worlds, such as the fax, telephone, television and computer screen, a new digitally transmitted visual and functional reality is arising that in turn has an influence on the production of real, architectural space. Transmissions in realtime make simultaneous presence in the here and now, possible giving rise (in addition to new forms of communication) to the parallel switchability of spaces. Face-to-face conversation in which both parties are physically present is now just one of many possible forms of communication. The digital world is in the process of becoming a new media for personal communication, experience and action. That these new forms of interaction effectively eradicate the physical distance between these real spaces represents a revolution for architecture, and more immediately for interior design in particular. A new design reality is arising in which spaces are decoupled from their location and for which the parameters need to be redefined. What kinds of design will this make possible? What new functional relationships can these new design realities bring forth? It is now down to us to embrace the revolutionary design parameters made possible by this new symbiosis of digital and analogue worlds that is already beginning to influence the future of mankind, and to create new functional and visual realities and with them new patterns of action.

The interspace can be regarded as just one possible, temporary reality. Currently, however, the designers of cyberspace are concentrating, with the help of digital helmets, data suits and in future probably also direct brain adapters, on reducing this interspace to zero. The design relevance of the window seats of the diverse interfaces is all but disregarded. The interspace, as a potential space of endless doors, makes it possible, for as long as mankind still exists as a biological being, to perceive the digital images that fly by in the data space. But why do we think of the images of these digital worlds as virtual spaces? It would certainly be wrong to speak of spaces in the conventional geometric sense of three-dimensional spaces with X, Y and Z axes. But the notion of three-dimensional spaces with the dimensions of surface and time can be seen as an adequate representation, if rather unusual and vague. The way we see these technical images is akin to watching a film, a film of digital images.

The conventional way we use real space is overlaid in the virtual realm with an electronically generated, multisensory impression of space. Interfaces arise – intermediary spaces that are more than just one point or one surface but describe the physical and intellection interaction space between man and electronic technology as a whole. Through the superimposition of the real and virtual, space and object, both in terms of materiality and in projection, become a new sphere of reality, an interspace, a three-dimensional periphery, an output and input place. These are realities that we already experience on a daily basis on the television, the telephone or in front of the computer. Epistemologically, these realities have long been addressed in the field of philosophy, but architecturally they have until now been largely ignored, which is striking because these new spheres of reality have in principle been with us since the invention of the telephone and the radio.

With the increasing digitisation of everyday activities and the changing built environment, the difference between outdoor and indoor space is gradually disappearing. If, as Le Corbusier claimed, architecture is the wonderful interplay of space and light, should not these new realities have a role to play in this drama?

Water – water and nothing else in the showroom for a sanitary ware producer.
Minamo for TOTO, Tokyo Designers Week 2011, Japan; Torafu Architects

FROM INTERFACE TO INTERSPACE

Interspaces are networks between virtual and material spaces. Using camera installations, wide-screen projections, microphones and loudspeakers, remote or physically separate locations are connected by data links with one another. The interspace is a virtual extension of real space.

Interspaces are an evolution of interfaces. While interfaces represent the link between humans and computers, interspaces are the link between environments and computers. As an extension of videophones or online conferences, interspaces communicate not just images (usually of the heads) of the respective participants but also images of the (entire) space in which the people, animals and interior exist. In a manner similar to the relationship between architecture and painting in the Baroque (perspective, *trompe l'œil*, mirrors, etc.), the virtual transmission of spaces creates entirely new spatial constellations – the interspaces. The creation of interspaces gives rise to new areas of work in their design and technology, and heralds a paradigm shift in the design disciplines and fine art.

Building structures will no longer be measured solely in terms of spatial density but also in terms of speeds, timeframes and communication frequencies. The current linearity that we are accustomed to will be broken apart by the extended availability of space, by the concomitant transformation of time and the potential for individual attention. The ability to operate in telematic space means that it will be necessary to redefine conventional design parameters such as density, orientation, lighting and access for the realms of urban design and architecture, and in particular for interior design, and to add to these the aspect of communication. The ability to overcome actual distances as a product of the telematic availability of space will become more widespread, that is social contacts may be embedded in the frequency patterns of their availability. Buildings will therefore become nodal points in a network of states of availability. High periods of telematic and physical availability create density in a communicative as well as spatial sense. In a manner similar to the structures in medieval building complexes in which very different spatial densities and information intensities cumulated, spatial constellations arise that through the content communicated, the frequencies of information and the patterns of use become multi-incidental containers, i.e. enriched with occurrences. The individual networking mechanisms, which serve as the basis for every provision of space, can be represented in the form of model scenarios, functional diagrams or circuit plans. Abstracted codes, determined by speed, events and spaces will, with the help of specially developed analogue test models, become spatially definable zone groups.

Where the probability of occurrence becomes as great as it can possibly be, at the point where it is about to become reality, one speaks of the virtual. The less probable the possibilities become, the more informative they are until they ultimately reach the point at which they cannot become reality. Virtual spaces are therefore most probably emergent time-surface continua. The point of the digital world is to be. Consequently, it is in essence pointless. Its point is therefore to be pointless. The ability to accept this apparent contradiction is a first step towards understanding the digital world. Anarchy is pointless. Anarchy follows a game strategy that more than anything serves to create a place for theisms and atheisms, for mythology and natural science, for art and ethics. Anarchy should be equated with the search, with the experiment in the context of prevailing variety and contradictions. Anarchy here is not Kant's definition of law and freedom without violence. Here anarchy means: every contradiction has its topos, or more than that: anarchy itself is the product of these contradictions. The point of anarchy is to be. The point of anarchy is therefore to be pointless. Anarchistic being is a self-controlled cybernetic network in which not the data clusters themselves but the simultaneity of the polylogues represents what is concrete. It is an anarchistic being of simultaneous contra-consensual decisions within a kind of cosmic brain.

→272

The magic box – the pulsating epicentre of a pavilion in which visitors are transported into imaginary spatial landscapes through the use of LEDs.
State Grid Pavillon, EXPO Shanghai, China; Atelier Brückner GmbH

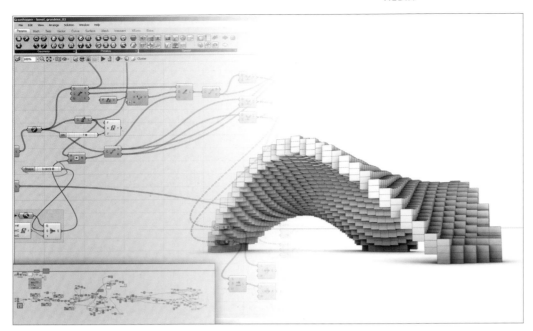

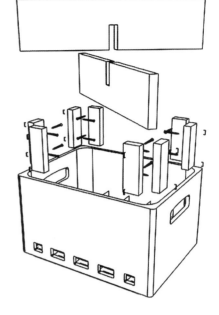

Software: approximately 2,000 beer crates were assembled into this expressive geometric free-form structure for a student project – without software an impossible feat.

Boxel, Detmold, Germany; design by Henri Schweynoch, supervised by Prof. Marco Hemmerling

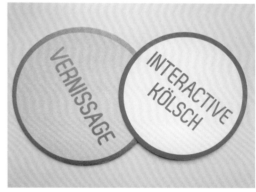

Kölsch: By moving around their pink and blue beer coasters on the table, guests at the bar can interactively control the LEDs of the room lighting.

Interactive Kölsch, Cologne, Germany; Mainz University of Applied Sciences

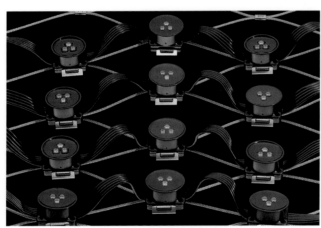

Medial: a transparent safety screen of woven wire mesh is transformed into a design element and attractive communication tool.
X-LED, Süssen, and Messe Frankfurt, Germany;
Carl Stahl Architektur

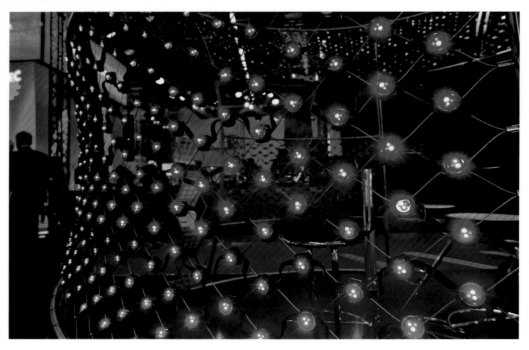

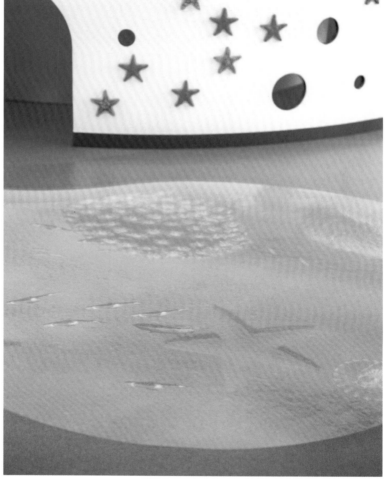

Interactive: a floor projection that responds to movement helps children while away time in the doctor's waiting room. Jellyfish swim and fish dart out of the way... and one can hear the splash of water.

"Zahnarium" Drs. Stammen & Partner
children's dentist, Grevenbroich, Germany;
100% interior Sylvia Leydecker

FROM INTELLIGENT TECHNOLOGY TO INTELLIGENT TYPOLOGY

Smart buildings are not a traditional building typology in which smart materials replace traditional building materials and the building is upgraded as it were with high-tech electronic features for security, climate control and the control of household appliances. Smart buildings are houses that are no longer primarily conceived, planned and assessed as an end result but instead reveal their qualities through their ability to accommodate processes. "The adaptive capabilities of smart materials mean that chronological processes in particular will be of increasing importance. A performative understanding of materials and technologies facilitates, and demands, a new approach to the architectural design process."[5] Smart buildings therefore refer to a future-oriented building typology, one that speaks of the relationship between the public, communal and private spheres and the use-oriented and climatic zoning of a building.

The development of smart skins is a further area of key importance. As the skin is the boundary and interface between one space and another, for example between inside and outside, it makes sense that it should contain a series of functional requirements: it can absorb light, be reflective, opaque, translucent, transparent, photovoltaic, insulating, thermally retentive, self-illuminating, multi-coloured, controllable, passive, active, interactive and reversible. At present, smart skins are mostly a multi-layered combination of various building elements made of different materials that are employed in different alternating constellations depending on the requirements the building skin needs to fulfil. In addition to materials that bear loads, bound spaces and thermally insulate, material combinations are also chosen for their visual effect. While smart technologies such as computer-controlled LED and OLED surfaces have a purely visual effect, smart materials are able to change their colour, form or shape reversibly in response to changing light conditions, temperature, electrical current, electromagnetic field potential or chemical reaction.

The Smart Treefrog project designed by SPLITTERWERK as part of the "Smart Material Houses" project in Hamburg is a building that makes use of these new technologies to create a new typology. The building employs a thick wall system based on the onion-skin principle in which the facade is made of multiple intelligent layers. The user can control several individual layers of the thick wall according to the function or filtering effect they provide – for example, special glass types, insulation panels, slats or blinds – and can switch them on and off as required. As a result, it is possible to finely control the degree of privacy or openness. In addition, the ability to reconfigure the thick wall

provides the basis for intelligently regulating and switching the indoor room climate. The outermost skin of this hybrid building is made of bioreactors supported on a hardwood skeleton that encloses the semi-public outdoor galleries and circulation and creates a climatic zone. This serves as an effective climatic buffer layer that reduces energy loss and provides the residents with a garden space that can be used all year round despite the cold Hamburg climate. This kind of highly networked functional and spatial system we have dubbed Supernature.

The process of creating these "case study houses" on a site of the IBA Hamburg provided an opportunity to explore and realise the typological potential of advanced technology – in the form of intelligent materials and intelligent technologies – and to relate this to the current state of research and development, to the possibilities of the building industry, to current issues in society, to insights in the field of cultural science and to architectural discourse. This has resulted in reconfigurable floor plans and switchable spaces. The flowing spaces created by Ludwig Mies van der Rohe, the open floor plans by Frank Lloyd Wright, Adolf Loos' *Raumplan* as well as the economical design of the Frankfurt Kitchen by Margarete Schütte-Lihotzky have all contributed in different ways to the contemporary design of the multi-incidental shell of the "Graz Apartment" and the "Hamburg Apartment": in the switchable structure of these new housing typologies, rooms are no longer interlocked but can change their function alternately or simultaneously on demand, for example to form a single large neutral space one moment and separate spaces the next. In the "Lightroom Apartment", entire functional units can be switched together to face into a light-filled central space. Adolf Loos' *Raumplan* concept gives way to an individually controllable, temporally-changing *Wohnplan* (one that responds to how one lives). The changing pattern of living and use requirements over the course of the day define what the apartment looks like according to the users' needs. This is the principle of Smart Spaces with different typologies of reconfigurable floor plans.

1 Flusser, Vilém, *Krise der Linearität* (Berne: Benteli, 1997).

2 Flusser, Vilém, *The Shape of Things: A Philosophy of Design*, (London: Reaktion Books, 1999), pp. 82-83.

3 Kelly, Kevin, *Out of Control: The New Biology of Machines, Social Systems, & the Economic World* (New York: Perseus Books, 1995).

4 Rötzer, Florian, *Die Telepolis. Urbanität im digitalen Zeitalter* (Cologne: Bollmann Verlag, 1997).

5 IBA Hamburg, *Dokumentation: Smart Material Houses*, Internationale Bauausstellung Hamburg, 2012, p. 10.

Separated and yet connected: the translucent glass wall is colour-printed on both sides, which in combination with the wall thickness creates a shift in perspective that makes the room beyond appear as if seen on a movie screen.
Vine Leaf Wall, Linz, Austria; SPLITTERWERK

2D and 3D: the ornamental motif covers all the surfaces of the stairwell, creating a complex and flowing space where surface blends into space. Junctions in the geometry of the space are carefully blended into the pattern.
Vine Leaf Sphere in the Black Treefrog, Bad Waltersdorf, Austria; SPLITTERWERK

A functionally neutral zone in the centre of the apartment is brought to life by opening sections of wall to attach adjoining spaces or functions – much like programme windows on a computer desktop.
Graz Apartment in the Black Treefrog, Bad Waltersdorf, Austria; SPLITTERWERK

In-house incline: special configurations temporarily fold out of the sloping surfaces into the horizontal.
Green Treefrog, St. Josef, Austria;
SPLITTERWERK

Fade to grey: the slowly moving projections obscure the boundaries of the room, causing the architecture to shift, disappear and reappear.
Performative light-space installation,
AIT-ArchitekturSalon Munich, Germany;
SPLITTERWERK

Light projections create
a contemplative space.
Performative light-space installation, Venice
Architecture Biennale 2008, Venice, Italy;
SPLITTERWERK

INFORMATION TECHNOLOGY

LARS GRAU

Digital projectors are now standard tools for teaching and presenting.

Office interior for ICADE Premier Haus, Munich, Germany; landau + kindelbacher

By definition, information technology pervades all areas of life within an information society. This is the type of society most of us live in. As a consequence, information technology is bound to have a major impact on our daily lives, an impact manifest to a great extent in the design of interior spaces. The integration of media and technology demands a close coordination of architects, interior designers, home automation engineers, media experts and craftsmen. With technology and media being integrated more and more into interior spaces, furniture, everyday objects, devices and materials, a deeper look into the impact of information technology from the interior designer's perspective seems essential.

The information society "is a society where the creation, distribution, diffusion, use, integration and manipulation of information is a significant economic, political, and cultural activity. The aim of the information society is to gain competitive advantage internationally, through using *Information Technology* in a creative and productive way."[1] Information technology is not only the Internet. Instead, it is a superordinate concept for the processing of information and the hardware and software required for this. Contemporary and future human-computer interfaces (HCI) need further detailed consideration within this field as well.

The information society started somewhere between the 1970s and today and is changing fundamentally the way societies work. Within the last three decades, information technology has transformed many areas of our lives by changing the way we use digital media and interact with our environment in almost any given context. As an example, automotive interiors have changed completely over the last 30 years in terms of the user's possibilities to interact. While cars in the 1970s were merely equipped with physical interfaces for very basic functionalities, vehicles today are moving supercomputers where the driver is surrounded by an overwhelming set of controls including tangible interfaces, voice control and touch-sensitive interaction, to be used in parallel in multimodal interaction. What is more, the automobile today not only interoperates with personal devices like mobile phones but also communicates with other cars and service operators, enabling for example much better traffic jam foresight and security.

One key driver of this change, obviously, is the continued miniaturisation and interconnectedness of technology, which now allows information technology to be integrated into everyday objects, fabrics and materials. Technology is moving away from single stationary devices that still make up our life today into a future where technology is ubiquitous and invisible – a permanently available virtual surrounding augmenting our physical environment. Highly integrated solutions like wearable computing are indicative of this trend. This vision of ubiquitous or pervasive computing is quite well understood by now and has become a large-scale research topic – being called "The Internet of Things". Ubiquitous computing refers to "invisible, everywhere computing that does not live on a personal device of any sort, but is in the woodwork everywhere".[2] Mark Weiser, a computer scientist and researcher at Palo Alto Research Center, predicted this (r)evolution 25 years ago by stating: "In the 21st century the technology revolution will move into the everyday, the small and the invisible."[3]

So, nothing new? What is rather new is that we are witnessing this utopia actually turning into reality. Many people see this upcoming reality as a threat to some extent – or at least they ask the question whether we really need this amount of "comfort". Do we need coffee cups that show us the exact temperature of the liquids they contain or seating furniture that charges our mobile phones? Obviously, new technologies arise because we are capable of inventing them, not because we need them. The question is: what makes sense? That is where designers come into play. Their role is to use given technologies in a reasonable manner to fulfil existing user needs. As Klaus Krippendorff puts it: "The etymology of *design* goes back to the latin 'de' + 'signare' and means making something, distinguishing it by a sign, giving it significance, designating its relation to other things, owners, users, or gods. Based on this original meaning, one could say: Design is making sense (to things)."[4]

Especially for the interior design discipline, information technology opens up undreamt-of possibilities. Technology can enhance our daily lives by increasing quality, adding comfort, security and efficiency while reducing maintenance time, costs and environmental pollution. But it all comes down to the user – the inhabitant – at the end. Technological systems get more and more complex, while their usability needs to get more and more simple for people to adopt them. This platitude is a logical side effect of the information society: people are overloaded with the amount and diversity of information and technology. As technology is also no longer transparent and comprehensible for end users, they need efficient and properly working solutions as they are no longer capable of repairing things. What is needed is comfort based on technology and made available by design.

See me: hotel guests now assume they will have a network connection during their stay.
W Hotel, London, England; Concrete Architectural Associates

SMART HOME

The interior design discipline currently faces the challenge to combine the physical and the virtual environment. Interior designers of today and especially of tomorrow need to cope with complex technological opportunities and fulfil central cross-linking design tasks in interdisciplinary teams to evolve and apply *sense* to rich user experiences in domestic, public and work environments.

Within the last years, terms like Smart Home or Connected Home became more and more popular. Smart Home solutions or Home Automation systems aim to simplify living at home and offer more quality of life, comfort and security. Multiple areas of applications exist. It is appropriate to distinguish the subsectors Home Entertainment, Energy Management and Household Controls. Home Entertainment addresses the users' need for all kind of media at home, available in multiple devices and in multiple locations. Energy Management concerns sustainability issues, ecological and economic aspects: heating, ventilation, air-conditioning, power consumption and so on. Household Controls contains all kinds of applications around the building: security systems, light control, assisted living, etc. This categorisation already indicates the major issue: the need for standardisation.

As often, North America is the biggest market worldwide, with most suppliers and the most technically mature solutions. In Europe, and especially Germany, holistic Smart Home systems have not yet reached the mass market as the back-fitting into existing buildings is mostly considered to be too complicated. In Europe, currently only 20 % of Smart Home solutions are installed in existing buildings, as 80 % are installed into new buildings.[5] Asian players mostly act as suppliers for Western companies, with only few European and American brands on the market. In this field, China will not belong to the key markets in the close future, which is also due to cultural differences, as for example Americans feel a much stronger need for security systems than Europeans or Asians, while in Asia, wireless solutions are preferred over wired ones.[6]

The Smart Home market is constantly growing and changing as user needs for comfort and connected solutions at home increase.[7] Being dominated by premium solutions before, many young innovative companies are entering the mass market and the do-it-yourself (DIY) market, offering simple "wireless plug & play"-products.[8]

While various players are pushing into the market, Smart Home is a complex story, especially for users. As always, the pitfall is within standardisation. Currently, technological aspects of standardisation drive the Smart Home discussion, but the next real challenge is within the area of user experience – providing simple and enjoyable user interfaces across multiple devices.

Smart buildings: digital control of the home from afar is no longer science fiction.

Flexible network in a smart home with battery-free radio communications; EnOcean

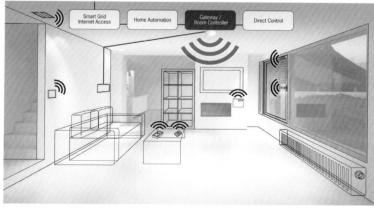

STANDARDISATION AND THE USER EXPERIENCE

From a technological perspective, "central intelligence" is the most promising approach: A "digital butler" has the knowledge about the devices and the different communication channels inside the house. "He" manages to connect different devices with different networks, supporting device-independent solutions. In principle, the exchange of one device will not change anything from the users' perspective. Systems are being developed in various countries on a national scope; in Germany, for instance, a partner network recently developed a technological standard called SerCho[9] – a software-based module toolbox to integrate devices into a manufacturer-independent network.

Obviously, the hardware device that connects all the other devices inside a building with the outside world (currently known as "the Router" and "the Internet") has the potential to fulfil this task as well. A leading networking hardware provider, Cisco recently released CloudConnect[10], a service that gives users "anytime, anywhere access to their home network" as a basis for further connected living scenarios.

There will be no universal, international standard for Smart Home solutions in the near future. Therefore, from a user perspective, the most important factor is device interoperability and usability. Large technology companies that offer a wide range of consumer devices for the digital lifestyle tend to create "closed" eco-systems wherein their devices interoperate very well while "foreign" devices are excluded. Such closed eco-systems of single suppliers in the Smart Home subsector will almost certainly become obsolete and replaced by open platforms for multiple devices, creating eco-systems to connect people, devices, their homes and cars in seamless, "ubiquitous" scenarios.

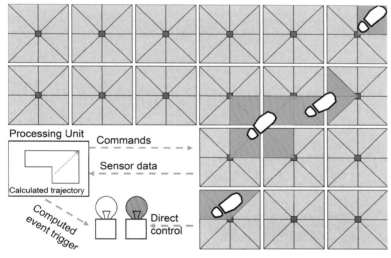

Fall detection: floor surfaces equipped with sensors and digital communication are able to help ensure the safety of elderly residents by registering and reporting falls.
SensFloor; Future-Shape GmbH

RESIDENTIAL APPLICATIONS

Residential buildings feature more and more information technology, making them complex "devices" with immense capabilities. According to Tom Rodden and Steve Benford,[11] "new challenges can be identified that will need to be addressed by those involved in designing them". In 2003, Rodden and Benford identified three different categories for appliances for ubiquitous domestic environments: Information Appliances, Interactive Household Objects and Augmented Furniture; a useful segmentation that seems still valid almost ten years later: "*Information Appliances* are stand-alone interactive devices that are self-contained with specific functionality[12].

Many of these have been realized in the home by layering interactive functions onto existing household appliances using standardized communication facilities. Examples of these include the Internet fridge[13] and handheld and mobile devices[14] supporting specific forms of interaction. *Interactive Household Objects* merge interactive capabilities with existing household objects to offer new forms of interaction. These often build upon the cultural values associated with existing artifacts. Examples of these include augmenting picture frames with new display and interaction facilities,[15] adding new communication capabilities to household notice boards[16] and augmenting cups.[17] *Augmented Furniture* adds interactive capabilities to the different furniture in the home. These include the DiamondTouch interactive table[18] and proposals to augment cupboards[19] and garden furniture.[20] These three different approaches vary in terms of the prominence of the digital technology and the ways in which the technology is made available to inhabitants. The technology is most intrusive in information appliances and then reduces in household objects and augmented furniture."[21]

Compared to devices and cars, domestic environments feature one major difference: they evolve over time according to user needs. Residential homes are open to continuous change. The ever-changing nature of buildings is the subject of the framework presented by Stewart Brand, which adds an interesting perspective to the design process. According to Brand, the core concept to understand how buildings change consists of six layers – the generic "six S's": Site, Structure, Skin, Services, Space Plan and Stuff.

Site, in this context, means the "geographical setting, location, and the legally defined lot, whose boundaries and context outlast generations of ephemeral buildings". Obviously the site is fixed and does not change easily. Structure refers to the "foundation and load-bearing elements which are perilous and expensive to change, so people don't. These 'are' the building. Structural life ranges from 30 to 300 years." Skin describes "the exterior surfaces" that "now change every 20 years or so, to keep up with fashion, technology, or for repair". Services are the "work-

ing guts of a building: communications wiring, electrical wiring, and plumbing", that resist replacement for 20 to 30 years as well. "Buildings are demolished early if their outdated systems are too embedded to be replaced easily." The Space Plan defines the "interior layout – where walls, ceilings, floors, and doors go. Turbulent spaces can change every 3 years or so; exceptionally quiet homes might wait 20 to 30 years". Finally, the Stuff changes continuously: "Chairs, desks, phones, pictures, kitchen appliances, lamps, hairbrushes; all the things that twitch around daily to monthly. Furniture is called 'mobilia' in Italian for good reason." According to Brand, "Site dominates Structure which dominates Skin, which dominates the Services, which dominate the Space Plan, which dominates the Stuff".[22]

Most of these six layers demand specialists like architects, civil engineers, service providers, designers, craftsmen or other experts to be built and maintained. Although information technology has developed much further since the early 1980s, Brand then already understood that the different levels are closely interwoven and that devices within the Stuff layer are closely tied to the underlying Space Plan layer. Unsurprisingly, interior design focuses on issues surrounding Space Plan and Stuff, leaving out the Service layer. Even more interestingly, the Service layer is the one to correspond to the notable changes by the emerging integration of information technology in terms of interoperability and connectedness.

To evolve compelling user experiences in ubiquitous domestic environments, the interior design needs to incorporate all three layers: Service, Space Plan and Stuff. The Service defines the core technological capabilities and acts as the foundation, whereas the Space Plan incorporates a flexible infrastructure for the Stuff to work properly, while allowing inhabitants to adapt in accordance to their individual needs.

PUBLIC AND COMMERCIAL ENVIRONMENTS

Unlike residential environments, public and commercial environments form a much broader field of applications, but the general considerations concerning the integration of information technology remain the same.

Within commercial spaces, especially corporate environments, retail spaces and industrial facilities can be distinguished. While corporate offices, training and manufacturing facilities, big retail facilities, shopping malls and department stores mainly demand large-scale standardised solutions for collaboration, marketing and communication, there is a high potential for individual innovative solutions in "spatial branding" – venues that make use of space as a medium to express the corporate brand. What is often developed for flagship stores, showrooms or single-brand stores most certainly can and will be applied to all kinds of corporate environments and therefore should be of high interest to "digital native" interior designers. These venues demand the brand values to be communicated in a holistic manner to raise the users' involvement. Here, innovative technology allows to stand out against the standard audio-visual media that people probably have seen before. This applies also to exhibition and event design for non-permanent spaces as well as institutional venues like museums.

Public environments share another distinct specificity: the user need for personalised services. This applies to healthcare environments (for example, hospitals, assisted living facilities and medical offices using electronic health records and telemedicine appliances) and also to hospitality and recreation facilities (hotels, resorts, cafés and bars, restaurants, health clubs and spas offering designated services, etc.). Even though they offer a different kind of service, this also applies to institutional venues like government offices, financial institutions, schools and universities, museums and congress venues.

The pitfall for seamless scenarios in public environments is that we do have multiple virtual identities that we share extensively, but we do not like to broadcast our real one, which means that interaction in public environments demands a standardised, safe and reliable authorisation method beyond what we call "Login" today.

Public venues and commercial spaces differ from residential buildings in a few simple yet challenging key issues:

1. Users have little or no control over the infrastructure. Those who set the requirements are not those who use the spaces, making it more difficult to define the actual needs and leading to more standardised solutions.

2. Privacy needs are different. Technology can be used in a personalised and an unpersonalised manner. In public spaces the relation of single-user scenarios versus multi-user scenarios is reversed compared to residential environments. This means that public spaces need further examination to cope with both private and public use scenarios, including issues of the integration of technology.

3. Instead of inhabitants, there are multiple user groups with multiple needs. Employees, customers, patients, visitors and foreigners have different user needs, hence the scenarios of use differ in terms of involvement, authorisation, service offers and information. Consider, for example, the user needs of medical staff, patients and visitors in a hospital in relation to a family in its home.

4. While the fields of application are identical, the focus differs according to the type of environment. The bigger the venues are, the higher is the need for building automation, energy saving, security and communication technology. By contrast, entertainment plays a subordinated role.

5. Last but not least, the interfaces are potentially more numerous than in residential buildings. Being the core topic for designers, interfaces can be both humans and technology here. In public and commercial environments, designers need to deal with more stakeholders and more technological interfaces in parallel.   →286

Interactive multitouch tables that can recognise multiple simultaneous users are gradually becoming more widespread as an information medium.
Old Fish Market Tourist Information, Ghent, Belgium; SAQ Architects

Fusion: furniture, walls, floor and multimedia fuse into a single modular landscape.
UIA Stylepark Lounge, Berlin, Germany; J. Mayer H. Architects

Stock exchange: shares are traded in realtime on the trading floor with the help of high-speed data feeds, while in the visitor areas, information is communicated digitally as part of the interior design.
German Stock Exchange, Frankfurt am Main, Germany; Atelier Brückner GmbH

Digital road surfaces of the future – sensors integrated into the roadway fuse sidewalk, traffic lanes and parking spaces and control self-steering vehicles.
Audi Urban Future Award, Berlin, Germany;
BIG – Bjarke Ingels Group, Kollision Aarhus,
Schmidhuber + Partner

The client's own digital imaging technology is integrated into a sculpture: light made into form transported by innumerable bundles of fibres that cross the room creating a new kind of screen of light and image.

Light Loom, Milan, Italy; Torafu Architects

SENSE AND SIMPLICITY

Now, what is the consequence and how to deal with it? In the past, the interior designer was in charge of the spatial quality by defining the space plan layout, surfaces, materials and furniture. Besides the atmospherical aspects, interior designers basically provided spaces and objects for technology to be integrated. Engineers, specialised planners and experts took care of the technical planning and installation. Device manufacturers came up with new intelligent hardware and media specialists provided their custom installations.

The design of domestic interiors is facing exactly the same challenge as automotive design, where 30 years ago engineers took care of the technical development and interior designers defined the car's inner "look and feel". Today, interdisciplinary teamwork and fundamental technological knowledge is needed. With the future scenario of ubiquitous environments as sketched above, a holistic user experience design process is called for to define the usability of interfaces and add sense and simplicity to the "connected" scenarios.

Interior designers need to gather the competences of, or join forces with, an adjacent design discipline that arose in parallel with the emerging information technology – interaction design. Profound technological knowledge, methodical interaction design competence and usability expertise are needed, along with interface competence. Fortunately interior design education has identified this need already.

In the words of Tom Rodden and Steve Benford: "We need to build our future ubiquitous environments in a manner that is sensitive to these forces and place our activities within this changing context. If we fail to do so then we may be constructing the 21st century equivalents of the 'homes of the future' that dominated the world trade shows of the 1950s."[23]

Light Loom, model.
Torafu Architects.

1 http://en.wikipedia.org/wiki/ Information_society, accessed on 6.02.12.

2 Weiser, Mark, "Ubiquitous computing #1", available at http:// www.ubiq.com/hypertext/weiser/ UbiHome.html.

3 Weiser, Mark, "The Computer for the 21st Century", *Scientific American* (1988), p. 265.

4 Krippendorff, Klaus, "On the Essential Contexts of Artifacts", *Design Issues* 5,2 (1989), pp. 9-39.

5 http://www.home-tech-design. com/press%20Networked%20 Home%20Audio%20Market%20 to%20Hit.pdf.

6 http://www.home-tech-design. com/press%20Networked%20 Home%20Audio%20Market%20 to%20Hit.pdf.

7 http://sap.sys-con.com/ node/938689.

8 http://www.cmtresearch.com/ details/report-94.htm.

9 http://www.connected-living. org/ziele/sercho_technologie/.

10 http://home.cisco.com/en-us/ cloud.

11 Rodden, Tom and Benford, Steve, "The evolution of buildings and implications for the design of ubiquitous domestic environ- ments", in *Proceedings of the CHI'03 conference on human factors in com- puting systems, CHI letter*, vol. 5, no. 1 (2003).

12 Norman, Donald, *The Invisible Computer* (Cambridge, MA: MIT Press, 1998).

13 Electrolux Inc., Electrolux screen Fridge, available at http:// group.electrolux.com/en/topic/ screen-fridge.

14 McClard, Anne and, Somers, Patricia, "Unleashed: Web tablet integration into the home", in *Pro- ceedings of CHI 2000* (New York: ACM Press, 2000), pp. 1-8.

15 Mynatt, Elizabeth D., Essa, Irfan, Rogers, Wendy, "Increas- ing the opportunities for aging in place", in *Proceedings on the ACM conference on Universal Usability 2000* (New York: ACM Press, 2000), pp. 65- 71.

16 Hindus, Debby, Mainwaring, Scott, Leduc, Nicole, Hagström, Anna Elizabeth, Bayley, Oliver, "Casablanca: Designing Social Communication Devices for the Home", in *Proceedings of CHI '01* (New York: ACM Press, 2001), pp. 325-332.

17 Gellersen, Hans-W., Beigl, Michael, Krull, Holger, "The Medi- aCup: Awareness Technology Embedded in an Everyday Object", in *Proceedings of International Sym- posium on Handheld and Ubiquitous Computing (HUC99), LNCS 1707* (Berlin: Springer-Verlag, 1999).

18 Dietz, Paul and Leigh, Darren, "DiamondTouch: a Multi-User Touch Technology", in *Proceedings ACM UIST 2001* (New York: ACM Press, 2001), pp. 209-216.

19 Cooltown, http://cooltown. hp.com/cooltownhome/.

20 Gaver, Bill and Martin, Heather, "Alternatives", in *Proceedings of the CHI 2000* (New York: ACM Press, 2000), pp. 209-216.

21 Rodden and Benford, op. cit.

22 Brand, Stewart, *How Buildings Learn* (New York: Viking Press, 1994).

23 Rodden and Benford, op. cit.

TECHNICAL SYSTEMS

JOHANNES STUMPF

Always listen to the B-side: a wall of air-conditioning units.
Singapore

Rooms can be thought of as being analogous to the body of a living being. Their surfaces are what we see and experience physically, but without the underlying systems – the bones, tendons, nerves and senses – the surfaces are just an empty shell.

The technical and constructional systems therefore give life to the rooms and make it possible to experience them as a whole. When the visual impression of the design of a space harmonises with the underlying systems, the whole can amount to more than the sum of its parts.

The role of an architect or interior designer in the form-finding process and technical realisation includes incorporating contributions from specialist planners and engineers into the overall design concept. To achieve this, a designer needs to understand their requirements and how they affect and relate to the interior design. The following text provides a general overview of the key aspects.

Technical systems are usually independently functioning sets of components that need to be incorporated into the overall concept. In most cases, the specialist engineers brought in to develop these systems only consider the aspects for which they are directly responsible. Architects or interior designers can only expect specialists to consider wider concerns if they are sensitive to the particular requirements of the different specialists in the context as a whole and can communicate the project aims adequately from the outset.

The fundamental purpose of all technical systems and building services is to transport energy or information to where they are needed. A few basic principles of physics apply in more or less the same form for all technical systems:

– The transport of heat in a solid, liquid or gaseous medium
– The transfer of electrical and electromagnetic energy
– The controlled transport of solid, liquid or gaseous substances to and from their point of use

HEAT

The degree to which a material is able to absorb and conduct heat energy depends on two material-related properties:

– The specific heat capacity of a material, which describes how much energy a material can absorb
– The specific conductivity of a material

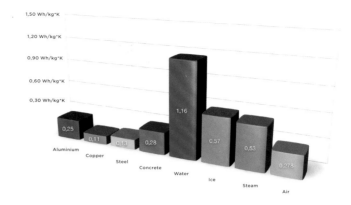

Of all the materials shown, water has the greatest capacity to store heat.
Specific heat capacity of selected materials

All technical facilities for transporting heat energy have to address three fundamental aspects:
– The energy needs to be created at a point in the system
– The energy needs to be distributed (via a medium)
– The energy needs to be given off in a controlled way

The oldest source of heat used by mankind is an open fire. Today, the vast majority of technical heating systems still employ combustion to convert an energy source into heat. However, in response to the depletion of fossil fuels and global warming caused by greenhouse gases, other forms of energy conversion are becoming increasingly relevant.

Heat can be obtained in a variety of ways:
– Combustion processes (for example by burning oil, wood, gas or coal)
– Solar energy (thermal solar energy systems, passive heat gain)
– Energy conversion, for example using heat exchangers
– Energy conversion from electricity
– Direct or indirect use of geothermal energy
– Utilisation of process heat given off from technical installations, agricultural processes, etc.

Heating (and cooling) is usually conveyed to where it is needed using water or air as a carrier medium. The advantage of water-based heating systems is the higher specific heat capacity of water compared with that of air. Energy can be transported using water-based systems much more efficiently and with less effort than using air.

ELECTRICITY AND SIGNALS

The term electricity covers a variety of physical phenomena and is hard to define categorically. However, the ways in which these phenomena operate follow a few basic principles.

All matter consists at a subatomic scale of smaller particles that together make up atoms. These particles attract or repel each other. The force (or charge) of these processes of attraction or repulsion is the basis for all electricity. In principle, an electrical signal results when subatomic elements (protons, electrons) start moving or are set in motion by others.

The flow of these subatomic elements resembles that of the flow of water, and the terms used to describe and measure this flow are derived from this:
- The "voltage" (measured in volts) describes the electrical pressure on a conductor, analogous to the pressure of water in a pipe
- The term "resistance" (measured in ohms) describes the extent of the forces that resist the flow of electricity
- The term "current" describes how many particles are actually flowing

These three terms – voltage, resistance and current – are proportional to one another: if the value of one of these changes in a given situation, the values of the others change accordingly.[1]

Electricity makes it possible to transfer energy quickly over long distances, and this energy can in turn be converted into kinetic energy and/or heat. All energy production and conversion processes using electrical energy involve a degree of energy loss, which in some cases can be quite considerable. As a rule of thumb, around a third of the primary energy used to originally produce electrical energy actually arrives at the end consumer.

WATER, GASES, AIR

The distribution or circulation of liquid and gaseous materials through pipelines follows more or less the same principles. To determine the dimensions of the distribution network, a few key parameters apply: the velocity of the material transport, the quantity of material to be transported to the part of the network where it is required and the pressure necessary to overcome resistances in the pipework or ductwork. The resistance of distribution systems is a factor of the material parameters of the surfaces of the pipework and of the material to be transported (e.g. surface roughness, material density) as well as the geometry of the system. Bends and changes in the cross section of piping cause a drop in pressure, which needs to be overcome for the material to be successfully transported to its destination. As a consequence, simple systems are generally more energy-efficient than complex structures. When dimensioning such systems, an engineer will determine the different pressures within the network and then choose the cross section and elements of the ductwork in order to determine the energy required to transport the medium. Typically, the pressure required for the distribution system is provided by an external energy source such as a pump or fan.

HEATING SYSTEMS

Heating systems are differentiated according to how their heat is:
- produced or converted
- distributed
- emitted

HEAT PRODUCTION

Most heat production systems employ combustion processes (wood, gas, oil) in which the energy of the combustion process is transferred via a heat transfer device (boiler, etc.) to a carrier medium (water or air). The better the design of this heat exchange process, the better the proportion of energy input to usable energy output (efficiency). The efficiency is heavily dependent on the quantity of energy to be transferred and drops significantly with higher-temperature heat transfer processes. Heat production systems that operate at low temperatures are therefore much more efficient, and in turn more compact and easier to integrate into a design. As a consequence, the less energy a building needs (i.e. well insulated), the more efficient and compact the heating system will be.

As the use of renewable energy sources becomes more important, other means of heat production are becoming increasingly relevant:

- Solar energy can be used to heat buildings directly (solar collectors, solar gain through windows, thermal retention elements in facades)
- Heat pumps can make use of solar energy stored in the ground, the air or watercourses
- Combined heat and power systems make use of excess heat generated by other processes
- Electricity from renewable sources (for example water or wind energy) can be used for heating

The efficiency of heating systems can be significantly improved, especially for systems with low heat demand, through the use of advanced thermal storage technology. The thermal energy store functions as a link between the different energy production systems and can, for example, make it possible to use solar energy from collectors in conjunction with oil, gas or solid-fuel fired boilers. In such systems, solar energy is used to preheat the heating water, reducing the energy required from combustion processes to raise the temperature of the heating water to the supply water temperature.

Thermal energy stores do, however, take up a lot of space and must be placed where there is sufficient load-bearing capacity for their considerable weight.

HEAT DISTRIBUTION

The type of distribution system depends on the heat transfer medium transporting the energy. Due to its high specific heat capacity, water is a good heat transfer medium and can also be transported through pipework with relatively small cross sections. Heat transfer using air requires much more space but is a feasible alternative where buildings already have cavities suitable for transporting air. The primary advantages of air heating systems are their quick reaction to a demand for heat (due to the low thermal inertia of air) and the lack of a requirement for radiators in rooms. In Europe, air heating systems are comparatively rare, but in America, they are a standard form of domestic heating.

Heat distribution networks are typically organised in tree structures. Groups of rooms that lie above one another can be linked together with vertical supply lines. In each group of rooms, the distribution network then runs horizontally between the individual heat emitters (radiators). Where possible, horizontal distribution systems should feed the radiators from the bottom so that it is possible to use the radiators to bleed air out of the heating system. When routing the heating pipes, the engineer needs to consider the release of air trapped in the system. The laws of physics dictate the positioning of air relief valves, and it can transpire that inspection openings are needed in walls or ceilings at positions that are less than ideal for the design concept. The simpler the horizontal circulation, with as few crossing points as possible, the less it is likely to impact on the interior design concept.

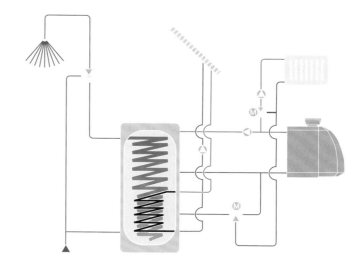

Heating system consisting of a solar plant, conventional boiler, storage system and circuits for heating and hot water provision.
A system for coupling energy produced from different sources

Storage heaters with two heating coils for use with different heat sources.
External view and schematic isometric view of the interior

HEAT EMISSION

How heat is ultimately transferred to the room depends on a large number of factors and system-dependent decisions. For the interior design of spaces, the heat emitter is the part of the system with the greatest impact on the interior. Which system is adopted, however, is subject to particular technical conditions.

Heat is transferred from an emitter to a room or space by two main physical principles:
- Convection: the heating of air as it passes over the emitter
- Radiation: the (infrared) radiation of warmth from the emitter

The proportion of heat transferred by radiation or convection depends on the material of the heat emitter, its form and the parameters of the underlying heat distribution system.[2]

Infrared radiation permeates what it falls on and warms, as it were, "from within". Most people find this a pleasant physiological sensation similar to that of an open fire. Radiative heat sources generally do not require such high temperatures to create the same sense of comfort. They also have a series of biological advantages as they reduce, for example, the incidence of mould formation because the walls, floors and ceilings are also warmed from within.

Convection by contrast has the advantage of being quicker to respond. The desired indoor temperature is generally reached more quickly using convection-based heating systems.

Most heat sources, including so-called "radiators", utilise predominantly the convection principle. The higher the operating temperature[3] of a radiator, the higher the proportion of radiated energy but also the lower the efficiency of the entire system.

The air outlets of air heating systems are a special case among convection-based systems. Their primary advantage is the speed with which they can provide warmth, but their disadvantage is the draughts that the system causes by circulating air at high speed. To heat rooms rationally using air heating systems, the arrangement of air diffusers is especially important, and these can have a number of implications for the design of the room.

Typical sources of heat radiation are underfloor heating and wall heating. A key advantage of these systems is that they are practically invisible. Their disadvantage is their comparatively slow speed of response: it can take a relatively long time to bring an unheated room up to a comfortable temperature level using only floor or wall heating. A further disadvantage is their higher general cost and the relatively large surfaces they require to be effective.

But once a sufficient temperature level has been reached, they do provide a good degree of thermal comfort.

The lower the feed and return temperatures are, the larger the surface required for the heating element, but at the same time the better the efficiency of the system. Heating entire elements in buildings can make sense when sufficiently large expanses of unobstructed wall, ceiling or floor are available and the building is well insulated. Radiation-based systems are generally more expensive than convection-based systems.

COOLING

In terms of energy and technical implementation, heating and cooling systems have much in common. There are even a number of examples in which the distribution network is used for heating in winter and cooling in summer. These include approaches in which the surfaces of building elements are heated or cooled, for example using pipework embedded in the construction of the ceiling. Such systems will become increasingly important for the sustainable operation of buildings in future. At present, however, cooling systems are still predominantly planned as part of the ventilation system or as freestanding cooling appliances.

COOLING SYSTEMS

All systems that provide space cooling also produce exhaust heat. In addition to the actual cooling unit, cooling systems therefore require additional recoolers to take the heat extracted from the interior spaces and ensure it is released into the atmosphere. These exhaust cooling units are often the largest part of the cooling equipment, and are usually positioned externally due to their large size, noise (fans) and dirt. The actual room cooling process on the other hand takes place in relatively compact installation units. These too are also noisy due to the pumps they contain, and produce condensation water that needs to be discharged. For this reason cooling systems should usually be placed away from areas with important functional requirements.

The primary energy source used for cooling is typically gas or electricity. Systems that make direct use of renewable energy sources are already available on the market but are currently not economical.

KOMPRESSIONSKÄLTEMASCHINE

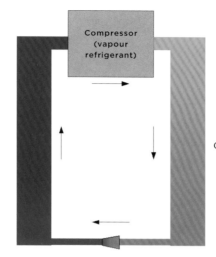

Schematic diagram of a refrigeration system.
Compression refrigeration system

A compressor used as a cooling unit. Large-scale installation.
Large-scale installation

Air-conditioning unit in room interior and heat exchanger on the outside of a building.
Conventional split system cooling unit

DISTRIBUTION AND PROVISION OF COOL AIR

The systems for the absorption and removal of extracted heat energy correspond in principle to those of heating systems. Due to the low temperature differential between the feed and return and the low temperatures in general (approx. 20–25°C), water-based room cooling systems require large surfaces to be effective, such as the undersides of ceilings and large homogeneous wall surfaces.

Systems that are retrofitted, such as split system appliances, generally use air as the carrier and transfer medium by setting the room air in circulation and pumping in cool air using integral fans. These systems are not very sustainable in terms of their energy use and are hard to incorporate unobtrusively into the interior design. Given the relatively low levels of cooling these systems provide, it can be more economical – and less visually intrusive – to install well-planned solar protection devices to reduce heat gain in the first place.

VENTILATION SYSTEMS

In addition to the temperature control of spaces through heating and cooling, ventilation systems can be employed to provide rooms with fresh air and to maintain defined levels of humidity. These systems also make it possible to fulfil a series of technical and hygienic requirements for the built environment.

The physical processes involved in ventilation systems are particularly complex and often entail extensive technical installations and energy input. The design of such systems is usually dependent on a large number of parameters and is generally less flexible. As such, it is advisable to consider the ventilation and air-conditioning systems as early as possible in the design process to minimise the need for costly revisions at a later stage.

The primary determining parameters for the design of a ventilation system are:
– The necessary air change rate
– The minimum and maximum room temperatures
– The maximum upper and lower limits for air humidity

In special cases, further parameters such as the need for particle-free environments or maximum levels of contaminants may apply.

HUMIDITY AND TEMPERATURE

Temperature and humidity are directly related to one another. A change in one parameter has a direct effect on the other. Depending on the temperature, air can only hold a certain quantity of moisture: the colder the air the lower the absolute quantity of moisture it can hold.[4] When liquids evaporate or when moisture condenses, energy (heat) is absorbed from or given off to the surroundings (the same principle as a refrigerator or a heat pump).

The complex relationship between temperature, moisture and energy is described by the Mollier H-S chart, which clearly illustrates the dynamic character of their interdependencies.

For some special types of buildings, such as museums, laboratories and treatment rooms in health care facilities, the upper and lower temperatures and humidity levels may only vary within tightly defined boundaries. Here, the design and technical planning requirements are correspondingly complex, as this has implications for the size and arrangements of windows, the space required for ductwork and installations, the placement and design of air supply diffusers as well as the design of the lighting concept as lighting can represent a heat load.

In many other cases, however, complex air handling requirements may not be necessary if requirements are discussed in advance with the client. The tighter the spread between the minimum and maximum permissible temperature and the minimum and maximum permissible relative humidity, the more elaborate the technical means required to achieve this.

AIR CHANGE RATE

Alongside temperature and humidity, a further parameter that determines the design of ventilation systems, and in turn affects the interior design concept, is the air change rate. The greater the volume of air in a space that needs to be ventilated, the greater the necessary cross section of ductwork will be. The required cross section is also influenced by the hygienic requirements and the number of people frequenting a space.

By way of example, here are some typical air change rates:

ROOM / FUNCTION	AIR CHANGES / H
Bathroom	4-6
Office	3-6
Canteen	6-8
Shopping store	4-6
Cinema	4-6
Kitchen	20
Operating room	15-20
Swimming pool	3-4
Conference room	6-8
Meeting areas	5-10
Workshops	3-6

HEALTH AND COMFORT LEVELS

Ventilation systems are repeatedly thought to be the cause of sick building syndrome, which describes the increased incidence of symptoms such as red eyes, irritation of mucous membranes and skin and other typical symptoms of a cold among the users of air-conditioned buildings. It would, however, be wrong to conclude that air-conditioning systems are fundamentally unhealthy. There are many factors that contribute to sick building syndrome and only some of these can be attributed to technical installations. Some possible causes for the development of such problems include:

- Insufficient maintenance of filters and plant equipment
- Outgassing of textiles, paints and furniture as well as volatile organic compounds (VOCs) in the air
- Poor hygiene
- Insufficient air change rates

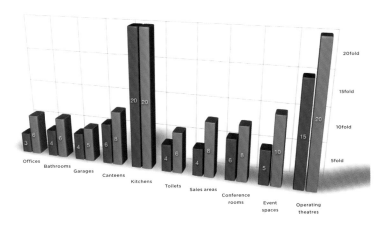

Hourly air exchange rates for selected room functions.

From minimum (blue) to maximum (green)

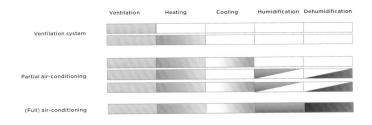

BASIC TYPES OF VENTILATION AND AIR-CONDITIONING SYSTEMS

Ventilation and air-conditioning systems are differentiated according to the thermodynamic functions provided by the system.

Simple mechanical systems ensure that the indoor air within a given area is changed at the required rate and only need fans to ensure sufficient throughput of air. These are termed mechanical ventilation systems. Systems that additionally heat the air are also termed ventilation systems. When, in addition to heating and ventilation, a system provides further functions such as cooling, humidification or dehumidification, these are then termed air-conditioning systems. Partial air-conditioning systems are installations that condition either only the temperature or the humidity of the air.

Air-conditioning systems contain a series of further components in addition to ventilation fans, including heating coils, cooling coils, humidifiers, dehumidifiers, heat exchangers and filters. To heat or cool the air, air heaters or coolers are used in which the air stream passes over heating or cooling elements in the form of plates or tubes. Because the relative humidity of a cold air stream falls as it is heated, it may be necessary to add moisture to the warmed air. This happens in a humidification chamber in which steam or a fine water spray is injected into the air stream. Conversely, cooling an air stream produces condensation water, which then has to be discharged. For situations with special indoor climate requirements, such as museums, it may be necessary to cool a warm air stream to dehumidify it, before reheating it again.

Unnecessary energy loss is reduced in simple systems using a cross-flow heat exchanger (recuperator) between the outdoor air and exit air. Rotary heat exchangers are employed in complex systems in which the humidity of the air also needs to be maintained.

Filters and filter sections remove contaminants and airborne particles from the air within the system. At which point filters should be used depends on the specific use requirements. The greater the degree of air purity required, the denser the filter has to be in order to remove even the very smallest particle of foreign matter from the air. The filter density also determines the degree of pressure loss (resistance) caused by the filters. Dense sets of filters will therefore increase the energy demand. A recurring problem is the premature wearing out of filters caused by dust left over from construction when the system is first put into use.

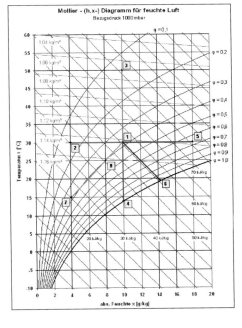

The three dimensions of air and their dependencies: temperature, humidity and energy.

H-S chart

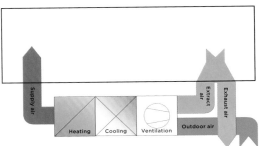

The four kinds of air.

DECENTRALISED VERSUS CENTRALISED AIR-CONDITIONING SYSTEMS

Traditional central air-conditioning systems require more space for their installations and equipment but are generally more economical to run and less complex to maintain. The higher the indoor air quality requirements, the more sense it makes to choose a centralised system.

An alternative approach, which has become increasingly widespread in recent years in office and administration buildings, is to distribute the task of air-conditioning among many individual decentralised systems. This is more flexible for the individual users and also helps avoid many potential causes of sick building syndrome. If well integrated into the concept for the facade, this approach can have a beneficial effect for the long-term sustainability of the building as a whole.

DUCT NETWORK

The duct network of a ventilation system follows a tree-like pattern. The closer the ductwork to the supply system, the more air it has to convey and the more space it takes up. Depending on the type of system, there can be duct networks for supplying air as well as for removing extracted air.

Ducts with large cross sections are obviously more difficult to incorporate into a design than smaller ones. The areas where ducts cross or meet are particularly sensitive zones, which impact on other trades and technical installations and on the interior design. Once the necessary air change rate and the volume of the space are known, it is possible to calculate approximate cross sections of the ducts that need to be incorporated in shafts or ceiling spaces. For example:

APPROXIMATE DIMENSIONING OF DUCT CROSS SECTIONS

- Determine room volume and air change rate
- Determine room volume and air change rate
- Define airflow velocity (3-5 m/s, higher rates are noisier)
- Calculate approximate duct cross section:
((Room volume * Air change rate) / 3600) / Airflow velocity

Example:
A canteen kitchen with a volume of 1500 m², an air change rate of 20 and airflow velocity of 3 m/s

((1500 * 20) / 3600) / 3 = 2.78 m²

The space required for a supply air or extract air duct is therefore approx. 3 m² if it is to be inaudible!

The duct network is divided into sections that distribute air to the rooms and sections that are specific to the plant equipment.

An important aspect to consider in the dimensioning of ventilation systems and the power of the fans required to propel the air stream through the system is the pressure loss in the system. Every junction, every additional component, every outlet and every bend in the ductwork causes a drop in the pressure of the system, which has to be overcome through the use of more powerful fans. As a consequence, a simple duct network with few bends is much more economical in terms of energy use than a complex network with many bends.

In areas where space is limited, the building services engineer can reduce the cross section of the ducts if the velocity of the airflow is increased, which however increases the noise level of the system. This can make the use of duct silencers necessary, but these also impact on the efficiency of the system, in turn requiring more power from the fans.

When evaluating the duct network, architects are advised to verify the vertical position of technical installations and their junctions in cross section and to ensure that there is sufficient leeway, especially where they meet central service ducts. This can help to identify critical areas for the interior design early on in the design process.

Typical sources of conflicts in the design include:
- Failure to take into account the necessary slope of ducts
- Failure to consider all relevant technical services in the estimation of cross sections
- Failure to consider changes in the use of spaces in the planning of technical services (for example, different air change rates required for new room uses)
- The location of necessary inspection hatches is not aligned with the demands of other trades, or access to them is blocked by interior fittings

The design of the duct network has a major impact on the design of other technical installations and building services as well as the interior fittings and should therefore be carefully considered as early as possible in the design process. Changes to the ventilation and air-conditioning duct network during the construction phase should be avoided as it can cause significant delays in the construction schedule.

ROOM VENTILATION FLOW SYSTEMS

Room ventilation systems typically follow one of the following principles:

- **Mixing ventilation** creates a circulatory flow of air through the whole of the area to be ventilated. The velocity of the supply air exiting the diffusers as well as the direction of the supply air diffusers determines the desired circulation pattern. In such systems, the designer has little influence over the location of the supply air vents but the positioning of the exhaust air inlets is more flexible. The diffusers are often located on the ceiling ("vertical discharge"), with some restrictions where rooms are more than 4 m high. It is also possible to locate diffusers in the wall ("tangential discharge"). Because the air velocity can sometimes be appreciable, diffusers should be located at least 2.50 – 3.00 m above finished floor level to avoid unpleasant air turbulence at head level.

- **Layered ventilation** arises when air is supplied to the ventilated area at slow speed, usually from below through vents with large cross sections to allow the slow passage of air with as little turbulence as possible. Layered ventilation systems are especially sensible in conjunction with heated room surfaces (underfloor or wall heating). The supply air vents are comparatively straightforward to integrate in the design concept as they are usually visually unobtrusive.

- **Displacement ventilation** involves the supply of a strong flow of air from below and is commonly used to effectively remove heat from areas subject to high heat levels.

AIR DIFFUSERS

Conditioned air is injected into a space through diffusers of different types, which depend largely on their purpose as well as a number of other preconditions. The building services engineer must first ensure that a jet of the required volume of air can reach the desired location without causing undesirable turbulence and high air speeds in the room. Different approaches are taken for systems that essentially provide cooling and those that provide air heating.

Building services engineers can employ the following basic types of diffusers:

- Simple rectangular wall or ceiling-mounted vents with blades to direct the air stream
- Round or square ceiling diffusers
- Linear slot diffusers
- Special forms, including supply air diffusers for especially slow air velocities (for use in museums, theatre foyers, trade fair halls as well as industrial workplaces) and filter diffusers for clean rooms

The choice of diffuser depends on the ventilation concept. The greater the volume of air flowing through a given cross section, the more limited the possibilities of controlling the airflow without changing its aerodynamic characteristics. Because air diffusers are generally visually prominent, the interior designer should discuss the possible implications of the ventilation concept with the building services engineer as soon as possible in the design process.

SOLAR PROTECTION

Solar protection systems are not normally regarded as being part of the building services. They can, however, fulfil a number of functions relevant to the building's operation. For sustainable approaches to facility management, this is especially relevant as an integral part of operating and control concepts because solar protection systems have the capacity to:
- Optimise the use of natural illumination
- Reduce the energy required for artificial illumination
- Reduce the energy required for cooling
- Provide additional energy for heating in winter

The integration of solar protection systems in building services concepts requires extensive consultation with the building services engineer. In many cases intelligent architectural solutions – judicious arrangement of windows, the use of shading devices, etc. – can considerably reduce the energy demand of an interior without the need to install extensive, maintenance-intensive mechanical systems.

A basic principle for planning solar protection systems is to locate them outside the thermal envelope of the building so that no undesirable heat radiation enters the building. Indoor solar protection devices are at best half as effective as external systems.

ACTIVE VERSUS PASSIVE SOLAR PROTECTION

For the sustainable operation of buildings, designers can choose between highly controllable technical systems on the one hand and traditional, non-mechanised systems on the other. Which of these options is more suitable is ultimately a question of the design approach and the particularities of the project in question. More mechanised systems are generally more prone to malfunctions and are more costly to repair and operate.

In any case, an intelligent solar protection concept can contribute significantly to improving the overall energy efficiency and sustainability of a building, and not just in warm climates. Because solar protection measures do not clearly fall within the remit of the building services engineer, architect or interior designer, it is especially important to carefully agree the aims, methods and effects of planning decisions in this regard.

WASTEWATER SYSTEMS

Of all the sanitary installations, wastewater facilities have the greatest impact on the design and construction of interiors. Wastewater installations require defined minimum gradients and large pipe cross sections, and junctions in sanitary pipework take up considerable space in walls and ceilings. For this reason the vertical location and horizontal routing of wastewater installations should be determined early in the design process. Because horizontal pipework always has to have a gradient, it is important to ensure that there is sufficient space in ceiling cavities to accommodate the pipework along with the necessary gradient in the flow direction of the wastewater. A minimum gradient of 1 % should be observed in all but the most exceptional circumstances. The building services engineer should rule out collisions with other building services such as ventilation ducts and electrical conduits by drawing sections through the system as early as possible.

Installations in wall cavities should be planned with sufficient margins for leeway, taking into account the space requirements for fixing elements such as pipe clamps and vibration dampers. Likewise sufficient space must be planned for where pipework crosses. The following minimum wall thicknesses should be observed for typical drywall systems where pipework does not cross:

INSTALLATION	CLADDING	INSTALLATION STUDWORK SUB-STRUCTURE	TOTAL
Drywall partition with washbasin	2 x 1.25cm x 2 = 5cm	15cm	20cm
Drywall partition with WC	2 x 1.25cm x 2 = 5cm	2x 5cm + 15cm Zwischenraum = 25cm	30cm
Drywall partition with washbasins on both sides	2 x 1.25cm x 2 = 5cm	2x 5cm + 20cm Zwischenraum = 30cm	35cm
Drywall wall lining with washbasin	2 x 1.25cm = 2.5cm	15cm	17,5cm
Drywall wall lining with WC	2 x 1.25cm = 2.5cm	5cm + 15cm = 20cm	22,5cm

As a rule: walls with wastewater installations should be made as thick as reasonably possible and never less than 20 cm overall.

Bends and curves in wastewater installations can also give rise to conflicts with other systems and the room design. 90° bends are not suitable for the free flow of wastewater and bends therefore usually have an angle of between 45° and 75°. An area where problems commonly arise is the junction between the wall and ceiling or the wall and floor. These cannot always be detected in the plans provided by the building services engineer, and it is advisable to draw or sketch a detailed section through the junction during the design stage to avoid problems arising during construction.

Mounting and utility connections for a washbasin in a plasterboard wall duct.
Waste water treatment

GAS INSTALLATIONS

Gas installations are usually found in buildings with special uses (laboratories, hospitals, etc.), catering establishments or for the gas supply for heating systems. Their basic structure is very similar to that of water supply installations. For the interior design concept, there are only a few particular aspects of such installations that need to be taken into consideration.

WATER PURIFICATION

A special form of water installation is the provision of demineralised water. Depending on the intended use, there are different degrees of technical water purification. For ventilation systems the use of demineralised water is advisable to minimise fouling in the ventilation systems. As demineralised water is chemically aggressive, non-ferrous metals or plastics are typically used for the pipework, but these can have fire safety implications, which in turn can require more space for the fire protection of technical installations.

HOT WATER AND DRINKING WATER INSTALLATIONS

Hygiene plays a central role in drinking water and hot water installations. For installations used irregularly by many different people, it is important to prevent the occurrence of legionnaires' disease. As the causative micro-organisms thrive in temperatures between 25–50°C, temperatures must be maintained above at least 60°C within the water pipes. With centralised hot water installations, this can result in significant temperature and energy losses and it can instead make more sense to install decentralised water heaters.

Pipework for drinking and hot water is much more flexible and easier to incorporate into an interior design than other technical installations.

For centralised systems, domestic water heating is usually provided by the central heating system. More modern storage heaters make it possible to simultaneously utilise heat provided by different primary energy sources, for example from a heating system in conjunction with thermal solar collectors or a geothermal heat pump. Renewable energy sources can quite easily cover 70 % or more of hot water provision.

ELECTRICAL INSTALLATIONS

In recent decades, the electricity market has shifted towards a handful of large multinational energy providers, both in regional and supra-regional distribution networks, as well as in the generation of electricity. The sustainability debate has, however, called these structures into question. As such, there is now increased interest in decentralised energy production systems located near to the consumers, and in the medium term it is foreseeable that these could acquire an appreciable share of the market. This will have an impact on the design of the built environment as buildings will no longer solely consume energy but also generate energy.

CENTRALISED ENERGY PRODUCTION AND DISTRIBUTION

As the distance between the electricity consumer and the electricity producer increases, the resistance of the network lines also increases, and with it the necessary cable cross section in proportion to the voltage of the transmission path. In Europe an interconnected grid of high-voltage electricity lines (220–380 kV, outside Europe as much as 750 kV) between large-scale power plants ensures that we have sufficient electrical energy regardless of variations in demand during the day. Electricity from other energy sources (e.g. wind and solar power stations, city power stations, industrial facilities with combined heat and power systems, etc.) is fed into the grid at electricity substations. The next lower level is the medium-voltage network (1–30 kV, in cities usually 10–15 kV), which distributes energy to local transformers. Local energy producers typically feed their energy into this network. The conversion of this electricity to 380 V / 220 V for end use takes place in transformer stations in the vicinity of the consumers. This is also where local energy production fed back into the system is offset against energy consumption.

DECENTRALISED ENERGY PRODUCTION

Consumers with consistently high levels of energy demand may often have their own energy production systems. These can range from emergency power generators to combined heat and power systems (CHP), for example for buildings that need to provide constant heating, such as hospitals. As energy prices increase, decentralised systems are becoming increasingly interesting for housing estates, single family houses and other small-scale consumers. In addition to using photovoltaic systems to generate electricity, micro-CHP systems, for example using gas-powered Stirling engines, now represent a viable alternative.

TRANSFER POINTS IN BUILDINGS

For large-scale consumers, the energy transfer point is usually located within the premises of the consumer. Energy from the medium-voltage grid located on the local road network or elsewhere nearby is passed via a switching station to a substation belonging to the consumer. Because these are high-voltage facilities, these must have restricted access and be adequately protected against the risk of explosion. Depending on the type of transformer, further regulations can apply: for example, oil-cooled transformers must be placed within chemical and oil-resistant basins to prevent contamination of the ground water.

These transformers then feed the consumer's low-voltage network. Usually this takes place in a low-voltage main distribution system within the consumer's own premises and ideally located not far from the medium-voltage substation. For systems with emergency power generators, a separate emergency power supply network exists alongside the general power supply network. Because it can take several seconds for an emergency power system to take over in the event of a power outage, critical systems need to be able to continue on battery or flywheel backup power. For this a battery or flywheel room must be provided, which is ideally located near to the low-voltage main distribution system and its size will depend on the necessary power output capacity of the battery/flywheel system.

The low-voltage system within the building usually has a tree-like structure. From the main distribution system, the system branches into subsystems for each storey and/or wing of the building. To minimise the voltage drop, thick cables are used for these connecting lines, which require special mountings and a firm supporting substrate to sustain the weight and stress of the relatively large bending radii of the cables. The routing of the necessary vertical and horizontal cableways should therefore be coordinated with the routing of other technical services and the interior design plans at an early stage.

The distribution of electricity to the final electrical circuits (lighting, power points, special appliances) is usually provided by floor- or ceiling-mounted cableways. The routing of such cables should avoid passing over door openings to avoid possible conflicts with the components of door fittings.

PUTTING IT ALL TOGETHER: MEASURING, CONTROL AND REGULATION SYSTEMS

The notion of the "intelligent building" dates back to the age of modernism, but today we are closer than ever before to turning this vision into reality.

Light fittings that order a new bulb when the bulb blows, or signal in advance that it will soon fail, and houses that turn on the heating when someone enters the room are just two examples of a series of new possibilities for the field of interior design. If the designed surface of the house is thought of as the user interface of a "machine house" that can communicate with its users, there is vast potential for new ideas and future concepts. Compared with the development of human-computer interfaces, the current state of the art of human-building interfaces is still very rudimentary: at present we are still in a time long before the invention of the mouse, in the dark ages of text terminals and punched tape.

Nevertheless, modern data technologies have played a role in building services for some time, most notably in the area of building automation. Here a so-called "level model" is used in which the individual components of a building automation system are categorised in functional areas of differing degrees of abstraction.

THE FIELD LEVEL

The field level concerns the sensors and actuators attached directly to the equipment to be monitored and controlled, as well as the signals they communicate. A variety of digital or analogue components are used, depending on the application area in questions and the product philosophy of the manufacturer. The degree of "intelligence" of these components can vary considerably. In addition to basic units that simply signal a physical event in the form of an electric resistance or an electric current, there are also more sophisticated "mini bus systems" that communicate with one another on the field level.

Using modern sensor technology, almost every physical condition of a technical installation can be measured. There are sensors for measuring the temperature, humidity, air pressure, pressure in fluids and solids, wind speed and direction, light intensity, gas concentration, electromagnetic and radioactive radiation, voltage, resistance and current. To control them, a series of motors, motor-driven valves, flaps and pumps are available.

One characteristic of the field level that offers room for design possibilities is that different kinds of signalling devices can be combined relatively freely. The sensors and actuators are connected to the data network on the next level via small microcontroller-driven direct digital control (DDC) modules that translate the signals coming from the sensors into a corresponding digital protocol. These modules are often manufacturer-specific and usually connected via proprietary protocols.

THE AUTOMATION LEVEL

The automation level concerns the data exchange between the DDC modules and the control and management level. In recent years various manufacturers have developed their own data communication protocols or so-called "bus systems" such as BACnet or LON-Bus. The resulting dependency on manufacturers for replacement parts and attachment of third-party products has led to an increased interest in open standards such as TCP/IP familiar from the IT sector. This is likely to expand in future, so that it will become possible to choose more freely between combinations of components.

THE MANAGEMENT LEVEL

The management level concerns the processing of the signals from the automation level, its visualisation using different methods, and its control through a variety of events. Control systems make it possible to couple different bus systems with one another via so-called "gateways". The output of data and its processing via control functions can take place through a series of different channels.

The management level is the level at which the user interface of building automation can be designed. It controls how the measured values from the field level are displayed and how the user can influence them. Over and above conventional control methods with screens for display and mouse and keyboard as input devices, a series of alternative control methods are also conceivable: gesture-based control, voice control, controls that respond to body movement and so on.

At present this field remains the domain of the building services engineer, and interior designers have yet to explore this aspect of communication between the user and the building. Sooner or later, however, interior designers will recognise the vast potential for design that these technological developments can offer.

**Everyday
fire prevention
measures.**

FIRE PROTECTION

Fire protection in the context of buildings usually refers to "preventive fire protection", which covers all measures intended to prevent fires occurring or spreading in buildings. An interior designer's scope of responsibility includes the implementation of fire protection measures that relate to the building's structure and construction, but the technical installations required for fire protection systems can also impact on the interior design in a number of ways. In addition, interior designers need to pay particular attention to inflammable building materials that may not have been evaluated by fire protection engineers or are not directly subject to statutory regulations.

THE FIRE PROTECTION CONCEPT

The first step towards implementing fire protection measures for a building is the drawing up of a fire protection concept summarising all the statutory requirements applicable to the project and the technical conditions under which these have to be fulfilled. The fire protection concept should include:

– An escape route plan and rescue concept
– The division of the building into logical fire compartments
– A table of fire protection requirements for wall and floor/ceiling elements, doors, portals and any other special elements, such as smoke barriers
– A description of the requirements for fire protection systems and the corresponding technical installations
– Concepts for any technical or special use-specific fire protection solutions, such as sprinkler systems or gas-based fire extinguishing systems

There are no specific stipulations regarding the form or extent of a fire protection concept and it can be drawn up by anyone with the relevant knowledge. For simple building projects this may be the interior designer or another construction professional with the requisite knowledge. In practice, however, there is an increasing trend towards specialisation. For larger and more complex projects, fire protection concepts are therefore almost always drawn up by specialist fire protection engineers, who should be consulted as early as possible in the design process.

The task of the interior designer at this stage in the project is to ensure that the design concept is possible within the stipulations of the applicable fire safety regulations. This covers the appropriate choice of materials as well as the determination of possible alternative protection objectives and ways of implementing them.

FIRE PROTECTION – BUILDING STRUCTURE AND CONSTRUCTION

During the planning process, the interior designer must ensure that the fire behaviour of the materials used conforms to the requirements outlined in the fire protection concept. In addition to the duration a material is able to withstand the effects of fire, it is also important to assess whether the materials themselves represent a fire hazard.

In Germany, building materials, building components (construction elements) and building products are classified in fire resistance classes that correspond to the duration in minutes they are able to resist the effects of fire, for example, F30 or F90 walls or T30 or T90 doors. In addition, building materials in Germany are also classified according to flammability denoted by terms such as "highly flammable", "hardly flammable" or "non-combustible".

A further criterion, particularly for doors and windows, is whether a building component is able to contain the spread of smoke and fumes. In addition to the fire performance of the element itself, it must be ensured that the door or window will be closed in the event of a fire. The simplest way to achieve this is with a door closer, but there are also more elaborate systems triggered by smoke detectors, which may require more detailed input from fire protection engineers during the planning process. Because in practice, the needs of the building's users often conflict with fire protection requirements, and doors that are held open can potentially be the cause of significant costs, the fire protection concept needs to consider the users' access requirements from an early stage.

Interior design concepts implemented at a later date, after the actual construction of the building has been completed, run the risk of undermining the original fire protection concept if they employ unsuitable materials. Interior designers should therefore responsibly evaluate any pre-existing fire protection requirements before embarking on the project design and make their material choices accordingly.

FIRE PROTECTION – TECHNICAL SYSTEMS AND INSTALLATIONS

In addition to many concealed fire protection building components, such as conduit and cable sealing systems and fire protection ducts, there are still a number of technical installations that may be visible in the interior. For example, inspection openings for fire dampers in ventilation ducts need to be clearly marked with notices. Similarly such inspection openings, covers and removable and replaceable access hatches need to be provided in the first place, and their location and size is often prescribed and not always easy to integrate harmoniously into the design. To minimise their impact, it is worth considering their requirements early on in the development of the design concept.

Another aspect that likewise needs to be considered from the outset is the integration of emergency escape route signage and fire detectors, which are usually planned by the electrical engineer. For example, depending on the size of the area in question, fire detectors usually need to be arranged in a 5 m grid.

To avoid unsightly fittings in a carefully designed ceiling, aspirating smoke detectors (ASD systems) can be used. While these are much more expensive than conventional smoke detectors, they offer a series of technical advantages, including the ability to combine them with other gas sensors and the low level of maintenance they require.

1   See Ohm's law.

2   Of particular relevance are the feed and return temperatures or rather the difference between the feed and return temperature.

3   Today, typical feed and return temperatures lie between 55° and 35°C, sometimes even less. In the past, systems such as the so-called "steam-powered heating" had feed and return temperatures of between 90° and 70°C.

4   See also the term "relative humidity", which describes precisely this relationship.

BUILDING IN EXISTING FABRIC

JOHANNES STUMPF

Prevention of falls: barrier-free rooms will become increasingly important as demography changes.
Hospice, Stiftung Marienhospital, Euskirchen, Germany; 100% interior
Sylvia Leydecker

BARRIER-FREE ACCESS

In today's democratic society, all people have a right to equal treatment, regardless of physical or mental ability or disability, gender or other factors. One aspect of this is the requirement that all buildings be accessible to more or less the same degree for all people, with as few restrictions as possible. For the design of the built environment, this means that one needs to take into account a large number of possible disabilities.

People in wheelchairs are just one of many groups of people to whom this applies. Nowadays the term accessibility has a much broader connotation and tends to refer to providing for the expected needs of the actual users rather than the more general "one-size-fits-all" principle. In the contemporary understanding of accessibility, this can therefore range from giving staircases sufficient contrast to help people with sight impairments to the avoidance of coarse-mesh metal gratings in areas where women are likely to be wearing high heels. As the number of older people in society rises, accessibility will increasingly become an issue we will need to address in the design of our environment. This applies to almost all developed countries around the world and will have a considerable impact on how new buildings are designed and without doubt also on the existing building stock. In many cases, existing buildings were not designed to take into account the particular needs of an aging society. As such, it will be necessary to retrofit buildings accordingly. This will involve adjusting floor plans (for example making bathrooms and kitchens sufficiently large to move around in) as well as introducing new fittings.

Since the mid-1980s, standards authorities throughout Europe have strived to introduce mandatory design principles for accessible buildings. In addition to regulations for improving accessibility in the public sphere with ramps, low threshold door sills, sufficiently wide entrances and the-provision of wheelchair-accessible toilets, there are now further regulations for all kinds of uses and physical handicaps. In Germany, the coming into force of DIN 18040 marked the introduction of mandatory regulations for the accessible design of buildings.

A central principle is the consideration of measures based on the possible physical or mental handicap of the user. A distinction is drawn between motor impairments and sensory or cognitive disabilities. In addition to fulfilling requirements for wheelchair access, the catalogue of potential design solutions encompasses a broad range of possible measures including:

- Tactile markings along routes for the visually handicapped
- Additional handrails or supports for the frail and infirm
- Alarm systems
- Wayfinding systems with legible, good-contrast typography
- Colour coding of zones in buildings to provide orientation for people with memory disorders

For the designer, it is important to know the anticipated user groups. As a matter of principle, this is dependent on the use of the building and is therefore an aspect that the client should clarify in the project brief.

The barrier-free design principles set out in national standards are predominantly for implementation in publicly accessible buildings, but can equally be applied to all kinds of buildings. Early on in the design process, the interior designer should agree with the client, and his or her accessibility compliance representative, which standards and guidelines apply. Likewise, all aspects of the design, such as the choice of colours, surface treatments and materials, should take into account accessibility requirements and where necessary be discussed with the client's representatives as early as possible.

Unfortunately, the degree of regulation in the field of accessibility has in some cases reached excessive levels, and well-meaning representatives or agencies sometimes stipulate demands that go far beyond what is actually necessary. For example, some accessibility recommendations define which typeface may be used along with type size and colour usage, all of which are unnecessarily restrictive. It is a matter for the responsible designer to work together with the client to determine and document which requirements need to be catered for and to what degree. With the appropriate justification, deviations from the regulations may often be permissible. → 310

Handrail in an elegant residence for the elderly.

Residence for the Elderly, Les Jardins d'Alysea, Roeser, Luxembourg; JOI-Design

Handrails provide a sense of security and are clearly visible for people with poor eyesight.

Hospice, Stiftung Marienhospital, Euskirchen, Germany (left and bottom left); Josephinum, Munich, Germany (bottom right); 100% interior Sylvia Leydecker

The reception desk features a low-level section for wheelchair users.
Gynaecological practice, Maria-Hilf Hospital, Brilon, Germany; 100% interior Sylvia Leydecker

The WC and handrails are visually differentiated to provide better support and orientation.
Sana Hospital, Bad Wildbad, Germany; 100% interior Sylvia Leydecker

Barrier-free accessibility is important for all areas of hospitals that patients have access to.
Benjamin and Marian Schuster Heart Hospital, Kettering, Ohio, USA; Jain Malkin Inc., LWC Inc.

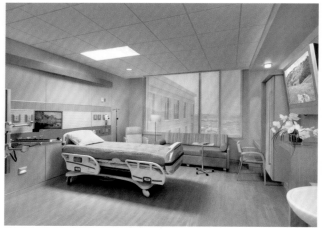

Barrier-free access is a recurring aspect in day care centres.
Day care centre Grevesmühlen, Germany; baustudio melchert+kastl

Mix: living, patina, urban life, old and new – all together in one neighbourhood.
Belgian Quarter, Cologne, Germany

Art Nouveau: the ornamental motif recurs in the shower door glazing and as a vastly-enlarged fragment on the floor of the patient lounge.
Josephinum Private Clinic, Munich, Germany;
100% interior Sylvia Leydecker

CONSERVATION OF HISTORIC BUILDINGS

In the Western world, the definition and practice of building conservation is a product of modern times. An awareness of the cultural achievements of times past first came about with the emancipation of bourgeois society in the 18th and 19th centuries and the search for a new identity after the decline of feudalism. The veneration of Greek and Roman antiquity as a humanistic ideal of a society and culture shaped by the sovereign people, as well as the "discovery" of the Middle Ages as national heritage would not have been conceivable without the social upheavals of the early modern age since the 15th century.

Even in the baroque, the grand edifices of the ancient world were little more than piles of stones. In fact, there was no consciousness of a "historical" dimension. The present and the past were seen as one, and it therefore made no difference if remnants of the old were replaced with the new without giving a thought to their conservation.

In Germany, it was Karl Friedrich Schinkel, who in his role as the Prussian Building Commissioner became one of the main proponents of preserving outstanding examples of artistry from earlier epochs. His report on "The Preservation of Monuments and Antiquities throughout our Country" in 1815 anticipated many of the systems we employ today for the conservation of buildings. Schinkel initiated the process of conducting surveys and drawing up inventories, establishing local "protection committees" to identify objects worthy of preservation, which included churches, city gates, castles and town halls as well as fountain sculptures, baptismal fonts, coats of arms, choir stalls, paintings and murals. However, Schinkel's definition of what was deemed relevant and what was not was somewhat arbitrary: for him, everything built after 1650 had no value as a monument.

That Schinkel himself was not so exacting in his restoration of buildings from the past is not as surprising as it might seem given the context of the day. Schinkel and his contemporaries had an idealised view of the past: if the reality did not measure up to the ideal, it would simply be "improved". An interesting example of this attitude can be seen in Schinkel's design for the rebuilding of the Moritzburg in Halle/Saale, which illustrates how this principle of idealisation overshoots the mark, eclipsing even its model.

The completion of Cologne Cathedral from 1823 onwards was undertaken in the same spirit: the building of the south facade followed historical drawings and was largely "faithful to the original" but the facades of the transept are reproductions.

The principle of "continuing on" from the historical situation reached its pinnacle in the work of Eugène Emmanuel Viollet-le-Duc, who was responsible for restoring Notre Dame in Paris, the reconstruction of Château de Pierrefonds in Picardy and the restoration of the city of Carcassonne in Languedoc. Viollet-le-Duc's theoretical elaborations on the preservation of monuments reveal this approach and justify the reshaping of the original with the aim of finding an "ideal" form.

Viollet-le-Duc and Schinkel were both more or less open proponents of an approach that regarded the historical substance merely as a point of departure for reinterpretation. Both architects were therefore aware of the risk of losing original building substance and of distorting the historical situation.

John Ruskin, whose strongly conservation-oriented theories have influenced conservation practice to the present day, put forward a different point of view. In his essay "The Seven Lamps of Architecture", published in 1849, he railed against the recreation ("restoration") of historical substance, in his eyes an impossible undertaking. He argued that the time embodied in the building, which was part of what needed preserving, was lost through restorative efforts. For him, the only true approach to dealing with historic monuments was their preservation ("conservation").

This fundamental dialectic between restoration and conservation continues to dominate the discourse on conservation practice to the present day. In the period between 1850 and the mid-1960s, the pendulum swung back and forth between these two viewpoints. This came to an end in 1964 with the introduction of the Charter of Venice – a formal framework of guidelines for the conservation and restoration of monuments and sites – drawn up by the Second International Congress of Architects and Specialists of Historic Buildings. Since then, ICOMOS, the International Council on Monuments and Sites, which was created as a result of the congress, has been responsible for carrying out and developing the charter on a regular basis.

The basic principles elaborated in the Charter of Venice can be summarised as follows:

Historic works should always be seen in their respective context and should be kept in their setting wherever possible.

In addition to their artistic value, the significance of works should also be judged in terms of their cultural, historical and historico-technological evidence. The conservation of works of cultural significance applies to all aspects of the work to the same degree. Modest works of the past should be given equal treatment to great works of art.

The conservation of a monument requires maintenance on a permanent basis. The best means of conservation is its continued and respectful use.

A monument should always be seen in its entirety. Traces of history on the monument should be preserved.

The aim of restoration is to preserve and reveal the aesthetic and historic value of the monument. The restoration of a monument as a special case can only be justified in exceptional circumstances.

Traditional techniques should always be given priority over modern techniques. The use of modern techniques for conservation should be undertaken and evaluated using scientific means.

The restoration concept should respect the contribution of all periods of a building. Unity of style is not the aim of a restoration.

Replacements or additions must be distinguishable from the original.

All works undertaken on a monument must be precisely documented in the form of reports, drawings and photographs and the results made available to interested researchers and the public.

These comparatively simple principles can, however, in practice lead to extraordinarily complex solutions. Interior designers who work in the field of conservation are regularly faced with the need to weigh up the individual requirements of a project and to find an answer to these that also respects the conservation requirements of the historic building. Depending on the kind of object, its history, condition and the intended use, the importance of these requirements can vary considerably and have a direct impact on the design concept. → 321

Without leaving a trace: this cultural exhibition in a world heritage site could not impact on the building at all and needed to be removable without leaving even the trace of a drawing pin.
"Ex Oriente – Isaak und der weiße Elefant" Exhibition, Aachen, Germany; 100% interior Sylvia Leydecker

Layers: the installations follow the structure of the building from the late Renaissance; photos of the modernisation can be seen as film strips applied to the suspended lighting with hand-lettered typography painted on the wall.
Josiger & Collegen, Saalfeld, Germany; 100% interior Sylvia Leydecker

Limit experience: the unspectacular entrance to the synagogue is poignant due to the photos of previous members of the community. The altar space has been left untouched by the interior designers, with only Hebrew typography applied to the ceiling as a contrasting design element.
"Grenservaringen" Exhibition, Roermond synagogue, Holland; 100% interior Sylvia Leydecker

The salon,
once the heart
of social life
in historical
buildings,
has been
inhabited by
a hairdresser
who has
chosen to
reinstate
a vintage
character.
Salon Nemetz, Munich,
Germany; DESIGNLIGA

Historical and oriental.
Sepia Lounge and Restaurant, Beirut, Lebanon;
Bachir Nader – Interior Architect

Interior designers renovate and modernise old buildings. This building from the late 1800s has been sensitively restored and radiates the glory of times past.
Conversion and renovation of a listed villa from 1900, Düren, Germany; FRANKE Architektur I Innenarchitektur

Inspired: modern-day product design that draws on historical patterns.
Tiles; IVANKA Concrete Design

Stimulating contrast: an old building is made more interesting through the insertion of an utterly new element.

Kyoto Silk, Kyoto, Japan; Keiichi Hayashi Architect

Shades of overseas: the director's office in this listed historical building exudes an aura of respectability and the history of shipping companies.

Offices for International Shipping Company, London, England; SHH

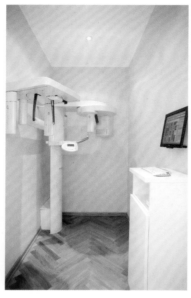

Parquet flooring: the necessary sterility of a practice is made more approachable by its historical surroundings.
Dr. Dux & Kollegen Orthodontist's Practice, Detmold, Germany; Stövesand Architektur

Slow: farmhouses and country life have a pace of their own.
La Finca, Mallorca, Spain; UXUS

Opulent: one of the most exotic palaces in Europe was built in the first half of the 18th century – Chinese, Indian, and above all eclectic.
The Long Gallery, The Royal Pavilion (built 1815–1822), Brighton, England; John Nash (*18.01.1752; † 13.05.1835)

Sign here: communicative staircase in an old warehouse.
Staircase, London, England

This hotel with a view over a small oasis in Tunisia is inspired by traditional architecture; it is not a replica but an experiment of our times.
Dar'Hi, Nefta, Tunisia;
Matali Crasset

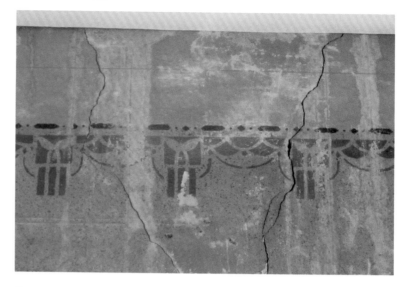

Pattern: an ornamental painted border in an old industrial building.
Bonn, Germany

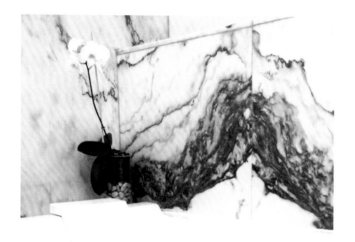

Pattern: marble around a bathtub gives a historical building an appropriately authentic touch.
DenkmalBad, Cologne, Germany; SEITENANSICHT – Innenarchitektin Martina Lorbach

TWO DIFFERENT APPROACHES TO CONSERVATION: NEUES MUSEUM AND ALTE NATIONALGALERIE IN BERLIN, GERMANY

The recent restoration of two buildings in Berlin, the Neues Museum and the Alte Nationalgalerie on the Museum Island, exemplify two contrasting approaches to the conservation of monuments. Both buildings are part of the Museum Island world heritage site, which was founded as a "Sanctuary for Art and Science" from 1830 onwards.

Unlike the Neues Museum, rebuilding efforts for the Alte Nationalgalerie began shortly after the end of the war so that it was possible to open parts of the building to the public in 1946. In the 1950s, the building was comprehensively renovated and the destroyed staircase rebuilt in a simplified form. There were few further alterations until German reunification. A general restoration programme, for which detailed plans had been drawn up in the 1980s, was not undertaken.

After reunification, the plans were re-examined in 1993. The commissioning of the architectural office of HG Merz to undertake the reconstruction work in the turbulent years after the reunification turned out to be stroke of good fortune: with a clear sense of form, colours and materials and a love of detail, he oversaw the renovation work for the Alte Nationalgalerie from 1997 to 2001.

In contrast to the Neues Museum, which had remained a ruin for 65 years and had changed little over the years prior to its renovation, the Alte Nationalgalerie was used more or less continually and went through several clearly identifiable periods.

The concept for the renovation of the Neues Museum developed by David Chipperfield Architects and Julian Harrap had two main aims: to reinstate the original volume through the construction of a new northwest wing and to repair and restore the parts that remained. In addition a range of new technical installations were necessary – lighting, air-conditioning and security measures – as a 21st-century museum has quite different requirements for the conservation of exhibits than a building in the 19th century.

The interior design concept uses the existing ducts and shafts to route the required technical installations to where they are needed. It was nevertheless necessary to make numerous openings in existing walls and ceilings that, after the installation of the necessary utilities, were then closed again using modern restoration techniques and materials that correspond as far as possible to the original material. The intention was – as can be seen throughout the building – to keep elements that show the building's own decay and damage and to allow this to remain as an aesthetic quality.

Chipperfield and Harrap employ this principle throughout the building. Damaged surfaces remain as fragments; lost sections of wall murals are not augmented with missing elements but simply filled in with the same basic colour and structure. All new elements have a subdued, refined and simple materiality that does not compete with the sumptuous colour of the original building. The design conserves the building, as it were, in the epoch of its destruction. It is always possible to tell apart the old from the new.

This approach, which in its essence follows the guidelines of the Charter of Venice, also succeeds in creating a quite individual and very deliberate aesthetic expression of a clarity and lucidity rarely seen – one that goes much further than the objective of conservation alone.

A contrasting approach to this can be seen in the concept for the general renovation of the Alte Nationalgalerie. As the building has been in constant use – with only one major interruption during the war – it has, over the course of its 125-year history, acquired layer after layer of temporal periods, each worthy of conservation. The war damage had been largely repaired and was no longer apparent to

visitors to the building. As such, the interior design task of the renovation was not to conserve the status quo but to work from the existing situation and add a new temporal layer. In contrast to the concept for the Neues Museum, therefore, the intention was not to articulate the breaks in time but rather to sensitively reorder and augment the existing situation in the same way that the interventions of the past had done.

In order to realise the extensive technical installations and the third exhibition floor required by the client, it was necessary to make major interventions in the existing building. In the region of the Great Hall on the second floor, all insertions were taken out to reveal just the structure so that a new floor and the ventilation ductwork could be installed. The original insertions were dismantled, placed in storage and then reinserted after the technical installations had been completed.

Following the idea of adding a new temporal layer, the heavily reconfigured areas of the central halls of the second floor and the new halls on the new third floor employ a vocabulary of forms and materials of their own that, rather than contrasting with the existing building, pick up its general colour and texture. In particular they reproduce the quality of light of the former top-lit halls through the insertion of an illuminated ceiling.

As a result the Alte Nationalgalerie makes a coherent impression on its visitors. The concept avoids dramatising the changes in period without eradicating the legibility of the different time periods.

The examples of the Neues Museum and Alte Nationalgalerie demonstrate clearly the difficulty of translating the "pure principles" of the Charter of Venice into architectural and interior design practice. In every design task in the field of conservation, it is necessary to carefully weigh up which of the respective conservation aims should be pursued and the means with which to achieve them. With this in mind, it is vitally important for the designer to communicate to other professionals and consultants in the team that a holistic design concept will always be an interpretation of the existing context. Measures such as "exposing" the "wounds" of history, the "completion of missing building fabric" or the "closure of defects" are all a form of design intervention that wherever possible should follow a consciously formulated strategy. As such, the sensitive and harmonising repair of a building as well as the conscious decision to articulate the different time periods are both possible valid approaches to renovating a building – an approach that should ultimately always be seen as a design task.

East facade of the Neues Museum.
Reconstruction of the Neues Museum, Museum Island Berlin, Germany; David Chipperfield Architects

View from the Niobe Hall in the North Dome Room – the museum is worth visiting for the rooms alone.
Reconstruction of the Neues Museum, Museum Island Berlin, Germany; David Chipperfield Architects

In the imposing staircase hall, the old fabric of the building contrasts with the contemporary architectural language of the new insertion.
Reconstruction of the Neues Museum, Museum Island Berlin, Germany; David Chipperfield Architects

Views of the museum showing the transformation.
Reconstruction of the Neues Museum, Museum Island Berlin, Germany; David Chipperfield Architects

HISTORICAL BACKGROUND

NEUES MUSEUM

The Neues Museum was built between 1841 and 1855 on the orders of King Friedrich Wilhelm IV of Prussia according to plans by Friedrich August Stüler. Even its process of development is historically significant as it employed numerous technologies that at the time were revolutionary, such as the use of steam engines, lightweight brick construction and cast iron.

The Neues Museum was originally conceived as a universal museum in which every epoch of human cultural history had a room of its own, arranged in evolutionary order. Stüler succeeded in incorporating the design of the respective interiors as well as the construction methods used into a unique cosmos of meaning. The construction method employed followed the epoch of the exhibition or reflected the items being exhibited. Egyptian history, which was exhibited in the lower storeys of the building, was presented in rooms with hypostyle-like heavy pillars, while the Roman exhibits were in rooms with arches and cupola constructions. The Niobid room and the Greek room, which contained a collection of sculpture plaster casts, are roofed over by a lightweight cast-iron construction. The integration of technical services in the mid-19th century is a further special characteristic of the building. Stüler planned an ingenious system of integrated ducts to provide the rooms with fresh air. The building was also one of the first to boast a combined central heating and hot water system.

Numerous rooms of the building also featured good-quality wall murals, which were only finally completed in 1866. A typical characteristic of the time was that original stone was only used sparingly due to the high cost of its procurement. Many surfaces were therefore finished using stucco techniques aimed to imitate the impression of stone.

In the years that followed, the building was subject to a number of minor alterations but overall remained in a near-original state until the Second World War. In the last few years of the war between 1943 and 1945 it was badly damaged. The main staircase was gutted by fire and the northwest wing destroyed entirely. Unlike the other buildings on the Museum Island, the Neues Museum was not reconstructed but was more or less forgotten and became a "romantic ruin". The rooms that were still intact were used as storage, but everything else slowly decayed over a period of 65 years. In the mid-1980s, the German Democratic Republic (GDR) finally decided to repair the building. However, with the exception of some initial repairs to the foundations, this had not progressed beyond the planning stage by the fall of the wall and German reunification in 1989.

The building therefore remained a ruin for almost 65 years. Plans for its reconstruction only became more real after the reunification of Germany. After a series of competitions, a design by David Chipperfield Architects was chosen in 1997 and realised between 1999 and 2009.

ALTE NATIONALGALERIE

The first designs for the Alte Nationalgalerie were drawn up in 1841 shortly after the plans for the Neues Museum. Based on a sketch by Friedrich Wilhelm IV, Stüler developed a concept for a large hall-like building that initially had no clearly defined purpose. The plans were not put into effect until 1861 when the Wagener collection was bequeathed, giving the building a concrete purpose, as the State of Prussia had agreed in return to construct a "national gallery" to house it. Stüler produced a design in 1862, which was accepted shortly after by the King. The building was realised with a few further modifications to Stüler's design between 1867 and 1876 by Johann Heinrich Strack.

Only the first and second floors were used for the actual gallery spaces. The first floor contained a large hall for sculptures while the second floor was reserved for paintings. The Great Hall on the second floor contained designs for frescos and a larger-than-life bust of the artist Peter Cornelius.

The first alterations to the building followed the appointment of Hugo von Tschudi as director in 1896 and his stronger focus on more modern and international artistic movements. The hanging scheme in the Great Hall was changed significantly for the first time, and Tschudi also transformed the monumental and somewhat gloomy sculpture hall into a gallery for paintings by introducing more intimate, cabinet-like insertions. Further alterations followed under his successor Ludwig Justi, who became director in 1909. The Great Hall on the second floor was sacrificed in favour of smaller halls with skylights and suspended ceilings, and the apse on the first floor was extendet through the so-called "Justi Cabinets", continuing the pattern begun by Tschudi. Under Eberhard Hanfstaengl, who replaced Justi in 1933 after his dismissal, the alterations were continued on the second floor. The rooms were given a light grey surround and were made generally more sober. Hanfstaengl retained the concept of the rooms with skylights.

Between 1943 and 1945 the building was heavily damaged. The second floor suffered a direct hit from an artillery grenade, destroying load-bearing walls and the floor, and the monumental staircase was destroyed in a bomb attack. In addition, the facade was badly damaged by infantry fire in the final days of the war.

Sensitive interventions: interior and exterior views of the monument *par excellence* during the renovation.

General restoration, renovation and conversion of the Alte Nationalgalerie, Museum Island Berlin, Germany; hg merz architekten museumsgestalter

PROJECT MANAGEMENT

JOHANNES STUMPF

"Tell me how your project started and I'll tell you how it ends."
(Quote from an unknown project manager)

All projects, regardless of their kind or size, involve the same activities:

- The project aim and the resulting requirements need to be defined
- A functional, economic and design concept needs to be developed to realise it
- The project must be reviewed to ensure it conforms to the necessary statutory requirements
- Technical details necessary to implement the concept need to be developed
- Contracts need to be agreed with contractors
- The work of the different trades and technical installations needs to be planned and coordinated
- The work needs to be undertaken
- The work undertaken needs to be verified and paid

The standards for undertaking these activities differ considerably depending on the cultural context, as does the point of transfer between planning and execution and between client and building contractor.

There are, however, a few key roles that are always required:
- The client, who defines the project aims, stays informed about the progress of the planning and execution of the project, makes decisions about possible necessary changes, reviews and accepts the final work and pays for the work undertaken.
- The designer/planner, who advises the client, develops an aesthetic, technical and functional concept based on the client's requirements and prepares all necessary plans and documentation for executing the project.
- The contractor, who undertakes individual services as specified in the documents prepared by the planner.

Each of these people is normally responsible for the activities they undertake, but they are not responsible for clarifying the handover points or for aspects outside their own sphere of influence. Misunderstandings between project participants can therefore arise unexpectedly and endanger the progress of the project. This is where qualified project management can play a role by establishing clear structures and procedures for the project that define responsibilities and handover points and by implementing a control system.

Modern project management serves mostly as a support function for the client, helping to keep track of the "magic triangle" of cost, time and quality. The extent of services provided and the means used vary considerably depending on the kind of project and its specific requirements, but in any case this should be determined by the client at the beginning of the project, i.e. when preparing the project. Project managers help in:

- The organisation, communication, coordination and documentation of all processes and aims
- Specifying and monitoring quality levels and quantities
- Defining and controlling the budget and financing
- Arranging and monitoring completion deadlines, the capacity of the project participants and any logistical requirements
- Drawing up and agreement of contracts with project participants and any necessary insurance policies

Modern project management[1] divides every building project into the following five key project phases:

- The preparation phase, in which the project aims are defined along with an outline of the envisaged budget and timeframe. The design and planning requirements are agreed and design contracts are signed. Important organisational instruments drawn up in this phase include the project handbook, organisation handbook and outline time schedule.

- The design planning phase, in which the results of the design plan are evaluated against the client's technical, economic and functional requirements, and contributions from other planners are coordinated and assessed. In this phase, a change management system is established in which deviations from the time schedule, costs or quality levels are documented and, where necessary, renegotiated.

- The construction preparation phase, in which contracts with building contractors are drawn up and negotiated. Contractual documents are assessed to verify that they are in line with the general project aims and the estimated costs.

- The construction phase, which is by far the most complex phase of project management because the majority of the project resources are deployed here and problems that arise impact directly on the time schedule and overall costs. Project management tasks in this phase include monitoring the construction process, building site quality management and cost controlling (management of additional cost). In addition, project management is responsible for preparing the inspection and acceptance of completed works and its documentation.

- The project completion phase, in which the technical and cost-related aspects of the project are documented with the aim of making the building ready for use. Project management activities in this phase include conclusion of all contracts and acceptance of the work undertaken and any necessary preparations required to make the building ready for use.

Project management makes sense for projects of any size, although smaller projects do not have a dedicated person solely responsible for the above tasks. Many clients assume that the architect or interior designer will undertake this role automatically. In certain circumstances this may also be a practicable solution, but it is then advisable to clearly define the specific areas of responsibility in a contract, along with the payment terms where applicable, as this usually exceeds the normal level of services provided by an architect or interior designer.

1 See "Projektmanagement in der Bau- und Immobilienwirtschaft" (Project Management in the Building and Real Estate Industries) by the German AHO Committee on Project Controlling and Project Management, from 2009.

Making of... behind the scenes on various building sites.
Germany

Interactive and on time – without effective project management the IFA Gala would not have been possible.
IFA (consumer electronics trade fair) Gala 2011, Messe Berlin, Germany; KINZO

Live wires – cable routing as graphic decoration on the ceiling.
Fashion-Store MAYGREEN, Hamburg, Germany; KINZO

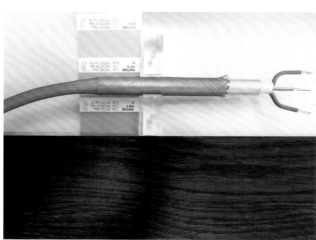

INTERIOR DESIGN WITHOUT FRONTIERS

THOMAS WELTER

Designing and building in a foreign country presents many opportunities, but also many risks. The different regional and national building traditions offer opportunities to create extraordinary projects, and it is stimulating for any creative professional to work in other cultural contexts. But what does the provision of cross-border interior design services actually entail?

The term export in this respect is not an accurate description: cross-border design services are not generally the one-sided sale of services abroad but cooperative projects where interior design offices at home and abroad work together for a foreign or internationally operating client.

CHALLENGES

Despite the multitude of opportunities that working internationally has to offer, it also bears considerable risks. Finding commissions abroad is often a more expensive and time-consuming endeavour than at home, and may very often be unsuccessful. Journeys abroad can be mentally and physically taxing, and misunderstandings caused by cultural differences can have financial consequences. Interior designers who design and build abroad must be prepared for unexpected setbacks because business cultures, decision-making structures and adherence to agreements in other countries can differ considerably from acceptable practice at home. In addition, interior designers who work abroad are often faced with the following major and minor difficulties:

- Problems with the language and culture
- Lack of support on site
- Difficulties in dealings with local authorities
- A lack of knowledge of local building and administration regulations and property rights
- High logistical overheads relative to the resulting profit

Knows no bounds. Similar furnishings, different contexts and different appearances – Europe and the United Arab Emirates.

Sana Kliniken AG Headquarters, Ismaning, Germany; 100% interior Sylvia Leydecker (top and opposite page). Emirates Lounge, Mumbai, India; JTCPL Designs (bottom)

PREREQUISITES

Not every interior design office will be in a position to successfully realise projects abroad. On the one hand, the size of the contract must as a rule be larger than a comparable project at home to justify the additional costs involved. In addition, supplementary costs such as travel and possible translation services impact on the fee income normally required to conduct similar work at home.

Interior designers who wish to work abroad should have the following prerequisites:
- The interior designer and one or more staff should have a good command of the client country's language
- Intercultural skills and an affinity with the people and culture of the client country
- Private contacts in the country to be able to settle in quickly and establish relevant formal and informal partners
- Ideally a member of staff from the client country with a good knowledge of the prevailing local conditions

A certain degree of additional organisational outlay is unavoidable when working across borders. A website in a suitable foreign language, for example, is essential for finding work abroad. Such expenses are more easily borne by large- and medium-sized firms than by one-man-bands or small design offices.

Whatever the case may be, a sound economic home base is essential in order to be able to cushion the effect of planning delays or outstanding fee payments with other income sources. Those who are already up to their neck financially at home should not even consider taking on a project venture abroad.

SERVICES

Interior designers develop general concepts and detail solutions for the interiors of buildings, and sometimes for temporary or mobile spaces. While there are no compelling grounds to commission an interior designer from another country, there are various reasons why it can be advantageous for internationally oriented clients to work with interior designers who also work internationally.

One important motive is the search for new and creative solutions to a design task. For example, designers and planners from other cultures typically bring a fresh interpretation to local design and building traditions. Sometimes a particular design needs to be transferred as accurately as possible from one country to another.

However, what attracts foreign clients to German interior design offices in particular is less the creative image of interior design from Germany than their technical and organisational expertise, and especially their ability to ensure projects are completed on time, without defects and within budget. These are the qualities and abilities of German design offices that are most highly valued and sought after abroad. Market research on the export chances of German architects repeatedly comes to the same conclusion: high-quality standards, the ability to realise technically innovative solutions and to organise the entire project is what people abroad associate with German interior design offices.

These secondary virtues of German companies – punctuality, reliability and the ability to complete projects on schedule and on budget – represent the added value that interior designers from Germany should be aware of and should highlight accordingly in their marketing initiatives.

International: 3 letter IATA airport codes used on the doors of toilet cubicles.
Samas Office Furniture Headquarters, Worms, Germany; 100% interior Sylvia Leydecker

Proper Tea. A luxurious tea salon in Kuala Lumpur makes reference to the country's past as a British colony.
Starhill Tea Salon, Kuala Lumpur, Malaysia;
design spirits co., ltd. – Yuhkichi Kawai

New York style Italian menu in Hong Kong – Blue Delft porcelain, that in its day mimicked Chinese porcelain, and sunflowers remind one of Holland and the design is by a Turkish firm.
208 Duecento Otto Restaurant,
Hong Kong, China; Autoban

FIRST STEPS

Projects abroad typically come about in a very private way: by far the largest proportion of cross-border projects are the product of private contacts. Periods of study or work experience abroad, office partners from other countries or bi-national partnerships are often a springboard for making international contacts that lead to projects abroad.

Another very common approach is the piggy-back strategy: businesses in Germany expanding their activities or investing abroad bring in offices with specific intercultural capabilities so that they do not need to worry about "translating" German qualities and standards to the destination country. For commissions of this kind, offices will be judged not by their own creative skills but rather by their ability to demonstrate intercultural competence and precise knowledge of the local conditions.

The choice of possible regions to work in is largely determined by language proficiency and cultural competence. Projects in other countries are not run-of-the-mill work. Instead, they require considerable personal commitment and a degree of affection for the people and culture of the country. Despite the tendency towards more complex organisational services, this rule applies equally for large interior design offices: the staff who are responsible for the task should have a thorough understanding of the cultural particularities of the job and the partner in the country.

First contacts can be made, for example, as part of a trade delegation to another country. These are usually organised by various governmental ministries or bodies such as chambers of trade or commerce at a regional or national level. A well-prepared visit to a trade fair, or even a dedicated trade fair stand can likewise be used to establish relationships. A further means of making relevant contacts abroad is to participate in professional events and conferences, for example as a speaker. Employing foreign members of staff can also lead to useful professional contacts abroad.

In Germany, there are a large number of sources of information and support for foreign trade relations. Besides governmental agencies, such as Germany Trade and Invest (www.gtai.de), professional associations and chambers, such as the Federal Chamber of German Architects' Network for Architecture Exchange programme (www.architekturexport.de) and its regional offices, can also offer assistance. The Worldwide Network of the German Chambers of Commerce (www.ahk.de) and the Federal Foreign Office (www.auswaertiges-amt.de) also provide assistance abroad.

OUTLOOK

Cross-border projects in the field of interior design offer a wide variety of opportunities but are also accompanied by considerable risks. For interior designers without any kind of connection to a foreign country, it can be an extremely difficult and risky venture. Although good support is now available in establishing foreign trade relations, considerable difficulties can be expected without some understanding of the language and culture.

For interior designers who already have personal contacts abroad, it is worth investigating whether these contacts can be built on for business purposes. Trade delegations, professional events or trade fairs offer a means of making contact with professional partners in other countries. It can, however, be complicated and time-consuming to maintain these contacts and very often years pass before a first contact leads to a concrete project.

According to many experts, the provision of design and construction services across borders looks set to increase in the coming decades as economic integration continues, especially within the European Union, and as digitalisation of planning services increases. Despite the difficulties and possible problems, cross-border projects can not only contribute to increased earnings but also offer new stimulus for work in the designer's home country. This could take the form of revised office organisational structures or modified working processes, the employment of staff from foreign countries and the opportunity for members of staff to work abroad for a while. Finally, working in several cultures can also lead to new ideas and directions in one's own creative work.

**Low-cost fusion with alpine
motifs in a Japanese office
building.**
Heidi House, Tokyo, Japan;
Klein Dytham architecture

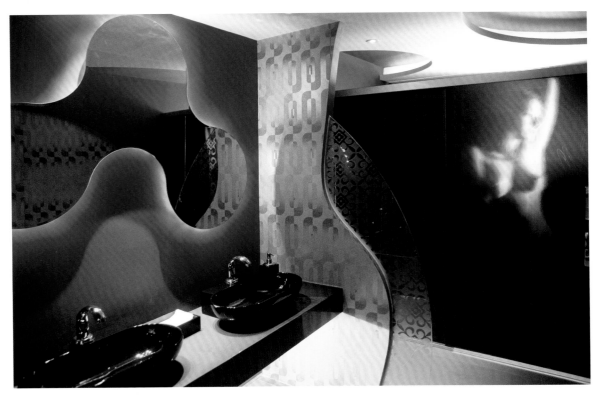

**Cultural differences
as seen in this public
toilet for men in Brazil.**
Banheiro Publico Masculino,
Vitória, Espírito Santo, Brazil;
Fabiane Giestas

Trattoria di Napoli, Istanbul.
Candido Restaurant,
Istanbul, Turkey; GOTWOB

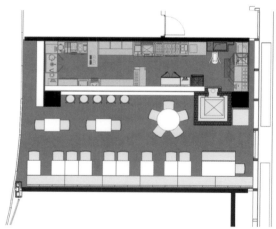

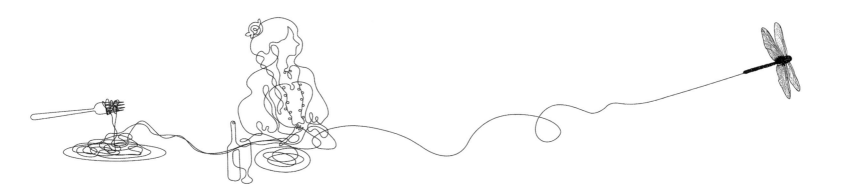

**Traditional Italian
pasta in Hong Kong.**
Spaghetti Tales Restaurant, Hong
Kong, China; Joey Ho Design Ltd.

The Royal China Restaurant with its roots in London – *haute cuisine* served in the high-class historical British Colonial Hotel in Singapore.
Royal China Restaurant, Singapore; Ministry of Design MOD

HOW INTERNATIONAL DO WE WORK?

SIMON HAMILTON

In writing this personal view about why to work internationally, I have looked at the various projects that have taken me abroad as well as asked the question more broadly. What is so attractive about working internationally and does it have to be as literal as physically leaving one's own country? As International Director for the British Institute of Interior Design (BIID) I am fortunate enough to travel to different countries on a regular basis. I have the task of meeting and connecting with a very wide variety of different design bodies and communities on a global scale. I visit numerous design shows and events to keep up-to-date with trends, styles and movements. The aim of this is to learn about differences but also to share ideas and experiences. It became clear very quickly that there are similarities in the way that design is carried out around the world, but it is the culture, wealth, education and history which shape the outcome of the design process.

A high-rise designed by the same practice in Tokyo will not look and feel the same as a similar project in Paris. Why is that? Beyond the obvious differences in landscape and surroundings, does it have more to do with issues of culture? In a year that has seen the world economy shift dramatically

from a peak to a trough overnight, I have experienced the effects of this development in all of the cities I have visited. For me the year of the Global Economic Crisis 2008 included visits to Berlin, Paris, Valencia, Toronto, Dublin, New Delhi and Milan. Wherever I visited, there has been a sense of hope that tomorrow will be better and that if we pull together this will be our way out of the difficult times. Despite strong competition in the trade there is also a strong sense of community and shared opinions with other designers, in whichever discipline or sector worldwide. Designers want to be recognised as individuals but realise that to achieve this we need to network and embrace each other.

On a trip to Berlin some years later to visit a new interior design show called "Qubique", I soon became aware that I had seen some of the exhibited products and suppliers before in London and Milan, but this did not devalue the event. The venue, the disused Tempelhof Airport building, was a big draw and also received a lot of pre-show PR. As this was the inaugural year of "Qubique", it was reassuring to see such a well-organised event with a balanced display of established names alongside unknown brands. → 343

Made in Germany: branded interiors of a German fashion label in Madrid and Shanghai.

Hugo Boss, Madrid, Spain; (top) and Shanghai, China (bottom and opposite page); RAISERLOPES

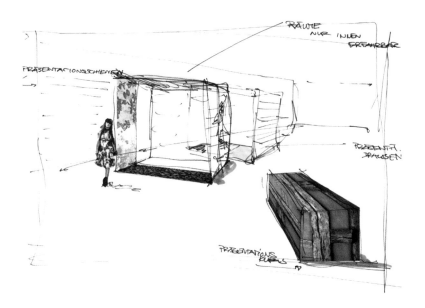

**Design of a German
high-street fashion
chain store
in Hong Kong.**
Esprit, Hong Kong, China;
Schwitzke & Partner

Working in another country gives everyone involved an opportunity for reinvention. You can be a new person abroad. No longer are you someone who plays safe in your own backyard. By taking a step away from your comfort zone you can give your work a boost. The attraction of being in demand by those who do not know you is also very hard to resist. On being contacted by an established practice from abroad your ego and self-image are refreshed. Such an opportunity arose for me in the summer of 2008, when an African architectural practice contacted me to create the interiors of a new twin-tower development. Although well versed in building 20-storey residential apartment blocks, they wanted to add something European and modern to the look and feel.

After some caution as the country was notorious for corruption and international financial scams, I met with the principal in London and decided to follow my gut instincts. After a positive start there was a breakdown in terms of interpretation of the design brief, mainly due to poor communication. The principal architect seemed to lose interest in the work we produced, despite our design team creating highly finished large-format presentation boards. The alpha male-dominated environment presented an unfamiliar and imbalanced scenario compared to working in London. There, the senior staff were represented by men and women alike. The experience taught me that you need to adapt to suit your environment in more ways than simple attire. Without a shadow of doubt the brief time I spent there was misrepresentative of a longer spell, as I was not exposed to the real poverty and huge divide in society there; being driven in a luxury SUV from hotel to office to bar gave me a sense of security but also dread. Nowhere in the world have I felt such impending potential violence. The mood of the meetings and communications changed as time went on, which gave me the feeling that this project was not going well for all concerned.

A different example of working abroad came about through a family connection. When my partner and his mother bought a house in southern France as an investment and to run it as a *chambre d'hôte*, it was a natural decision to appoint me as the interior designer. The team we assembled was truly international as the project manager was Danish, the builders were Polish and subcontractors French. Although not spoken fluently by all but the natives, the common language was French. In addition we used sign language and *impromptu* sketches to communicate ideas, explanations and the meaning of drawings. As with any mix of strangers there were some mild disagreements about methodology and process. A number of compromises were made due to the lack of regular communication, which was down not so much to language problems but rather to not being on site all the time. However, the project was successfully completed, providing a luxury holiday house.

The most exciting and creatively rewarding project abroad for me was the 947 Rooms boutique hotel in Venice, Italy, which opened for business in 2008. The name is derived from the client's father's restaurant, established in 1947 and situated on the floor below the hotel. This commission came about when I advertised for an interior designer. When I interviewed Matteo Bianchi he mentioned he might be able to bring this project to work on. Although he was not exactly the candidate I was looking for, I followed my instinct and once we began working together it became clear we were going to have a very positive, mutually beneficial relationship. The combined input of an Italian designer who had the essential language, both culturally and emotionally, and of my English perspective was appealing to the client. We were both very excited to be working on something we saw as highly glamorous. The client was very involved in the design development, which made the process more intimate and personal for such a commercial project. The results of this 18-month project were a life-long friendship and a beautifully designed hotel, which has a distinctive non-Venetian feel and style while still managing to relate well to its surroundings.

The issue of human rights has also been a subject to be addressed because in some emerging markets such as China and Russia, there are whole groups of the population who are suffering while all this high-design work goes on around them in a bubble they cannot burst. Any growth has victims and they must not be forgotten in the rush to exploit the new markets. Design should be applied so that it is of benefit to all. This is where international design work really has an important role to play. Good design should be brought to the masses to enhance life. One such project is underway for victims of the 2011 Tsunami in Japan with the Wallpaper Project led by London-based Japanese interior designer, Noriko Sawayama. The initiative provides rolls of wallpaper to decorate the accommodation of those whose homes have been destroyed, as a way of giving the occupants some hope for the future. Wallpaper suppliers and designers alike support this internationally. →346

Unmistakably Japanese!

Arata Restaurant, Tokyo, Japan; SWeeT co.,ltd.

Inspired by Mexico: the Mayan deity Kukulkan – the feathered serpent – winds its way through the rooms of this restaurant.

Hacienda del Cielo Restaurant, Tokyo, Japan; SWeeT co.,ltd.

"Neo Bistro": Italian food inspired by the quartier de l'Odéon in Paris and the age of European discovery.

Rigoletto Spice Market, Tokyo, Japan; SWeeT co.,ltd.

By pooling knowledge, experience and resources I have learnt a great deal, and it has created opportunities that would not have existed. I feel it is important to nurture unions with other industries and organisations so we can share and benefit. Defining links with established brands and foundations is a very healthy way to connect. Traveling to Japan, Australia, the USA, Europe and India in the past 24 months clearly demonstrated that there is a common desire to improve quality, understanding and dialogue in all design disciplines. Among others, the BIID, UKTI, DBA, CSD, Chicago Architecture Foundation and IIDA are champions of creating discussion and exchange of ideas. As fashion designers recognised a long time ago, the transition is obvious and workable. Theatre, textiles, graphics, film, engineering have become even more inter-related, too. All you need to do is look at the interiors of the Boeing 787 Dreamliner or Airbus A380. These now have intimate, tactile spaces similar to a study or bedroom as well as more public spaces similar to a hotel lobby or restaurant with mood lighting.

International work comes about in several ways. The sim-plest, but still successful route can be via a client's initial contact on noticing the designer's work in an article or visiting an exhibition. A number of means such as design awards, magazine editorials, advertising, exhibiting, net-working and working locally for clients with a global reach support this approach. Another major source of inter-national commissions is collaboration. Teaming up with a practice that has clients in other countries instantly increases the potential for work abroad and at the same time provides the opportunity to learn and share expe-riences, skills and knowledge. Repositioning your own company within a team can lead to raising the profile for all, which may be extremely attractive for potential clients.

Key factors are the kudos, expertise, differences in approach, culture and methods as well as bottom-line results in the form of realised projects. Track record is ultimately the biggest factor, especially in the commercial design sectors of retail and hospitality.

The current mood is one of numerous independent col-laborations. As people work in more flexible ways and have multiple roles, the definition of a designer is changing. By assuming some creative element in design work, it could be said that the role of a designer is not simply to produce original ideas but to curate, nurture and coordinate. In the age of social media, communication has become as instant as one-to-one conversation, but endowed with a potential for a much larger audience participating in what would have been limited to a personal exchange in the past. Today, designers from different countries and disciplines get together without restrictions by convention or labels. Getting together can now be an online experience as tech-nology is so fast and easy that there is no longer a need to leave your studio to work across borders. In order to make a relationship work, most find it essential to have at least one face-to-face meeting. This instills trust and confidence while giving each person an emotional point of reference. As sophisticated as webcams can be, there is nothing like shaking hands in person and sharing the subtle reactions and interaction in a close environment.

The power of digital design allows us to enter a new eco-nomic age, with the developing world gearing up to become leaders in the next decade. Digital design is the largest growth area in the fields of advertising, packaging, product design, exhibition design, interiors and graphics. Indicative of this trend is the expansion of start-ups and small-scale operations that maintain low overhead costs by outsourcing to the developing world. Filmmakers and fashionistas work with graphic designers, ceramicists get together with fine artists and product designers. One Dot Zero is an interna-tional moving image and digital arts organisation which commissions, showcases and promotes innovation across all aspects of moving image, digital and interactive arts. Founded by Shane Walter, this is one such company that demonstrates on a regular basis, with its Annual Festival, how graphics, film, web, animation and art come together to produce unique results that appeal to a global audience.

In this form, international design is not in another country but "in your own backyard". Designing for overseas inves-tors has another and different perspective. Getting local designers to engage in an international team is a clever way of making the most of the available talent with reduced risk, thereby having the kudos of working for an interna-tional client without having to set up a new branch office. In a different business model, global design groups such as WPP and Omnicom, who own several well-established design practices, focus on fast-growing emerging markets, which bolsters their fee income as they can afford to spread their risk in this way.

Retail and hotel interior design constitute the largest and most obvious sectors in international design cooperation. Richmond International, United Designers and Woods Bagot, an Australian practice with global offices, to name just a few, are working on hotel developments in the Middle East. There is a large demand for hotels in emerging markets. As new middle classes expand in numbers, they are demanding the comforts of Western nations. In terms of income, top UK retail interiors practices such as Checkland Kindleysides are doing well with roughly a 30 % increase in fee income year on year, not least through their offices in Mumbai and Shanghai, where British retail design expertise is highly prized.[1] Other retail design experts, such as Dalziel & Pow, are also benefitting from foreign investment in the UK, with ten retail concepts realised in the Australian-owned Westfield Shopping Centre in Stratford, East London. This development happens to be the gateway to the Olympic Park, the focus of global attention for a few special weeks in the summer of 2012. Trends play a role in international business and design is no exception: in tandem with the Queen's Diamond Jubilee, the 2012 Olympic Games saw an onslaught of Britishness and caused a ripple effect in that design from London is now more than ever seen as cool and in demand.

1   Design Week Top 100 Survey, May 2011, p. 35, Specialisms: Interiors & Exhibitions UK Top 10.

AFTERWORD AND ACKNOWLEDGEMENTS

In this book I wanted to reveal the complexity and sophistication of interior design. It was not our intention to create another coffee table book or a technical manual. Instead, the conceptual idea for this internationally oriented publication on interior design is based on two main components: contributions from a careful selection of professional authors from as far apart as Germany and Australia, illustrated with examples of interior design from around the world. Rather than showing individual projects in the form of case studies, the book features compilations of projects that highlight and illustrate specific themes.

The choice of authors and the selection of projects was entirely my own. The authors as well as the originators of the works shown are not exclusively interior designers but also come from the realms of product design, architecture and other design disciplines concerned with the built environment. This transdisciplinarity reflects the global situation of those working in interior design and the spectrum of their work.

The field of interior design is becoming both ever more complex and ever more specialised. But despite the increasingly varied and less uniform structure of the field, the activities of those practising in it still relate to "interiors" as a whole. This can be seen in the range of different approaches and ways of conveying the information that the authors take, coupled with their willingness to work within the systematic framework of the structure of this book, ranging from education and design inspiration to international practising in the field. Deciding which projects to choose to illustrate the topics was a seemingly endless task, as new, interesting and exciting projects are continually surfacing all over the world, making the selection even harder. In the end, we elected to set a cut-off point, which in this case is 2012. The result is a book with two parallel layers, one of texts, the other of images, that are distinct from one another but at the same time complement each other.

The authors I chose first and foremost for their professional competence and also my personal knowledge of them. I would like to extend my heartfelt thanks to them all, for their contributions but also for staying the course over the protracted and at times uncertain development of this publication. The same goes for my editor Andreas Müller, who at all times held the reins firmly but calmly, and contributed (yet again) with helpful and competent suggestions to the success of this book. Those who created the projects shown and/or made images of them provided us with a wealth of material, and they are to be thanked for making it possible for us to present such a rich and varied selection of projects to illustrate the topics.

While personal relationships, trustworthy partnerships and functioning networks in the real world still remain as valuable as ever in the digital age, advances in information technology did help to make the entire project much easier to manage. Whereas in 2008, when working on my previous book, I received large quantities of data on CD by post, this time the contributors and participants busily uploaded and transferred data online. One should nevertheless not forget that there are colleagues in countries whose virtual boundaries are tightly controlled and for whom communicating online is practically impossible. The task of sorting, structuring and selecting projects was, of course, that much more difficult because we had requested and received much more material than we were able to use. This is where I would like to thank my own office crew, including Sabrina Wolters, Nina Kröncke, Rena van den Berg and especially Florian Kast, who were entrusted with handling the project, experienced various ups and downs, and also relieved me of much work.

Managing and writing a book project "on the side" while also working as a practising interior designer and running an office means you need to be well organised and to enjoy doing this. Where global processes are concerned, a degree of openness also helps – the exchange of cultures has, after all, as much to offer in the realm of interior design as it does in other fields. But not only the authors and projects are international; the book itself is an international coproduction by my esteemed editor Andreas Müller in Berlin, the delightfully British translator of the German texts, Julian Reisenberger in Weimar, and the magnificent Austrian graphic designer Rein Steger in Barcelona – where we had a most enjoyable meeting over glasses of Cava discussing the final layout of the book. Thank you all for your work on the book.

Finally, I would like to extend special thanks to the sponsors for making this book possible in the breadth and depth that we have achieved.

It is my hope that this book does justice to the complexity of the profession, that it inspires readers to reflect on and explore the subject in greater detail and, last but not least, that it encourages people to work together with professional interior architects and designers.

I would like to end with the words of Robert Smith, front man and leader of The Cure, who said (taking the words right out of my mouth): "I do a job I really, really love and I kind of have fun with. People think you can't be grown up unless you're moaning about your job."

Sylvia Leydecker
Spa / Cologne in January 2013

LITERATURE, TRADE FAIRS, ASSOCIATIONS/ORGANISATIONS AND OTHER USEFUL LINKS

INTERIOR DESIGN

Ballast, David Kent, *Interior Detailing. Concept to Construction* (Hoboken, NJ: John Wiley & Sons, 2010).

Binggeli, Corky, *Building Systems for Interior Designers*, 2nd edition (Hoboken, NJ: John Wiley & Sons, 2009).

Brooker, Graeme and Weinthal, Lois, *The Handbook of Interior Architecture and Design* (London: Berg Publishers, 2013).

Caan, Shashi, *Rethinking Design and Interiors* (London: Laurence King, 2011).

Dohr, Joy Hook and Portillo, Margaret, *Design Thinking for Interiors: Inquiry + Experience + Impact* (Hoboken, NJ: John Wiley & Sons, 2011).

Hausladen, Gerhard and Tichelmann, Karsten, *Interiors Construction Manual. Integrated Planning, Finishings and Fitting-Out, Technical Services* (Munich / Basel Boston Berlin: DETAIL / Birkhäuser, 2010).

Kiedaisch, Petra (Ed.), Samesch, Stéphanie (Ed.), Beyrow, Matthias and Daldrop, Norbert W., *Corporate Identity / Corporate Design* (Ludwigsburg: avedition, 2007).

Meel, Juriaan van, *The European Office – Office Design and National Context* (Rotterdam: 010 Publishers, 2000).

Pile, John, *A History of Interior Design*, 3rd edition (London: Laurence King, 2009).

Taylor, Mark (Ed.) and Preston, Julieanna (Ed.), *Intimus: Interior Design Theory Reader* (Hoboken, NJ: Academy Press, 2006).

Taylor, Mark (Ed.), *Interior Design Critical and Primary Sources* (London: Berg Publishers, 2013).

Yelavich, Susan, *Contemporary World Interiors* (London: Phaidon Press, 2007).

Zeisel, John, *Inquiry by Design: Environment/Behavior/Neuroscience in Architecture, Interiors, Landscape and Planning,* revised edition (New York: W.W. Norton & Company, 2006).

MATERIALS

Beylerian, George M., Dent, Andrew and Quinn, Bradley (Ed.), *Ultra Materials: How Materials Innovation is Changing the World* (London: Thames & Hudson, 2007).

Glasner, Barbara, Schmidt, Petra and Schöndeling, Ursula, *Patterns 2. Design, Art and Architecture* (Basel Boston Berlin: Birkhäuser, 2008).

Lefteri, Chris, *Making it*, 2nd edition (London: Laurence King, 2012).

Leydecker, Sylvia, *Nano Materials in Architecture, Interior Architecture and Design* (Basel Boston Berlin: Birkhäuser, 2008).

Peters, Sascha, *Material Revolution: Sustainable and Multi-Purpose Materials for Design and Architecture* (Basel Boston Berlin: Birkhäuser, 2011).

Schmidt, Petra, Tietenberg, Annette and Wollheim, Ralf, *Patterns in Design, Art and Architecture* (Basel Boston Berlin: Birkhäuser, 2007).

DATABASES ON MATERIALS

www.materia.nl

www.materialarchiv.ch

www.materialconnexion.com

www.materio.com

www.materio.es

www.raumprobe.com

DESIGNERS

Adam, Peter, *Eileen Gray, Architect/ Designer – a Biography*, 2nd revised edition (London: Thames & Hudson, 2000).

Dixon, Tom, *The Interior World of Tom Dixon* (London: Conran Octopus, 2008).

Lange, Christian, Maruhn, Jan and Mácel, Otakar, *Mies and Modern Living: Interiors, Furniture, Photography* (Ostfildern: Hatje Cantz, 2008).

Rüegg, Arthur and Spechtenhauser, Klaus, *Le Corbusier. Furniture and Interiors 1905–1965* (Zurich: Scheidegger & Spies, 2012).

Ziesemer, John, *Studien zu Gottfried Sempers dekorativen Arbeiten am Außenbau und im Interieur* (Weimar: VDG Verlag und Datenbank für Geisteswissenschaften, 1999).

APPLICATIONS

Azur Corporation, *M² Interior Design vol. 4: Residential, Retail, Dining, Public* (Tokyo: Azur Corporation, 2012).

Banks, Abby, *Punk House: Interiors in Anarchy: Anarchist Interiors* (New York: Abrams Image, 2007).

Bichard, Jo-Anne, Ehrlich, Alma and Myerson, Jeremy, *New Demographics, New Workspace* (Surrey: Gower Publishing, 2010).

Englich, Guido and Remmers, Burkhard, ed. by Wilkhahn, *Planning guide for conference and communication environments* (Basel Boston Berlin: Birkhäuser, 2008).

Feddersen, Eckhard and Lüdtke, Insa, *Living for the Elderly. A Design Manual* (Basel Boston Berlin: Birkhäuser, 2009).

Häupl, Rainer, Marinescu, Sabine and Poesch, Janina, *Trade Fair Design Annual* (Ludwigsburg, Germany: avedition – Verlag für Architektur und Design, 2012).

Hudson, Jennifer, *Restroom. Contemporay Design* (London: Laurence King, 2008).

Inglis, Kim and Kawana, Masano, *Asian Bar and Restaurant Design* (Hong Kong: Periplus Editions, 2007).

Martin Pearson, Sarah, McNamara, Carmel and Van Rossum-Willems, Marlous, *Night Fever 3. Hospitality Design* (Amsterdam: Frame Publishers, 2012).

McNamara, Carmel, Van Rossum-Willems, Marlous and Schultz, Sarah, *Powershop 3. New Retail Design* (Amsterdam: Frame Publishers, 2012).

Neufert, Ernst and Peter, *Architects' Data*, 4th edition (Hoboken, NJ: John Wiley & Sons, 2012).

Office 21, *Office 21 – Push for the Future, Better performance in innovative working environnments*, Fraunhofer Institut für Arbeitswirtschaft und Organisation (Cologne: vgs Publisher, 2003).

Raizman, David, *History of Modern Design* (Upper Saddle River, NJ: Prentice Hall, 2003).

Van Rossum-Willems, Marlous (Ed.) and Schultz, Sarah (Ed.), *Grand Stand 3. Design for Trade Fair Stands* (Amsterdam: Frame Publishers, 2011).

Vickers, Graham, *21st Century Hotel* (London: Laurence King, 2005).

ENVIRONMENT

Parr, Adrian, *Hijacking Sustainability* (Cambridge, MA: MIT Press, 2012).

Schwartz, Hillel, *Making Noise: From Babel to the Big Bang and Beyond* (New York: Zone Books, 2009).

BREEAM – Environmental Assessment Method of the Building Research Establishment
www.breeam.org

DGNB Deutsche Gesellschaft für Nachhaltiges Bauen (German Sustainable Building Council)
www.dgnb.de

LEED – Leadership in Energy and Environmental Design
www.usgbc.org

World Green Building Council
www.Worldgbc.org

MAGAZINES

AIT *Architecture | Interior | Technical Solutions;* Germany

bob *Monthly international magazine for global design;* Korea

build *Das Architekten-Magazin*; Germany

Contract; USA

d+a: *design and architecture;* Singapore

detail *Zeitschrift für Architektur + Baudetail / Review of Architecture and Construction Details; Germany*

dezeen – architecture and design magazine; *UK*

Domus; *Italy*

Dwell *At Home in the Modern World: Modern Design & Architecture; USA*

Elle Decoration; *Germany and UK*

Frame; *Netherlands*

Häuser *Das Magazin für Architektur und Design; Germany*

Intramuros *International Design Magazine; France*

livingetc, uk *The homes magazine for modern living; UK*

MD Interior, Design, Architecture Germany

Monitor; *Poland*

Schöner Wohnen *Europas größtes Wohnmagazin;* Germany

Wallpaper* Magazine: *design, interiors, architecture, fashion, art*; UK

TRADE FAIRS

100% design, London, UK, Singapore, Tokyo, Japan
www.100percentdesign.com

ARCHITECT@WORK INTERNATIONAL, various countries
www.architectatwork.de

Architecture Biennale, Venice, Italy
www.labiennale.org

BAU, Munich, Germany
www.bau-muenchen.com

Clerkenwell Design Week, London, UK
www.clerkenwelldesignweek.com

Design Miami, Miami, USA / Basel, Switzerland
www.designmiami.com

EuroShop, Düsseldorf, Germany
www.euroshop.de

Furniture Fair, Stockholm, Sweden
www.stockholmfurniturefair.com

Hong Kong Business of Design Week, Hong Kong, China
www.bodw.com

ICFF International Contemporary Furniture Fair, New York, USA
www.icff.com

imm cologne – The international furnishing show, Cologne, Germany
www.imm-cologne.com

Interieur, Kortrijk, Belgium
www.interieur.be

ISH – International fair for bathroom design, heating and air-conditioning technology, renewable energies, Frankfurt am Main, Germany
www.ish2013.com

Light and Building, Frankfurt am Main, Germany
www.light-building.com

Maison et Objet, Paris, France
www.maison-objet.com

NeoCon, Chicago, USA
www.neocon.com

Orgatec Modern Office & Facility,
Cologne, Germany
www.orgatec.com

Salone Internazionale del Mobile,
Milan, Italy
www.cosmit.it

ASSOCIATIONS/ORGANISATIONS

Bund Deutscher Innenarchitekten
www.bdia.de

Bundesarchitektenkammer
www.bak.de

European Council of Interior
Architecture
www.ecia.net

International Federation of Interior
Architects / Designers
www.ifi-world.org

International Interior
Design Association
www.IIDA.org

world-architects
www.world-architects.com

NICE TO KNOW

ACTIVATED SPACE
www.activatedspaceblog.com

Archello – The Business
Networking Platform for the
Built Environment,
www.archello.com

Architonic, The independent
resource for architecture and
design
www.architonic.com

BauNetz, Online-
Architekturmagazin
www.baunetz.de

The Cool Hunter
www.thecoolhunter.com

Design Your Way
www.Designyourway.net

DESIGNSPOTTER
www.designspotter.com

DETAIL, Das Architekturportal
www.detail.de

Kinetic Architecture
www.kineticarchitecture.net

Stylepark, Design Culture
at Stylepark
www.stylepark.com

Treehugger
www.treehugger.com

ABOUT THE EDITOR AND THE AUTHORS

SYLVIA LEYDECKER (Dipl.-Ing.) is a practising interior architect and runs the studio 100% interior in Cologne, Germany. She studied interior design at the Wiesbaden University of Applied Sciences and Trisakti University in Jakarta, Indonesia, graduating from Wiesbaden in 1996. Before setting up her studio as an interior architect, she gained many years' experience working internationally for Lufthansa, including extended periods spent abroad in Manchester, UK, and Paris, France. Today her office designs corporate interiors with special focus on interiors for healthcare environments as well as the design of offices and products. She is voluntary Vice-President of the Union of German Interior Architects/Designers (BDIA) and is a delegate of the International Federation of Interior Architects (IFI). She is also a member of the German Designer Club (DDC) and the Hospital and Healthcare Design Committee (AKG) of the Association of German Architects (BDA). First and foremost, she is a passionate interior architect, designer and author of numerous publications. Sylvia Leydecker has established an international reputation as an expert on the application of nano-materials in the built environment and is author of the book *Nano Materials in Architecture, Interior Architecture and Design* (with forewords by Harold Kroto and Michael Veith), published in 2008 by Birkhäuser.

MARK BLASCHITZ, born in 1965 in Graz, Austria, co-founded the SPLITTERWERK Label for Fine Arts in 1988, whose work has won numerous awards and been featured in several renowned exhibitions, including the Biennales in Venice and São Paolo and the documenta in Kassel. Mark Blaschitz studied architecture, philosophy and sociology, graduating from the Graz University of Technology in architecture and urban design. He has lectured since 1989 on architecture, urban design, art and design and was Visiting Professor for space&designstrategies at the Linz University of Art and Design in 2009 together with heri&salli, before being appointed to Full Professor at the Stuttgart State Academy of Art and Design (ABK). In 2010 he became Director of the Chair of Housing, Fundamentals and Design at the ABK Stuttgart and was a Visiting Professor at the Centro de Estudios Superiores de Diseño de Monterrey (CEDIM) in Mexico in 2012. In 2012 he became Dean of the Faculty of Architecture at the ABK Stuttgart.

MICHAEL CATOIR, born in 1966 in Essen, Germany, is an industrial designer. Following an apprenticeship as a carpenter, he studied industrial design at the Folkwang University of the Arts in Essen. After two years of collaboration with Andrée Putman in Paris, France, he was head of the Interior Design and Styling Department at the studio of Matteo Thun & Partners, Milan, Italy, from 2000–2008. Since 2008 he runs, together with his wife Elisa, the Studio Catoir in Milan and Paris, carrying out projects for international clients in the field of interior design, product design and graphics. With a focus on residential and hotel projects, Studio Catoir provides design services across the full spectrum from objects to interiors and facade design, as well as corporate identity.

JOANNE CYS is Associate Professor of Interior Architecture and Dean: Teaching and Learning in the Division of Education, Arts and Social Sciences at the University of South Australia (UniSA). She has also held positions as acting Dean of Research and acting Dean of Graduate Studies at UniSA. Joanne Cys is a Life Fellow of the Design Institute of Australia and was its National President from 2008–2010. She is an executive board member (2011–2013) of the International Federation of Interior Architects/Designers (IFI) and is co-chair of IFI's Global Interiors Education Open Forum (GIEOF). Joanne Cys is Australia's representative to the Global Design Network (GDN) and the Asia Pacific Space Designers Alliance (APSDA). She is a founder of the Australian Interior Design Awards program and has been the jury convenor of the program since its inception in 2004. She has been invited to speak at international and national conferences, curate design exhibitions and is regularly invited to write for professional design journals. She has published over 50 academic papers in scholarly journals, conference proceedings and chapters in edited books.

LARS GRAU is a designer and educator focusing on interactive technologies. He is Professor of Media and Communication Design at the Macromedia University for Media and Communication (MHMK) in Hamburg, Germany, and runs the user experience design agency MOKIK in Berlin. He has worked since 1999 on the development of holistic user experience concepts for mobile applications, web applications, digital television and spatial interaction. His special field lies in the integration of strategy, design and technology and research into embedded interaction. He is a regular speaker at events and a jury member of the annual DDC Design Prize.

SIMON HAMILTON, London-born with an interior design degree from Nottingham, UK, has established himself as an interior designer with a career spanning over 20 years in the design industry. Running his own interior design consultancy, Simon Hamilton & Associates in London since 2002, has provided opportunities to design for a wide variety of projects across workplace, residential, retail and hospitality sectors in the UK and abroad. In his position as International Director for The British Institute of Interior Design (BIID), he is an ambassador for the best of British design, networking at high level on a global scale.

PETER IPPOLITO studied architecture in Stuttgart, Germany and Chicago, USA. During his studies he worked as an assistant to Professor Ben Nicholson in Chicago and gained practical experience in the office of Daniel Libeskind in Berlin, Germany. In 1999 he co-founded zipherspaceworks, which in 2002 became the Ippolito Fleitz Group, run together with Gunter Fleitz. Peter Ippolito was a Visiting Professor at the Stuttgart Academy of Art and Design (2001–2002) and taught from 2004–2008 at the University of Stuttgart and in 2009 at the Biberach University of Applied Sciences. He has served in numerous competition juries and is regularly invited to speak at conferences.

CHRIS LEFTERI was born in London, UK, and studied industrial design at Central Saint Martins College of Art and Design, completing his MA under Professor Daniel Weil at the Royal College of Art, London. He is recognised throughout the world as an authority on materials and their application in design. For over a decade his studio work and publications have been pivotal in changing the way designers and the materials industry consider materials. In 2001 he published the first of eight books on materials and their application in design ("Materials for Inspirational Design" series, RotoVision, UK, 2001–2007), which have been translated into six languages. Subsequently his studio, Chris Lefteri Design, has worked with bluechip corporations and major design studios across Europe, the USA and Asia, implementing a broad range of strategies for effective materials integration in the design process.

KEES SPANJERS is an interior architect and architect and lives and works in Amsterdam and New York. He is the Director of Zaanen Spanjers Architects in Amsterdam, The Netherlands, specialising in cultural buildings and public interiors, and the recipient of numerous awards, including the Architectural Record Interiors Award. Kees Spanjers was the President of the European Council of Interior Architects (ECIA) and served as co-opted board member of the International Federation of Interior Architects/

Designers (IFI). He is a past President and now honorable member of the Dutch Association of Interior Architects (BNI). He has written many professional articles and has been active on many international panels and juries.

JOHANNES STUMPF, born in 1963, lives and works in Berlin, Germany, as a freelance architect. His office, Büro Stumpf, specialises in the management of complex building projects, both for new buildings and conservation projects, and acts as an international consultant for institutions and enterprises on issues of sustainability in building construction. In 2007, he became Vice-Chairman of the Regional Competition Committee of the Berlin Chamber of Architects, where he is instrumental in the ongoing development of competition and tendering procedures. Since 2008, he contributes as part of an international development cooperative to the establishment of training concepts for local energy-use auditors in countries such as Romania and Georgia. In his capacity as an author, he also writes for a number of German architecture magazines and journals.

DR. MARINA-ELENA WACHS, born in 1966, is a qualified industrial designer, dressmaker and pattern cutter, and works as a design consultant for companies and architects, and as an author, curator and educator at universities and academies of art and design. In her doctorate (2003–2007, Braunschweig University of Art), she undertook interdisciplinary research into the use of new materials in design, art and architecture, culminating in the publication of her book *Material Mind* (Dr. Kovač Verlag, Hamburg, 2008). In 2010 she was appointed Professor of Theory of Design at the Niederrhein University of Applied Sciences. She has worked with architects, lighting designers and designers in the field of lighting and furniture design and contributes actively to professional federations and associations such as the German Fashion Institute (DMI), the network fashion textile (nmt), the German Society for Design Theory and Research (DGTF) and the British Design History Society. She lectures and publishes widely, most recently in the book *Nachhaltiges Textiles Design / Sustainable Textile Design* (Schaff-Verlag, Hamburg, 2013).

DR. THOMAS WELTER, born in 1969, is Managing Director of the Association of German Architects (BDA). He studied economics and North American studies at the Free University of Berlin, worked freelance for the German Institute for Economic Research (DIW) in Berlin and taught at various educational institutions. After completing his doctorate in economic sciences (Dr. rer. pol.) in 2000, he joined

the Federal Chamber of German Architects (BAK) as Head of Economic Affairs, becoming Managing Director of D.A.V.I.D., the association's publishing wing in 2002 where he was responsible for the Network for Architecture Exchange (NAX). He lectures widely, chairs discussions and contributes to numerous publications.

LILIANE WONG, born in Hong Kong, China, is Professor and Head of the Department of Interior Architecture at the Rhode Island School of Design, where she has taught since 1998. She earned her MA in architecture from the Harvard University Graduate School of Design and her BA in mathematics from Vassar College. She is a registered architect in Massachusetts, USA, and has practised in the Boston area including in her firm, MWA, where she focuses on the design of libraries. She is a co-designer of the library furniture system *Kore*. A long-time volunteer at soup kitchens, her teaching emphasises the importance of public engagement in architecture and design. She is a co-founder and co-editor of the *Int|AR Journal*, which promotes creative and academic explorations of sustainable environments through exemplary works of reuse.

I find all books too long.
Voltaire

APPENDIX

ILLUSTRATION CREDITS

11 Nendo / photo: Daici Ano
12 3deluxe / photo: Emanuel Raab
13 (centre right and bottom) CUBIK³ / photos: Nele Martensen, Hamburg
14 (top) 3deluxe / photo: Sascha Jahnke
14 (centre) Artillery MCG, © smg
14 (bottom) Pudelskern / photos: Markus Bstieler
15 UBIK – Philippe Starck
15 UBIK – Philippe Starck
16 (top) Frank Sinnaeve Interieur Architectuur – Belgium (www.franksinnaeve.be) / photos: Karel Moortgat, Belgium
16 (left bottom) Innenarchitektur-büro Eva Lorey
16 (centre bottom) Innenarchitek-turbüro Eva Lorey / photos: Christine Buhl
18 100% interior Sylvia Leydecker / photos: Karin Hessmann
19 Ab Rogers Design / photo: Todd Eberle
21 3XN architects / photos: Adam Mørk
22 (top left and centre left) 100% interior Sylvia Leydecker / photos: Karin Hessmann
22 (centre right, bottom) Vonsung
23 Penson
24 (top and centre) null2elf Dischek | Eitner GbR
24 (centre right) Ministry of Design MOD
24 (centre left and bottom) Ministry of Design MOD / photos: CI&A Photography, Edward Hendricks
25 (top left) Ministry of Design MOD / photo: CI&A Photography, Edward Hendricks
25 (centre right) spek Design / photo: Andreas Keller, Altdorf
25 (bottom) Schmidhuber
26 (top left) Tjep. / photo: Xander Richters, Tjep.
26 (top right) Tjep.
26 (centre left) UXUS / photo: Dim Balsem
26 (centre right) UXUS
26 (bottom) Klein Dytham architecture / photo: © Benny Chan
27 (top) Gisbert Pöppler / photos: Wolfgang Stahr
27 (centre right) dan pearlman Markenarchitektur GmbH / photo: diephotodesigner.de
27 (bottom left) Klein Dytham architecture / photo: © Nacása & Partners Inc.
28 (top) UNStudio / photos: Iwan Baan
28 (bottom) A1Architects / photo: A1Architects – MgA. David Maštálka
29 100% interior Sylvia Leydecker / photos: Karin Hessmann
30 (top) Jean de Lessard, Designer Créatif
30 (bottom) i29 interior architects
31 (top) 100% interior Sylvia Ley-decker / photo: Karin Hessmann
31 (bottom) Uta Cossmann (www.cossmann-jacobitz.com), Claudia de Bruyn (www.two-design.com) / photos: Stefan Schilling
33 (top and centre right) Karl Huss-mann von Karl's Werkstatt / photo: Manos Meisen, Karl Hussmann

33 (bottom) Sylvia Leydecker, DDC and global:local / photos: Erika Koch, Shoichi Maruyama
34 (top and bottom) SAQ Archi-tects / photos: Dave Vandebruel
34 (centre) SAQ Architects
35 Source Interior Brand Architects
36 (top left) camp Innenarchitek-tur. Markenentwicklung, Munich / photo: Frank Straßmann
36 (bottom right) i29 interior architects / photo: Jeroen Musch
37 (top left and bottom) Karim Rashid / photos: Iwan Baan for M.N. Metropolitana di Napoli S.p.A.
37 (top) Karim Rashid
38 (top) Kengo Kuma & Associates / photo: Marco Introini
38 (bottom) Lepel & Lepel / photo: Jens Kirchner
39 (top) Keggenhoff | Partner
39 (centre right) r2_innenarchitek-tur und design / photo: Frank Welke
39 (bottom) Sinato – Chikara Ohno / photo: Takumi Ota
41 Gisbert Pöppler / photos: Wolfgang Stahr
42 Jean de Lessard, Designer Créatif / photo: David Giral
43 3deluxe / photos: Emanuel Raab
44 (top) Concrete Architectural Associates / photos: Ewout Huibers
44 (bottom) Tjep.
45 SHH / photos: Gareth Gardner
46 (top) tools off.architecture
46 (bottom left) ZMIK / photo: Eik Frenzel
46 (bottom right) ZMIK
47 (top) Universal Design Studio
47 (bottom) Pieter Vanrenterghem Interior Architecture / photo: Tom Vanryckeghem
48 (top) NC Design & Architecture Limited / photo: Dennis Lo Designs
48 (bottom right) Klein Dytham architecture / photo: © Kouichi Torimura
50 (top) Nakayama Architects
50 (bottom) Nendo
51 (top) Silvia Pappa – Innen-architekten
51 (bottom) Achille Salvagni Architetti / photo: Sean Gleason
53 (top right) Ministry of Design MOD / photo: CI&A Photography, Edward Hendricks
53 (bottom left) Simone Micheli Architetto
53 (bottom right) Simone Micheli Architetto / photo: Jürgen Eheim
54 (top) RAISERLOPES / photos: Frank Kleinbach, Stuttgart
54 (bottom right) Concrete Architectural Associates / photo: Ewout Huibers
55 (top left) Architetto Pierluigi Piu / photo: Giorgio Dettori
55 (right centre and right bottom) Jennifer Worts / photos: Ted Yarwood
56 (top) bahlsconcepts
56 (bottom) andernach und partner
57 (top and centre) 100% interior Sylvia Leydecker / photos: Reinhard Rosendahl
57 (bottom) Vonsung
58 (top centre) eins:33 GmbH / photos: Bodo Mertoglu
58 (bottom) Klaus Bürger Architektur

59 (top) Schwitzke & Partner
59 (centre) Philipp Mainzer Office for Architecture and Design / photo: ERCO GmbH
59 (bottom) © ROW Studio / photos: Juan Marcos Castañeda – ROW Studio
60 (top and centre left) Atelier Brückner GmbH / photos: Mac Tanó
60 (centre right and bottom) Atelier Brückner GmbH
61 (top) Curiosity / photo: Nacása & Partners Inc.
61 (centre left and centre bottom) Concrete Architectural Associates / photos: Jeroen Musch
61 (bottom right) JOI-Design GmbH
66 Robert Harvey Oshatz / photo: Cameron Neilson
68 (top) Robert Harvey Oshatz
68 (centre left and bottom left) Robert Harvey Oshatz / photos: Cameron Neilson
68 (bottom right) HASSELL / photo: © Earl Carter
69 (bottom) 100% interior Sylvia Leydecker / photos: Karin Hessmann
71 (top right and bottom) Klab Architecture – Konstantinos Labrinopoulos / photos: Panos Kokkinias
71 (top left) Klab Architecture – Konstantinos Labrinopoulos
72 Raumkleid – Anke Preywisch
73 (top left and bottom left) Con-crete Architectural Associates / photos: Frank Pinckers
73 (right) Torafu Architects / photo: Daici Ano
74 Wiel Arets Architects / photo: João Morgado
75 IVANKA Concrete Design
76 © LAVA – Laboratory for Visionary Architecture
77 ateliersv Innenarchitektur Munich / photos: Christine Schaum
78 sculp(IT) / photos: Luc Roymans
79 (top and bottom) TRIAD / photos: Jian Wen Kang / Zhenglin Wenig
79 (centre) TRIAD
80 (top right) LTL Architects / photo: Michael Moran
80 (left bottom) de-spec – Farnaz Mansuri, Tom Shea / photo: Frank Oudeman
80 (left centre) de-spec – Farnaz Mansuri, Tom Shea
80 (bottom right) LTL Architects / photo: Michael Moran
82 LTL Architects / photo: LTL Architects
84 (top right and centre right) Edwards Moore / photos: Tony Gorsevski
84 (left and centre left) Edwards Moore
84 (bottom) Campaign
85 (top right) Adam Kalkin
85 (centre right and bottom) Adam Kalkin / photos: Luca Campigotto
86 (top) Caterina Tiazzoldi – L. Croce, F. Rizzo, R. Musso, A. Primavera, M. Pianosi, M. Fassino, Z. Ujhelyi, M. Rosso with Illy Art Direction
86 (centre and bottom) Caterina Tiazzoldi – L. Croce, F. Rizzo, R. Musso, A. Primavera, M. Pianosi, M. Fassino, Z. Ujhelyi, M. Rosso with Illy Art Direction / photos: Luca Campigotto, Federico Rizzo

87 Caterina Tiazzoldi / Nuova Ordentra / photos: Sebastiano Pellion di Persano, Hélène Cany, Davide Giglio
88 Maurice Mentjens / photos: Arjen Schmitz
89 b-k-i / brandherm + krumrey interior architecture
90 (left top) AllesWirdGut / photo: Michael Dürr
90 (left bottom) AllesWirdGut
90 (right bottom) Snøhetta Oslo
91 Snøhetta Oslo / photos: diephotodesigner.de
92 EDGE Design Institute Ltd.
93 EDGE Design Institute Ltd.
94 Pablo Zamorano
95 (top and bottom) The Principals – Drew Seskunas / photos: Matthias Weingärtner
95 (centre) The Principals – Drew Seskunas
96 Steinert & Bitterling
97 Steinert & Bitterling
99 Takashi Kuribayashi
100 (top) Concrete Architectural Associates
100 (bottom) Bachir Nader – Inte-rior Architect (www.bachirnader.com) / photos: Diane Aftimos
103 (top right) UBIK – Philippe Starck
103 (bottom) Nils Völker
104 Yayoi Kusama
105 (top left) Marco Hemmerling / photo: Frank Vinken
105 (top centre and top right) Marco Hemmerling
105 (bottom left) Bachir Nader – Interior Architect (www.bachirna-der.com) / photo: Fares Jammal, Art Director Mr. Mohammed Ezo
105 (bottom right) Bachir Nader – Interior Architect (www.bachirna-der.com)
106 bluarch / photos: ADO
107 (top) GFG Gruppe für Gestal-tung / photos: Tom Kleiner, GFG Gruppe für Gestaltung
107 (bottom) barmade ag / photos: Markus Muther
108 Leong Leong
109 (top and centre left) Studio Fabio Novembre / photos: Pasquale Formisano
109 (bottom) Studio Fabio Novembre
111 (top left) NC Design & Archi-tecture Limited, Laboratory for Explorative Architecture & Design Ltd. / photo: Dennis Lo Designs
111 (centre right) J. Mayer H. Archi-tects / photo: Constantin Meyer Photographie
111 (bottom) 3GATTI / photos: Daniele Mattioli
112 (top) 100% interior Sylvia Ley-decker / photos: Karin Hessmann
112 (bottom left) dan pearlman Markenarchitektur GmbH / photo: Dan Pearlman
112 (bottom right) Architetto Pier-luigi Piu / photos: Giorgio Dettori
112 (centre right) Architetto Pierluigi Piu
113 (top) 100% interior Sylvia Ley-decker / photos: Karin Hessmann
113 (bottom) Architetto Pierluigi Piu / photo: Giorgio Dettori
114 (top left) MARC FORNES / THEVERYMANY / photo: François Lauginie

352

114 (bottom left) MARC FORNES / THEVERYMANY
115 ICD/ITKE Stuttgart University
116 ICD/ITKE Stuttgart University
117 Snarkitecture / photos: Snarkitecture, Peter A. Lee, David Smith
118 Snarkitecture / photos: David Smith
121 Nema Workshop / photo: David Joseph
122 Studio Catoir / photo: Michael Catoir
123 (top) Concrete Architectural Associates
123 (centre) Concrete Architectural Associates / photos: Ewout Huibers
123 (bottom) 100% interior Sylvia Leydecker
124 Studio Catoir / photo: Michael Catoir
125 Studio Catoir / photos: © Richard Powers
127 (top and centre right) Adam Lay Studio
127 (bottom) Anne Batisweiler / photo: Wolfgang Pulfer
129 Nendo / photos: Daici Ano
130 JOI-Design GmbH
131 (top right) Koichi Takada Architects / photo: Sharrin Rees
131 (top left) Koichi Takada Architects
131 (bottom) DRDI – regina-dahmeningenhoven / photos: Holger Knauf
133 Tina Aßmann Innenarchitektur / photo: © Florian Holzherr, Munich
134 (top left and bottom) Takeshi Hosaka / photos: Koji Fujii, Nacása & Partners Inc.
134 (top right) Takeshi Hosaka
135 (top left) 100% interior Sylvia Leydecker
135 (top right and centre) © AGROB BUCHTAL / photo: Jochen Stüber Objektfotografie
135 (bottom) Gisbert Pöppler / photo: Hiepler Brunier
137 Birgit Hansen
138 (top right) Simone Micheli Architetto / photo: Jürgen Eheim
138 (top left and bottom) Berschneider + Berschneider
139 (top left) Simone Micheli Architetto / photo: Jürgen Eheim
139 (top centre) Simone Micheli Architetto
139 (bottom) Simone Micheli Architetto / photo: Jürgen Eheim
140 (top left) atelier zürich gmbh / photo: Martin Guggisberg
140 (bottom) Anne Batisweiler / photos: Wolfgang Pulfer
141 (top) ateliersv Innenarchitektur Munich / photos: Christine Schaum
141 (bottom) innen-architektur. Daniela Haeck / photos: Malte Wandel
143 (top left and bottom) atelier zürich gmbh / photos: Martin Guggisberg
143 (top right) atelier zürich gmbh
144 büro uebele visuelle kommunikation
145 (top) andernach und partner
145 (bottom) Supermachine Studio: Pitupong Chaowakul, Suchart Ouy-pornchaisakul, Peechaya Mekasu-vanroj, Santi Sarasuphab / photos: Wison Tungthunya
146 (top) Lepel & Lepel / photo: Jens Kirchner

146 (centre left and left bottom) Claudia de Bruyn (www.two-design.com), Uta Cossmann (www.cossmann-jacobitz.com) / photos: Nicole Zimmermann
146 (bottom right) Claudia de Bruyn (www.two-design.com), Uta Cossmann (www.cossmann-jaco-bitz.com) / photo: Bernd Haugrund
147 (top) ruge + göllner raumconcept
147 (bottom) Moho Arquitectos / photo: David Frutos
148 100% interior Sylvia Leydecker / photos: Karin Hessmann
149 100% interior Sylvia Leydecker / photos: Karin Hessmann
150 atelier zürich gmbh / photo: Martin Guggisberg
151 (top) Raumkleid – Anke Preywisch
151 (centre and bottom) Studio Catoir / photos: Michael Catoir
152 Studio Catoir / photo: Michael Catoir
153 Studio Catoir / photos: Michael Catoir
154 Studio Catoir / photo: Michael Catoir
155 Studio Catoir / photos: Michael Catoir
156 © Holzer Kobler Architekturen Zürich / photo: Jan Bitter
158 (centre right) 100% interior Sylvia Leydecker / photo: Reinhard Rosendahl
158 (bottom) 100% interior Sylvia Leydecker / photo: Karin Hessmann
159 (top and bottom right) 100% interior Sylvia Leydecker / photos: Karin Hessmann
159 (bottom left) 100% interior Sylvia Leydecker / photo: Friedhelm Krischer
160 (top right) 100% interior Sylvia Leydecker / photo: Karin Hessmann
160 (bottom and left) 100% interior Sylvia Leydecker / photos: Karin Hessmann
160 (centre) 100% interior Sylvia Leydecker
162 (top left) innen-architektur. Daniela Haeck / photos: Malte Wandel
162 (top centre) atelier zürich gmbh / photo: Martin Guggisberg
162 (top right) A1Architects / photo: A1Architects – MgA. David Maštálka
162 (bottom) Plan2Plus, Munich – Ralf Peter Knobloch, Ursula Regina Förster
163 (top left) 5AM / photo: © Thomas De Bruyne
163 (bottom) i29 interior architects / photos: Jeroen Musch
164 (top, centre left and bottom left) Tina Aßmann Innenarchitektur / photos: Florian Holzherr
164 (bottom right) SAQ Architects
165 Architetto Pierluigi Piu / photos: Giorgio Dettori
166 (top left) Ply Project – Kenichi Sato / photo: Masatoshi Mori
166 (centre right) Robert Harvey Oshatz / photo: Cameron Neilson
166 (bottom) Tjep. / photos: Yannic Alidarso, Tjep.
167 (top and centre right) RDAI – Dominique Hebrard, Sybil Debu, artistic director Denis Montel / photos: Michel Denancé

167 (bottom left) Susanne Kaiser
168 (top left) ROW Studio
168 (centre left and bottom left) ROW Studio / photos: Sófocles Hernández
168 (top right) Department of ARCHITECTURE Co. Ltd. / photo: Wison Tungthunya
168 (bottom right) © ROW Studio / photo: Jorge Silva – ROW Studio
169 (top) Torafu Architects
169 (centre and bottom) Torafu Architects / photos: Daici Ano
170 (top) Koichi Takada Architects / photos: Sharrin Res
170 (bottom) design spirits co., ltd. – Yuhkichi Kawai / photos: Toshihide Kajiwara
171 design spirits co., ltd. – Yuh-kichi Kawai / photos: Toshihide Kajiwara
173 (top and centre left) sinato – Chikara Ohno
173 (centre right and bottom) sinato – Chikara Ohno / photos: Toshiyuki Yano
174 (top left) Hooba Design / photo: © Parham Taghiof
174 (bottom right) Hooba Design
175 (top and centre) Archiblau & Partners / photos: Karel Moortgat
175 (top right) Lepel & Lepel / photo: Jens Kirchner
175 (bottom left) Vonsung
177 Concrete Architectural Associates / photos: Ewout Huibers
178 (top left and right) Graft
178 (centre left and right) Graft / photos: Ricky Ridecos
178 (bottom) 100% interior Sylvia Leydecker / photos: Karin Hessmann
179 100% interior Sylvia Leydecker
180 design spirits co., ltd. – Yuhki-chi Kawai / photos: Barry Johnson
181 (top) design spirits co., ltd. – Yuhkichi Kawai
181 (bottom) Elliat Rich / photos: Steve Strike
183 (top) Kengo Kuma & Associates
183 (bottom) ZMIK / photos: Eik Frenzel & ZMIK
184 (top) NAU Architecture / photo: Jan Bitter
184 (bottom) NAU Architecture
185 Institut für Textiltechnik (ITA) der RWTH Aachen University / photos: M. Cetin, B. Glauß, T. Gries
186 Gisela Stromeyer Design / photo: Michael Moran
187 Gisela Stromeyer Design
188 (top right) Boel Andersson / photo: Pär Hugosson
188 (bottom) 100% interior Sylvia Leydecker / photos: Karin Hessmann
189 (top) Department of ARCHI-TECTURE Co. Ltd. / photo: Wison Tungthunya
189 (bottom) Joey Ho Design Ltd. / photos: Wu Yong Chang
190 (top) bluarch / photos: Oleg March Photography
190 (centre) bluarch
190 (bottom) LAVA – Laboratory for Visionary Architecture / photo: © Gee-Ly
191 (top left) Photo: Heiko Gruber
191 (right top and right bottom) Studio Fabio Novembre / photos: Pasquale Formisano

191 (bottom left) Studio Fabio Novembre
192 (top) 100% interior Sylvia Leydecker / photo: Karin Hessmann
192 (bottom) 100% interior Sylvia Leydecker
192 (bottom) 100% interior Sylvia Leydecker
193 Photo: Sylvia Leydecker
194 i29 interior architects
195 Karim Rashid / photos: Lukas Roth
196 SWeeT Co., Ltd.
197 (top) Supermachine Studio: Pitupong Chaowakul, Suchart Ouy-pornchaisakul, Peechaya Mekasu-vanroj, Santi Sarasuphab / photo: Wison Tungthunya
197 (centre left) bluarch / photo: ADO, Scott G. Morris Photography
197 (bottom right) two_Claudia de Bruyn / photo: HG Esch
198 UXUS / photos: Dim Balsem
199 Sabine Hartl Architektur + Raumdesign, Switzerland / photo: René Rötheli
200 (top left) Wobedo Design / photo: Anna Diehl
200 (centre and bottom) i29 interior architects
201 (bottom) Mika Barr
202 (top) McBride Charles Ryan Architecture & Interior Design / photos: John Gollings
202 (bottom right) Architetto Pier-luigi Piu / photo: Giorgio Dettori
202 (bottom left) Joey Ho Design Ltd. / photo: Graham Uden, Ray Lau
203 Uzin Utz AG
204 Studio Fabio Novembre / photo: Pasquale Formisano
205 (top) Photo: Sylvia Leydecker
205 (centre) INM Leibniz Institute for New Materials
205 (bottom) Photo: Sylvia Leydecker
206 (top) 100% interior Sylvia Leydecker
206 (bottom upper and central photo) Photo: Sylvia Leydecker
206 (bottom) Photo: Dr. Dietmar Stephan, University of Kassel
207 (top left) 100% interior Sylvia Leydecker
207 (top right) 100% interior Sylvia Leydecker
207 (bottom) Fred Mafra Architect / photos: Jomar Bragança
208 (top, centre and bottom upper row) Photo: Sylvia Leydecker
208 (bottom lower row) sto AG
209 Photo: Sylvia Leydecker
210, 211 100% interior Sylvia Ley-decker / photos: Karin Hessmann
213 Photo: Sylvia Leydecker (sample: Lafarge Beton)
214 (top) Jay Watson design
214 (bottom) Philips
215 (top) J. Mayer H. Architects
215 (bottom) Photo: Sylvia Leydecker
216 SAQ Architects / photo: © Florian Licht
218 (centre and bottom) Re-Make/Re-Model Architecture / photos: Johanne Fick
218 (top) Re-Make/Re-Model Architecture
219 (top) Monz + Monz | Innenar-chitektur und Design

219 (centre and bottom) landau + kindelbacher / photos: Christian Hacker, Werner Huthmacher
221 (top right) Vonsung
221 (bottom) Achille Salvagni Architetti / photo: Massimo Listri
222 Meyer en Van Schooten Architecten (MVSA) / photos: Jeroen Musch Photography
223 (top left) 3deluxe
223 (centre right and bottom) Concrete Architectural Associates / photos: Frank Pinckers
224 (top and centre) bluarch / photos: ADO
224 (bottom) Ippolito Fleitz Group / photos: © Zooey Braun
225 (top and bottom left) Studio DRIFT
225 (bottom right) Studio DRIFT
226 Andy Martin Architects (www.andymartinarchitects.com) / photo: Vangelis Paterakis
227 Andy Martin Architects (www.andymartinarchitects.com) / photos: Vangelis Paterakis
228 (top) planungsbüro i21
228 (bottom) Vonsung
229 Atelier Brückner GmbH / photos: Marcus Meyer
230 Plan2Plus, Munich – Ralf Peter Knobloch, Ursula Regina Förster
231 (top) Níall McLaughlin Architects
231 (bottom) Hollin + Radoske / photo: Ludger Paffrath
232 (top and centre) Department of ARCHITECTURE Co. Ltd. / photos: Wison Tungthunya
232 (bottom) Hollin + Radoske / photos: Ludger Paffrath
233 Department of ARCHITECTURE Co. Ltd. / photos: Wison Tungthunya
235 (top) SOM
235 (bottom right) 100% interior Sylvia Leydecker / photo: Karin Hessmann
235 (centre left) Bachir Nader – Interior Architect (www.bachirnader.com) / photo: Diane Aftimos, Art Director Mr. Mohammed Ezo
236 Klein Dytham architecture / photos: © Nacása & Partners Inc.
237 (top and centre) 100% interior Sylvia Leydecker / photos: Karin Hessmann
237 (bottom) 100% interior Sylvia Leydecker
238 (top) Meyer en Van Schooten Architecten (MVSA) / photo: Jeroen Musch Photography
238 (bottom) Yi Architects / photo: Stefan Müller
239 Bates Smart Architects / photo: Peter Hyatt
240 Nendo / photo: Daici Ano
243 (top right) i29 interior architects
243 (bottom) Klein Dytham architecture / photo: © PACIA
245 (top and centre) Zaha Hadid Architects / photos: Luke Hayes, Joel Chester Fildes
245 (bottom) Zaha Hadid Architects
246 landau + kindelbacher / photos: Werner Huthmacher
247 Studio Pacific Architecture in association with Warren and Mahoney / photos: Patrick Reynolds

249 (top and centre left) i29 interior architects
249 (centre right) 100% interior Sylvia Leydecker / photo: Friedhelm Krischer
249 (bottom) Penson
250 Ply Project Kenichi Sato / photo: Masatoshi Mori
251 (top) JOI-Design GmbH
251 (centre and bottom right) 100% interior Sylvia Leydecker / photos: Karin Hessmann
251 (bottom left) 100% interior Sylvia Leydecker
252 (top and centre left) Ippolito Fleitz Group / photos: © Zooey Braun
252 (centre right) Ippolito Fleitz Group
255 Ippolito Fleitz Group / photos: © Zooey Braun
256 Photo: Sylvia Leydecker
257 ART+COM AG
259 (top and centre) E/B Office / photos: Peter Katz
259 (bottom) The Principals – Drew Seskunas / photos: Nicolo Bianchi
260 ART+COM AG
261 (right and bottom left) 100% interior Sylvia Leydecker / photos: Karin Hessmann
261 (top left and centre left) 100% interior Sylvia Leydecker
263 SAQ Architects
265 Torafu Architects / Graphic design: TAKAIYAMA / Sound-Lighting technical: LUFTZUG / photos: Daici Ano
266 Atelier Brückner GmbH / photo: Roland Halbe
267 Atelier Brückner GmbH / photo: Roland Halbe
268 (centre left and bottom) Marco Hemmerling, Henri Schweynoch / photos: Dirk Schelpmeier
268 (top) Marco Hemmerling, Henri Schweynoch / visualisation: David Lemberski
269 (top and centre left) Mainz University of Applied Sciences
269 (centre right) photo: Sylvia Leydecker
270 Carl Stahl Architektur / photos: Fotodesign Kissner
271 (top right) 100% interior Sylvia Leydecker
271 (top left, centre and bottom) 100% interior Sylvia Leydecker / photos: Karin Hessmann
273 (top and centre) SPLITTERWERK
273 (bottom left) SPLITTERWERK / photo: Paul Ott
273 (bottom right images) SPLITTERWERK
274 (top) SPLITTERWERK / photos: Paul Ott
274 (bottom) SPLITTERWERK
275 SPLITTERWERK
276 landau + kindelbacher / photo: Christian Hacker
277 Concrete Architectural Associates / photo: Ewout Huibers
278 EnOcean
279 (top and bottom) © Future-Shape GmbH
279 (centre) © Witex Flooring Products GmbH
282 (top left) SAQ Architects
282 (centre) J. Mayer H. Architects
282 (bottom) J. Mayer H. Architects / photo: Uwe Walter

283 Atelier Brückner GmbH / photos: Uwe Dettmar
284 BIG – Bjarke Ingels Group (partners-in-charge: Bjarke Ingels, Andreas Klok Pedersen, Project Leader: Daniel Kidd, Team: Søren Martinussen, Kuba Snopek, Daniel Selensky, Chris Brown)
285 Torafu Architects / photos: Daici Ano, Daisuke Ohki, Daisuke Shimokawa
286 Torafu Architects / photo: Daici Ano, Daisuke Ohki, Daisuke Shimokawa
288 Photo: Sylvia Leydecker
289 Dipl.-Ing. Johannes Stumpf
291 Fa. Buderus
293 (top and centre) Creative Commons
293 (bottom), 294, 295, 296, 298, 301 Dipl.-Ing. Johannes Stumpf
302 Photo: Sylvia Leydecker, taken in Berlin
304 100% interior / photos: Karin Hessmann
306 (top left) JOI-Design GmbH
306 (centre) 100% interior Sylvia Leydecker
306 (bottom) 100% interior Sylvia Leydecker / photos: Karin Hessmann
307 100% interior Sylvia Leydecker / photo: Karin Hessmann
308 (top left and centre right) Jain Malkin Inc. / photos: Ed LaCasse Photography
308 (bottom) baustudio melchert+kastl
309 (top) Photo: Sylvia Leydecker
309 (bottom) 100% interior Sylvia Leydecker / photos: Karin Hessmann
311 100% interior Sylvia Leydecker / photo: Karin Hessmann
312 (top) 100% interior Sylvia Leydecker / photo: Karin Hessmann
312 (bottom) 100% interior Sylvia Leydecker / photos: Karin Hessman, Sylvia Leydecker
313 DESIGNLIGA / photos: Pascal Gambarte
314 (top left) Bachir Nader – Interior Architect (www.bachirnader.com) / photo: Diane Aftimos, Art Director: Mr. Mohammed Ezo
314 (bottom right), 315 FRANKE Architektur I Innenarchitektur
316 IVANKA Concrete Design
317 (centre right) Keiichi Hayashi Architect
317 (top) Keiichi Hayashi Architect / photos: Yoshiyuki Hirai
317 (bottom) SHH / photo: Alastair Lever
318 (top) Kieferorthopädische Fachpraxis, Dr. Dux & Kollegen
318 (bottom) UXUS / photos: Dim Balsem
319 (top) © Royal Pavilion & Museums (Brighton & Hove)
319 (bottom right) Photo: Sylvia Leydecker
320 Matali Crasset / photos: Jérôme Spriet
321 (top) SEITENANSICHT – Innenarchitektin Martina Lorbach / photos: Marco Lorbach
321 (bottom) Photo: Sylvia Leydecker
323 (centre right) © SPK / David Chipperfield Architects / photo: Jörg von Bruchhausen

323 (top right) © Ute Zscharnt for David Chipperfield Architects
323 (centre left) © SMB / David Chipperfield Architects / photo: Ute Zscharnt
323 (bottom) Christian Schittich, Munich
325 Photos: Johannes Stumpf
328 Photos: Sylvia Leydecker (image bottom right: Blütenrausch, Cologne)
329 (top) KINZO
329 (bottom) KINZO
330, 331 (top) 100% interior Sylvia Leydecker / photo: Karin Hessmann
331, 332 100% interior Sylvia Leydecker / photo: Karin Hessmann
333 (top) design spirits co., ltd. – Yuhkichi Kawai / photo: Toshihide Kajiwara
333 (bottom) Autoban / photo: George Mitchell
335 (top) Klein Dytham architecture / photos: © Ryota Atarashi
335 Fabiane Giestas / photo: Cacá Lima
336 GOTWOB
337 (bottom) Joey Ho Design Ltd. / photo: Graham Uden, Ray Lau
337 (top) Joey Ho Design Ltd.
338 Ministry of Design MOD
340 (top and bottom left) RAISERLOPES
340 (bottom right) © RAISERLOPES / photo: Martin Grothmaak, Stuttgart
341 © RAISERLOPES
342 Schwitzke & Partner
344 (top left) SWeeT Co., Ltd. / photos: Nacása & Partners, Inc.
344 (bottom) SWeeT Co., Ltd. / photos: Nacása & Partners, Inc.
345 SWeeT Co., Ltd. / photos: Nacása & Partners, Inc.
348 style:FREE / photo: Kim Bierbrauer

INDEX OF BUILDING TYPES

Trade Fair Design
Audi Exclusive Lounge at the Geneva Auto Salon 2011, Geneva, Switzerland
Audi Urban Future Award, Berlin, Germany *284*
FutureCare at CeBit, Bitkom with Deutsche Messe Hannover 2010, Germany *261*
Garment Garden, Messe Frankfurt, Germany *111*
IFA (consumer electronics trade fair) Gala 2011, Messe Berlin, Germany *329*
Palace of International Forums, lobby, Tashkent, Uzbekistan *254, 255*
Panasonic Convention, Munich, Germany *60*
Performative light-space installation, AIT-ArchitekturSalon Munich, Germany *274*
Sci-Fi Trade Fair Stand, Cornicon, San Diego, California, USA *178*
Siemens Trade Fair Stand for the Interkama 2007, Hannover Messe, Germany *56*
State Grid Pavilon, EXPO Shanghai, China *266, 267*
Tent, London, United Kingdom *57*

Transport Buildings
Metronapoli – Università Station, Naples, Italy *37*
Schiphol Airport Lounge 3 / House of Tulips, Amsterdam, Netherlands *26*
Wellington Airport International Passenger Terminal ("The Rock"), Wellington, New Zealand *247*

SUSTAINABLE AND BEAUTIFUL: FURNISHING TEXTILES MADE OF TREVIRA CS

As a manufacturer of polyester fibres, Trevira is committed to sustainability in all its activities, not just in the production of fibres. All Trevira products bear the Oeko-Tex Standard 100 Certificate and the company conforms to certification standards for quality assurance and environmental and energy management systems. Trevira's advantages are apparent from the moment they are put to use. For example, unlike materials made of natural fibres, textiles made of Trevira CS need no additional fire-retardant surface treatment because the flame-retardant properties are already built into the fibres themselves.

From 2013, a recycling concept for Trevira CS materials will be available for manufacturers and users to return discarded textiles for recycling into other products such as lagging or insulation material.

Modern office architecture is increasingly recognising that communicative open-plan work environments must also provide areas for concentration and peace and quiet. Acoustic elements made of textile materials are not only effective sound absorbers but can also be used as variable and decorative elements that are easy to integrate into the office's interior design. Textiles made of Trevira CS

can be used to make acoustic dampeners in the form of panels, room dividers, suspended ceiling sails and wall coverings.

Sliding panels, roller blinds, vertical vanes as well as room dividers and wall cladding made of flame-retardant hybrid yarns offer a range of design possibilities for clean and minimalist room elements. The stiffened material keeps its shape and hangs much better than conventional materials.

left: Procedes-i-d interior design centre: abinitio right: Coulisse

trevira® CS

Trevira GmbH
Philipp-Reis-Str. 2

65795 Hattersheim, Germany
www.trevira.com

HOME: UNIVERSAL DESIGN AT ITS BEST

The HOME ceramic tile series provides comfort with functionality and design whatever one's age or phase of life. Additional decorative elements and floor tiles are available to match the colours of the wall tiles.

EMOTION: CREATIVE FUNCTIONALITY

Inspired by slate, Emotion floor tiles are available in a range of expressive surface variants, and are complemented by a creative palette of wall tiles and decorative elements.

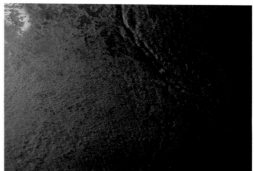

URBAN STONE: ELEGANT STONE LOOK

With a subtle, fine-grain structure, the surface treatment of the Urban Stone porcelain stoneware tiles lends them a natural appearance reminiscent of natural stone.

GEO 2.0: A SUCCESS STORY CONTINUES

A new range of colours of subdued natural grey tones expands the successful range of GEO tiles for public spaces. With through-coloured particles, each tile has structure, depth and a natural feel.

PATINA: THE FASCINATION OF TRACES OF TIME

The fascination of traces of weathering in a ceramic tile – a mineral mixture is applied layer on layer to create a tile with an organic surface texture. Decorative CRAQUELÉ wall elements complement the overall feeling of authenticity.

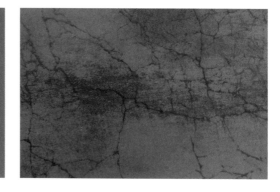

Buchtal 1
92521 Schwarzenfeld
Germany

www.agrob-buchtal.de
agrob-buchtal@deutsche-steinzeug.de

 DEUTSCHE STEINZEUG AGROB **BUCHTAL**

ARCHI TONIC

THE INDEPENDENT RESOURCE FOR ARCHITECTURE AND DESIGN

WWW.ARCHITONIC.COM

www.architonic.com/PRODUCT CODE

5100047   1106579   1071278   1118971   1089277   1102366   1020541   1104105   1106588   1121487

1001279   1110673   1106150   1123457   1101896   1015612   1093117   1169954   1083010

1095680   1085023   1103997   1034567   1128498   1088650

1085494   1126116   1099491   1106828

1111534   1106276   1003803   5100389   1092688

1083715   1096225   1104019   1165416   1117017   1131166   1102367   1101957   1101218

1103454   5100155   1035384   1048792   1081783   1085083   1170307   1068155   1101389   1125597

1068781   1141664   1116943   1109250   1105604   1101995   1103729   1167633   1073872

1070669   1106724   1102349   1092689   1164867   5100399   1055766   1130809   1127725   1102618

1099628   1104939   1104265   1009329   1103838   1085027   1170625   1106285   1176577

1106905   1105150   1098989   1168577   1162230   1103161   1003339   5100358

1166414   1106246   5100015   1003430   1103616   1092697

Maximum insulation effect, minimum thickness

The innovative internal insulation system StoTherm In Aevero

Never before has internal insulation been so thin and yet so effective: the new, innovative internal insulation system StoTherm In Aevero is exceptionally thin and made of high-tech aerogel particles. Thanks to the board's thermal conductivity of just 0.016 W/(m·K) it already meets the requirements specified in EnEV 2009 with a thickness of only 30 mm. **StoTherm In Aevero** – an intelligent and vapour-permeable insulation system.

www.sto-aevero.de

THE FUSION OF WALL
AND FURNITURE

burgbad

Morsbacher Straße 15 – 91171 Greding
T +49 (0) 8463-901-0 – F +49 (0) 8463-901-143 – info@burgbad.com – www.burgbad.com

Bathrooms are becoming more and more like living rooms both in terms of furnishings and materials as well as the way they are used. Nevertheless, bathroom designers are still restricted in where they can place their sanitary fittings – at the very most, a bathtub is occasionally placed in the room as a freestanding element. The desire for design freedom is still hampered by a lack of practical solutions for realising creative designs. burgbad has made it its business to resolve this shortcoming.

The first important step in this direction was made in 2005 with the introduction of the rc40 system, where "rc" stands for room concepts. rc40 turns the bathroom into a room for living. What at first glance seems little more than a wall cupboard system with added extras, can actually be used to line, subdivide and enclose entire rooms and bathrooms, creating a single living interior. The series offers a wealth of options: the flexible range of sizes, wall-high panel systems and a wide range of integral modules such as washbasins, bathtubs, mirror cabinets and front panels as well as the vast range of perfectly flat, freely combinable surfaces in qualities ranging from wood to high-gloss lacquer finishes. Invitations to break out of the bathroom and redefine one's living space!

Where does the bedroom begin and the bathroom stop? Do you control the multimedia wall from the bathroom or from the reading niche? Is that just a walk-in wardrobe or a salon with dressing table and washbasin? Why even differentiate between wall and cupboard, shelving unit or shower when shelves and hanging cupboards with drawers merge invisibly into the wall panelling, when cupboards, wardrobes and consoles can be integrated into the system and when mirrors, tall units and sanitary wall installations meld seamlessly into one another. Like a set of building blocks or Lego bricks, the rc40 tempts the creative designer in us – whether professional or amateur – to explore the endless possibilities of creating new spaces. Just the way you dreamed them – for the luxury of spending time in an aesthetically pleasing environment, where you can enjoy yourself and for a moment forget the world around you while you delight in the gentle splash of water.

THE *FEELGOOD* FLOOR

noraplan® sentica feels good and looks good – in 38 new colours.

Life is colourful. Colours reflect our moods and influence how we feel. Architects know this and use colour to design creative and atmospheric environments, for example for buildings such as hospitals, universities and offices. nora systems knows this too and has developed a corresponding innovative new rubber floor covering. The result speaks for itself, is available in 38 inspiring colours and is called noraplan® sentica.

Experience noraplan® sentica, the feelgood floor: www.nora-sentica.com/uk

To find out more, scan the code with your smartphone.